Ralph J. Poole
Queer Turkey

Ralph J. Poole is an American-German researcher who teaches as professor of American studies at the University of Salzburg, Austria. Amongst his publications is a book-length study on the avant-garde tradition in American theater, a book on satirical and autoethnographical cannibal texts and an essay collection on dangerous masculinities. His main research interests are gender and queer studies, popular culture, and transnational American studies.

Ralph J. Poole
Queer Turkey
Transnational Poetics of Desire

[transcript]

An electronic version of this book is freely available, thanks to the support of libraries working with Knowledge Unlatched. KU is a collaborative initiative designed to make high quality books Open Access for the public good. The Open Access ISBN for this book is 978-3-8394-5060-4. More information about the initiative and links to the Open Access version can be found at www.knowledgeunlatched.org.

This publication was made possible with financial support from the University of Salzburg.

Bibliographic information published by the Deutsche Nationalbibliothek
The Deutsche Nationalbibliothek lists this publication in the Deutsche Nationalbibliografie; detailed bibliographic data are available in the Internet at http://dnb.d-nb.de

This work is licensed under the Creative Commons Attribution 4.0 (BY) license, which means that the text may be remixed, transformed and built upon and be copied and redistributed in any medium or format even commercially, provided credit is given to the author. For details go to http://creativecommons.org/licenses/by/4.0/
Creative Commons license terms for re-use do not apply to any content (such as graphs, figures, photos, excerpts, etc.) not original to the Open Access publication and further permission may be required from the rights holder. The obligation to research and clear permission lies solely with the party re-using the material.

First published in 2022 by transcript Verlag, Bielefeld
© **Ralph J. Poole**

Cover layout: Maria Arndt, Bielefeld
Cover illustration: Verena Laschinger, Erfurt

Print-ISBN 978-3-8376-5060-0
PDF-ISBN 978-3-8394-5060-4
https://doi.org/10.14361/9783839450604
ISSN of series: 2703-1365
eISSN of series: 2703-1373

Contents

Introduction 9

I. Queer Istanbul

1. Istanbul: Queer Desires Between Muslim Tradition and Global Pop 29
12 points 29
Turkey's Transitional Periods: Kemalist Modernization,
Military Coups, Queer Activism 32
Sex Between Men: Ottoman Tradition and Turkish Everyday Life 36
Istanbul at Night: Queer Literature, Arabesk Music, and Gay Bars 46

2. Architecture of Seduction, or: What (Really) Goes On in the Hamam? 65
Travelers' Hamam Fantasies 67
Lady Montagu Visits the Hamam 76
Harem Suare: Fictions within Fictions 81
Hamam: The Official Tour Guide Version 85
After Sex Is before Sex: The Hamam as Sacred Space of Transition 90
Hamam: Architecture of Seduction 96
Archives of Feeling: *Hamam*'s Queer Temporality 102

II. Istanbul and the Queer Stage

3. "But we are all androgynous:" James Baldwin's Staging America in Turkey .. 113
Speaking from Another Place 113
The Reluctant Queer 116
Stranger in the City 118
Freaks at the Welcome Table 121

4. **"Built for Europeans who came on the Orient Express:"**
   Queer Desires of Extravagant Strangers in Sinan Ünel's *Pera Palas* 129
   "a fucking palace:" Grand Hotel 129
   "Where memory is, theatre is:" Harem as Memorial 136
   "a place without a place:" Queer Space.. 142
   "A kiss is just a kiss?" Extravagant Strangers 150

III. Transnational Queer Poetics

5. **"The Wonder of Thy Beauty:" Bayard Taylor's *Poems of the Orient***
   as an Intermediary Between German Romanticism and American Gentility .. 163
   The Arabian Indifference to Time—Moving From East to West 163
   From West to East to West—Cross-Cultural Counterpoints 165
   "Wahlheimatliteratur"—Taylor Reading Rückert Reading Goethe 168
   "Unwinding the Turban:" *Poems of the Orient* as American Pastoral 174
   Emblematic Male Oriental Beauty—Emulating Hafiz 181
   Taylor's Travels to the Orient—Expanding Genteel Expectations 185

6. **Bastardized History: Elif Shafak's Transcultural Poetics** 193
   Comic Survival or the Endless Repeat Melody 193
   Elegiac Metropolis or "A Bridge in Between" 199
   Edible City, or the Etho-Poetics of Food and Sex 206

IV. Performing Queer Turkish Cultures

7. **Precarious Masculinities in the New Turkish Cinema** 217
   From Yeşilçam to New Turkish Cinema:
   Black Turks and Nationalist Masculinity 219
   Precarious Masculinities in the New Turkish-German Cinema:
   The Melodramatic Penis and Trans-Masculinity 224

8. **Arabesk: Nomadic Tales, Oriental Beats, and Hybrid Looks** 237
   Arabesk's Impurity: From Anatolia to Istanbul 238
   From Tatlıses's Nostalgic Anatolian Machismo to Emrah's Sexed-Up Hard Body 242
   Flamboyant Transgression? Bülent Ersoy.. 245
   Orientalized Pop-Export: Tarkan 249

This book is dedicated to my Istanbulite friends and students.

Introduction

Early June 2016. I was invited to attend a symposium on Turkish-American Studies in Istanbul.¹ Reluctantly, I agreed to join. My reluctance was not because of disinterest or bad time management, on the contrary. I longed to return to Istanbul, where I had spent four of the most challenging but rewarding years of my life. I also wished to reconnect to some of my friends and colleagues from that period. My reluctance, instead, was due to the political situation in Turkey. I had heard rumors—soon substantiated—about Turkish colleagues being discharged, some of them having to clear their desks overnight. I know of at least two of my former colleagues—one from Bulgaria, the other from the United States—having had to leave the country, or even having been threatened with imprisonment. It was unclear to me what the reasons for such sudden and drastic measures were, but I was aware of a sense of imminent threat that many of my colleagues in Turkey felt, unrelated to any specific action that would bring them under political suspicion. I asked myself whether I had done anything that would bring me in danger if I were to reenter the country. Might scholarly writing about Turkey have turned into a risky business?

At the last minute, I did attend the conference. Without regrets. It was a happy reunion with old friends, and an opportunity to make new ones. Istanbul to me seemed not very changed. I registered a heightened military presence, but I had seen that before. I could move freely. Istikal Avenue was thriving with tourists and shoppers, and the nightlife was booming in Cihangir. All

---

1   The symposium took place at the Istanbul Office of the American Research Institute in Turkey (ARIT) in June 3-4, 2016. It was organized by Belma Baskett, Anthony Greenwood, Louis Mazzari, and Gönül Pultar on behalf of ARIT and the Cultural Studies Association of Turkey. The proceedings were published as *The Turkish-American Conundrum: Immigrants and Expatriates between Politics and Culture* (2019), which includes my own contribution on James Baldwin's theatrical endeavors in Istanbul, reprinted here.

seemed the same from what I had seen a decade before. And yet, the people I met at the conference confirmed that colleagues of theirs had been dismissed without notice and that they worked under the constant strain of surveillance and suspicion. Former colleagues from the university I had taught at were in fear of losing their jobs and were already looking for new ones. Soon after, on 23 June 2016, the university—one of 15 universities across the country to be impacted by the "biggest purge in Turkey's modern history" (Lowen)—would be closed down altogether due to alleged entanglements with the Fethullah Gülen Movement, which had been declared a terrorist organization by the government and therefore a threat to national security.[2] The closure led to issuing detention warrants for more than 170 university employees and the displacement of all of its students ("Fatih University Report;" "More than 50").[3]

July 2016. During the night of July 15th, only a month after I hesitantly attended the symposium, another coup d'état would be added to the long list of military coups in the Turkish republic's history. The military instigated an unfortunate and futile revolt on the Bosphorus Bridge, and five days after the failed coup President Recep Tayyip Erdoğan declared the state of emergency, which would enable him to eliminate internal enemies. In this speech, he moreover announced: "We will also build the historical replica of those barracks in Taksim, whether they want it or not" ("Erdoğan Topçu Kışlasında Israrcı," qtd. in Çıdam 370), implicitly acknowledging that after three years and even after the coup attempt, "he still considered the democratic protest that took place in Taksim's Gezi Park as the most significant challenge to his popularly supported authoritarian rule" (Çıdam 370). The state of emergency officially ended in 2018, but the legacy of that 'emergency'—the toxic climate of fear and retribution with its reinforced political measures and continuing

---

[2] Gülen, the supposed mastermind behind the 2016 coup, has lived in self-imposed exile in the United States since 1999. As Lowen explains, the Gülen Movement "was once close to President Recep Tayyip Erdogan—Islamists reshaping a constitutionally secular country. But from 2013 they fell out badly. Gulen followers within the police and intelligence services were blamed for orchestrating phone leaks that appeared to implicate Mr. Erdogan and his inner circle in corruption." Fatih University was closed and the institution's assets seized based on a decree "ordering the closure of 15 Turkish universities, in connection with a state of emergency declared by the government following the failed coup attempt on July 15" ("15 Universities Shut Down").

[3] At least one former professor of Fatih University and journalist of the *Zamam* daily newspaper, Ahmet Metin Sekizkardeş, was sentenced to nine years and is still in prison ("Former Professor;" "In a Secret Document;" "Ahmet Metin Sekizkardeş").

arrests and purges—still now holds the country in a tight grip. As I am writing this introduction, press releases continue to inform about discriminatory measures by the Turkish government against women, artists, regime critics, and queers.[4]

Based on my 4-year-stay in Istanbul (2004-2008), working at a very conservative private university, and witnessing the climax of queer visibility before Erdoğan's repressive politics took hold, this book reflects on various manifestations of queer culture and their interaction with transnational, especially European and American cultural contexts. Turkey, seemingly forever on the verge of joining the European Union and yet as far away from succeeding as ever, has become a symbol of how the West perceives the Muslim Orient. And while there are several books treating German-Turkish cultural relations (especially with a focus on Turkish-German immigration), there are

---

4   The stage actor and theater director Genco Erkal (winner of the Silver Bear—Special Jury Prize at the 33rd Berlin International Film Festival 1983), for example, is one of 174.000 persons and one of the latest victims being accused of insulting the Turkish president ("Acclaimed Turkish Actor;" Höhler). Cenk Özbay mentions as example of the "state homophobia" in Turkey the shutdown of the LGBTI Student Club at Boğaziçi University early 2021 as policing measure against protests that called on the rector Melih Bulu—newly appointed by President Erdoğan—to resign. Press announcements by the Istanbul Governorship linked the protests to terrorism and detained students from the protests. Özbay, however, also asserts "participatory and resilient queer politics" emerging in Turkey that give reasons "to be cautiously optimistic" ("Boğaziçi University Protests"), amongst them are queer representatives in the opposition Republican People's Party (CHP) and People's Democratic Party (HDP), numerous municipalities celebrating Pride Week in their official social media platforms, popular activism through hashtag "#LGBTIhaklariinsanhaklaridir" (#LGBTIrightsarehumanrights), and the increasing number of sociological and historical publications on queer lives in Turkey. (On the history of the queer movement and its representation in political parties in Turkey, see Çetin 25.) Also, in view of rising homophobia and gender-based violence in Turkey, the country's decision early 2021 to leave the Istanbul Convention against women and domestic violence gave cause for concern and was seen as pointing to a terrifying trend across Europe: "10 years ago, Turkey was the first country to sign the convention. But the continuing ban on Pride Month since 2015 and subsequent public threats have caused growing violence against the LGBTQ+ community. [...] Unfortunately, the argument that LGBTQ+ people are [a] threat to traditional values, has been rehashed and emulated by politicians in the EU such as in Hungary and Poland where symbols of LGBTQ+ pride are increasingly subject to political weaponisation" ("Turkey Leaves the Istanbul Convention"); see also "Council of Europe Leaders;" "Turkey to Pull Out."

very few dealing with Turkey in a broader Euro-American cultural perspective, and even less with a focus on queerness. Therefore, this book wants to contribute to a still new, but expanding field of interrogation.

While my own view as German-American scholar—although in itself bicultural—necessarily remains Western and thus presumably unwillingly culturally biased, my approaches take on various standpoints, sometimes closer to a Turkish perspective, at other times closer to a Euro-American perspective, sometimes more based on personal experience, at other times with a more distanced scholarly stance. In each of the chapters, however, the intercultural relations—both in terms of standpoint and subject matter—will be stressed. Questions that I will concern myself with include: How are Turkish artists representing themselves within their own culture as well as within a foreign setting? How do Westerners depict their encounters with Turkish culture, and how do Turks perceive those very same encounters in their homeland and abroad? What stereotypes are at work in both instances? What efforts in intercultural negotiation and transnational understanding are being made to understand and overcome such stereotypes?

With my scholarly background in literary criticism, cultural studies, and genderqueer theory, this book reflects both my established academic interests, and my scholarly and sociocultural experience in Istanbul. So there are chapters where my my specific circumstances as a gay man living in a country where homosexuality is not officially illegal but only precariously subsists, come into play.[5] The film and literature analyses, in contrast, are based on and interact with both Eastern and Western gender and cultural theories, and are deliberately written from more distanced, theoretically induced perspectives. This mixed approach hopefully appeals to a diverse audience cutting across the borders of academe alone. My specific aim therefore is to come to an understanding of how to negotiate obvious differences and hidden similarities between East and West in the realms of culture and ethics, gender and sexualities.

---

5   In a study on the views of young adult learners of English regarding homosexuality, Ordem and Ulum reveal that although there seems to be an increasing openness towards homosexuality and willingness to discuss queer issues on the side of students, the "Council of Higher Education (CHE) in Turkey banned discussing gender diversity at universities in 2019 by stating that negotiating gender diversity might be a threat to Turkish culture and family culture [...]. Therefore, Islamic values are often reinforced in education systems of Turkey" (35).

Like other transnationally oriented works on Turkey, *Queer Turkey* does not take 'Turkish' "to represent a timeless, static, or essential ethnic category," as Verena Laschinger writes in her introduction to a special journal issue on Turkish-American literature. Instead, it understands Turkish, Turkish-American, or German-Turkish "as social constructs, which are carved out of political, social, and ideological conflicts [...], (re-)imagined, negotiated, embraced, or dismissed, which hence leaves them continually developing and changing" (Laschinger 117). Furthermore, *Queer Turkey* does not claim any such thing as Turkey being queer, becoming queer, or coming out as queer. 'Queer,' instead, points to "lapses and excesses of meaning" within an "open net of possibilities," as queer theorist Eve Kosofsky Sedgwick (8) famously articulated. Challenging notions of the 'normal' and thus sexual and gendered labelling and taxonomies, *Queer Turkey* partakes in queer theorists' effort to view the sex/gender system as contextual and changeable. In this book, I aim to take objectives of queer theory to consider moments and effects of Turkish queerness. Such objectives, as Michelle Marzullo explains, include "to examine and critique the social processes that shape and normalize sexual and gendered identities, social relations, and expectations around culturally salient power axes such as gender, race, class, religion, ethnicity, and nationality" (696). 'Queer,' as Judith Butler reminds us, relies on its instability, on being called into being ("outness") and at the same time questioning that being by asking questions such as: "For whom is outness a historically available and affordable option? [...] Who is represented by which use of the term, and who is excluded? [...] What kinds of policies are enabled by what kinds of usages, and which are backgrounded or erased from view?" (227).

In my queer agenda, I might be subject to a discourse of the "Gay International" that, according to Joseph Andoni Massad, in its missionary and liberatory agenda aims to "liberate Arab and Muslim 'gays and lesbians' from the oppression under which they allegedly live by transforming them from practitioners of same-sex contact into subjects who identify as homosexual and gay" (362). For Massad, organizations such as the ILGA (International Lesbian and Gay Association) and the IGLHRC (International Gay and Lesbian Human Rights Commission, since 2015 called OutRight Action International) partake in this Orientalist impulse and crusading efforts that "continue[] to guide all branches of the human rights community" (362) to provide "proof of cross-cultural, cross-class gay identity, but in reality there is no evidence of gay movements anywhere in the Arab world or even of gay group identity outside of the small groups of men in metropolitan areas such as Cairo and

Beirut" (373). H. Burcu Baba, however, takes note of Massad's admonition as a dangerous discourse when she writes that "under the guise of 'Gay Global'" (59) dissident sexualities around the world are depicted as emanating from the West. She cites Massad as an example of those "who [criticize] the LGBT organizations in the Arab World and without distinguishing among organizations, their demands and efforts [...] have a destructive effect on LGBT people in those countries" (63, Fn 22).[6]

I am aware that many consider "LGBT" an outdated acronym that no longer represents the range of individuals that the rainbow coalition is supposed to serve. As legal scholar Marie-Amélie George comments, for "queer, intersex, asexual, and other identity groups, the LGBT initials that once signaled solidarity and intersectionality have come to seem limiting because they only identify certain subgroups" (245-246). In this book, I will use LGBT mostly when referring to activism, social movements, and human rights issues. Moreover, since I consider myself a researcher who from its onset in the 1990s has embraced queer theory, I like to stick to the term 'queer' in its expansive meaning, applicable to anyone—like myself—who is non-normative, not heterosexual or cisgender, including lesbians, gay men, asexual, transgender, and intersex people. I have always felt comfortable with reclaiming the slur "queer" as a liberating term for someone—myself—who does not conform to traditional gender roles. I do realize, however, especially when being occasionally addressed by students, that people still continue to be negatively affected by the term 'queer' as a derogatory expression meant to hurt. It is clearly not my intention to cause discomfort to anybody identifying with the LGBTQIA2S+ community. On the contrary, as an avowedly queer researcher, my scholarly agenda includes raising and addressing issues that have caused harm to queer people in different times and places as well as highlighting advocates, artists, writers, individuals, who in their own ways—and there are many!—have fought sexual and other forms of discrimination, have chosen non-normative life-styles, have made queerness essential to their art. Accordingly, the chapters of this book deal with various, highly selective—and thus not encompassing—facets of Turkish queerness, and especially with the ways that artists from different realms of cultural production reclaim and shape such queerness within and through their works.

---

6   For a comparative analysis of (distorted, scandalizing, and uninformed) representations of queerness in Turkish and German journalism, see Bayramoğlu.

Some of the artists that are discussed in *Queer Turkey* join those artists who even reclaim "queer" as a necessity not only to deal with LGBT themes in their work, but to make art that is quintessentially queer. As Megan Carney, About Face Theatre's artistic director in Chicago, states: "I think of queerness as a way to disrupt, reimagine, and liberate our bodies and minds—we need to tell more stories that reveal the nuances of our identities and desires." She continues: "We must remember that not all queer people benefited from the recently won policy battles, especially trans-folks and queer people of color. That said, I think everyone in our extended communities feels vulnerable and galvanized to act right now" (qtd. in Small 69). Similarly, Manhattan-based writer-performer Diana Oh sees a queer aesthetic as fighting against silencing and belittling, as countering queerphobic language and rhetoric: "We are innovators, trailblazers, and out-of-the-box thinkers. We know what it's like to live in a society that chokes us, and our art is pushing back by screaming for liberation. The queer aesthetic is not quiet" (qtd. in Small 70). Self-described "queer fate babe and *bruja*" theater artist Cristina Pitter even pushes queer aesthetics into the realm of the utopic, when in her personal manifesto she puts the call for a queer ideology in extravagantly florid words: "Queer aesthetic—what a whirlwind of color, vibrations, exhilaration, raw energy, and magic. The power of a fist held high, wrapped in fishnet glory and boots strapped up, or the fierce walk of a sleek black suit, heels, and mischievous eye. The soft femme fur of legs unshaved or the perfect polish on his fingernails. Queerness is more than sexuality and gender. I believe it's a political statement, a way of living and loving relentlessly, of knowing pain and violence and our history of existence—but still fighting for a better world" ("cristinapitter"). While all these statements come from North American artists, they reflect concerns that I see mirrored in the Turkish artists I discuss in this book. In his Hop-Çiki-Yaya series, for example, about a fabulous, unnamed transvestite detective, Mehmet Murat Somer, whom I briefly mention in chapter 1 and who would deserve much more consideration, has created a character that is truly queer. Somer reclaims "Hop-Çiki-Yaya," a Turkish derogatory term for queer people derived from a cheerleading chant popular in Turkish colleges in the 1960s. In this sense, Somer employs "Hop-Çiki-Yaya" in a way similar to LGBT activists, who have reverted the word 'queer' from an insult used to oppress and terrorize into a term of empowerment and subversion. I also invoke the highly disputed film *Hamam* by Turkish-Italian director Ferzan Özpetek as an example of the productive ambiguities that queer approaches can offer when discussing contexts that transcend an East-West chasm. I agree with Bill Marshall's assessment that such a film reminds us "that all identities are lived and indeed created in a tension between forces, and that political or other assertions or strategies are always dialogic" (7). As contradictory as "queer" may be, employing queerness as a critical lens need not lead to a regressive 'cultural imperialist' stance that takes West and East as oppositional, non-contradictory cultural, social, and political entities. Rather, queering the contexts of such a film through spatiotemporal considerations reminds us of the "different embeddings of modernity and tradition [and] the ways in which symbolic formations such as nations, ethnicities and diasporas are marked by hierarchical (hetero)sexual binaries whose normativities can be disrupted and undone, and realities reformulated and rewritten" (Marshall 7).

Queer Turkey assembles impressions, notes, and essays of the last fifteen years. The first part "Queer Istanbul" contains two interlinked chapters on aspects of queer lives in Istanbul. These chapters are the most personal, since partly based on my own experience, and as in the case of the chapter on the hamam grown over the years from various earlier versions. The first chapter starts with experiencing the Eurovision Song Contest in a gay bar in Istanbul and continues with thoughts about the history of Turkey's queer community. Ever since Turkey's inception as a modernized, secular nation, political efforts to forge a national identity were at odds with social practices that successfully subverted such efforts. Istanbul's LGBT community managed the paradoxical feat of embracing transnational notions of queerness while staking out sites of resistance, exemplified in this chapter in the vagaries of Istanbulite night life. This blending and interlacing of subversion alongside tradition instead of against it has led to a precariously flourishing, but greatly contradictory queer capital—Istanbul—where the modern and tradition, the rural and the urban, the margin and the center, and above all gay and straight merges into a hotbed of contemporary queerness at the crossroads of East and West. The following chapter enquires into what (really) goes on in a Turkish bathhouse. Taking the film *Hamam* by Turkish-Italian director Ferzan Özpetek as starting point, this chapter aims at examining the emergence and status quo of queer Istanbul. When the film *Hamam* was screened in Turkey, there was a great outcry claiming that this was a totally distorting, Orientalizing, and wholly untrue account of what goes on in a traditional Turkish bath, namely illicit sexuality between men. The movie's true scandal, however, was not the depiction of male nudity and intimacy as such, but the public disclosing of a strictly tabooed homosocial and indeed longstanding homosexual practice. While homosexuality is not forbidden by law in Turkey, it nevertheless still does not exist in an acknowledged social space, unless perhaps in the very marginalized and stigmatized practice of cross-dressing and transsexuality. Recent developments like the emergence of a queer club scene in cities like Istanbul, Izmir, and Bodrum notwithstanding, the fact remains that coming out of the closet proves to be an extremely painful, if not impossible act for many Turks. The chapter traces the history and discourse of same-sex male sexuality in Turkey by also considering historical and contemporary examples of depictions of same-sex female intimacy such as Lady Mary Wortley Montagu's eighteenth-century *Turkish Embassy Letters* and Özpetek's historical film *Harem suare*.

The section "Istanbul and the Queer Stage" looks at two examples of staging Istanbulite queerness, both viewed from a transnational perspective. The first of the two chapters follows James Baldwin's years in Istanbul that have left tangible traces in both his works written during that period and his interactions with local culture and people. Especially his engagement with theater while in Turkey led to the creation of Leo Proudhammer, the actor-protagonist of his novel *Tell Me How Long the Train's Been Gone*, the conception of his last play *The Welcome Table*, and the staging of John Herbert's *Fortune and Man's Eyes* in Istanbul. All three instances are imbued with Baldwin's notion of sexuality being intricately linked to race and nation. Contrary to many criticisms concerning his assumed political ineptness resulting from his geographical distance from American affairs, it is precisely through his self-chosen removed perspective that Baldwin could stay in touch with his Americanness. Only by a self-declared "seeing from a distance" could he emerge as key player in commenting on the American racial condition, and during much of the 1960s it was Istanbul that served for him as a transatlantic queer space where he could successfully juggle the intricacies of identity politics. The second chapter of this section centers around the Pera Palace Hotel in Istanbul that has long been a site of transnational interest. Already its original intent when built in 1892 was to host passengers of the Orient Express and its nickname as the "oldest European hotel of Turkey" aptly reflects this heritage. It has been the setting of Anglophone world literature such as Ernest Hemingway's "The Snow of Kilimanjaro," Graham Greene's *Travels with My Aunt*, and perhaps most famously Agatha Christie's *Murder on the Orient Express*. But the hotel also reflects Turkey's own turbulent history from Istanbul's luxurious Belle Époque to the oftentimes nostalgic luxury of a postmodern metropolis with Room 101 being converted into a memorial for Atakürk, the founder of modern Turkey, thus designating the space as museum-hotel. *Pera Palas* (1998), the play by Turkish-

American playwright Sinan Ünel that is the centerpiece of this chapter, is a complex spatiotemporal interlacing of the hotel's/nation's history with that of a Turkish family and their Anglo-American friends and lovers encompassing the 1920s via the 1950s to present time. Intermingling East and West, past and present, Islam and Christianity, traditionalists and feminists, hetero- and homosexuality, this play is at once a multifarious love story and a polylogic diasporic tale.

The third section "Transnational Queer Politics" features two writers' transnational queer poetics regarding their portrayal of Turkey: Bayard Taylor and Elif Shafak. A traveller from America to Arabian countries could very well pass through Germany. It is this track that nineteenth-century travel writer and poet Bayard Taylor took. Not only did he physically pass through Germany on his way east; in his ethically and aesthetically envisioning the Orient, he also fundamentally relied on Germany's Oriental reception. His Oriental travel accounts and above all his own Oriental poetry thus reflect Taylor's actual encounter *with* the East as well as his engagement with German literature *on* the East. Addressing his home audience from abroad (and later at home with lecture tours), Taylor through his writing held a prominent position in mid-nineteenth century as mediator in the triangular constellation America, Germany, and the Orient. At the same time, through his employing the cultural standards of Genteel America, Taylor managed to sidestep the condescending colonial and imperialist attitude that characterized much of European Orientalist literature of the nineteenth century. With her fifth novel of 2004, *The Saint of Insipient Insanities*, Turkish writer Elif Shafak entered the plane of transnational literature, since this novel is not only originally written in English, it also is set mainly in east-coast metropolitan North America. She has continued writing in English and her highly disputed sixth novel of 2007, *The Bastard of Istanbul*, with its predominantly urban setting of Istanbul but also of Tucson, Arizona, and San Francisco could be said to be a counter piece to *The Saint* in its Turkish-American connection. In both of these English-language novels, Shafak deals with the questioning of ethnicity and nationality from postcolonial and global perspectives, and thus on the one hand departing from her narrower focus on Turkish cultural history of her earlier novels, but on the other hand suggesting to read post-Ottoman Turkey's national setting against the backdrop of postcolonial national histories across the world.

The final section "Performing Queer Turkish Cultures" returns to some of the issues raised in the first section and continues concerns of raising issues of desire and ethics within trans-Turkish settings. The first of the two chapters looks at the development of the New Turkish Cinema. The enormous media attention attributed to the prize-winning film *Gegen die Wand* (*Head-On*) by German-Turkish director Fatih Akin has drawn critical attention to the diversity of cultural perceptions both from a European and a Turkish perspective. Whereas former and solely German productions like Hark Bohm's *Yasemin* still rely on stereotypical representations of clannish Turkish families and the influential films of Turkish director Yücel Çakmaklı aim at emphasizing a national Anatolian-Muslim morality, recent co-produced films like the ones by Italian-Turkish director Ferzan Özpetek and Fatih Akin deliberately question fixed notions of Turkish identity in an increasingly mobile, migrant and 'Europeanized' Turkey. Through their films, these directors take part in the popular culture movement of the so-called New Turkish Cinema that with its Arabesk, urban visual style distances itself from earlier dominant, rural and traditionalist Turkish film productions. Central to an understanding of the agenda of this cinema in particular and of the general changes in Turkish society, it implies the changing representation of male honor from a long-established protective nationalist principle toward a more flexible, tolerant attitude. This change in turn stands for a gradual dissolving of deep-rooted generational as well as class and gender-based family ethics, thus speaking for a broader cultural hybridization of Turkish traditions. The final chapter continues the discussion of Arabesk in its transnational appeal. Turkish pop music has entered the international charts, having progressed from Oriental sounds to dance-pop. Tarkan, whose music style and performance mixes belly-dance, rap, break-dance, Turkish classical music and Western pop, is but one example of a booming pop-culture in Turkey, centered in Istanbul's clubbing scene and present in every household throughout the country. And yet, as unlikely as it may seem when viewed solely from a Western perspective, where Tarkan figures as thoroughly Westernized and highly sexualized Orient-export, his music is actually rooted in the Turkish tradition of Arabesk culture. This culture has emerged on the fringes of Istanbul, where the traditional culture of immigrants blends with urban culture. The epithet Arabesk at first described a hybrid musical genre in the early 1970s and acquired immense popularity among low-income populations in Istanbul. Arabesk then was used as derogatory label; the music was banned from state radio and television for defying the established—and pure—canons of both folk and classical Turkish music by intermixing rhythms and instruments from poplar Western and Arabic, especially Egyptian music. With Arabesk singers like Orhan

Gencebay, Ferdi Tayfur, Müslüm Gürses, and Mahsun Kırmızıgül soon acquiring cult status, the label has come to denote not only a musical genre, but a film genre as well as the cultural habitus and lifestyle of its fans. Thus, today Arabesk means impurity, hybridity and bricolage, and it even designates a special kind of kitsch. In anthropologist Mary Douglas's terms, this is a polluted and polluting style, and in literary critic Susan Sontag's terminology, its banal, trashy and kitsch style would qualify as camp. Arabesk, therefore, has become a postmodernist phenomenon *par excellence* with its mixture of high and low styles, its mass-consumption, its transgression of class and race distinctions, and its overriding the division between rural and urban culture. Bemoaned by many as expressing the significant identity problem of contemporary Turkish society, it is hailed by others as symbolizing the Turkish success story of merging East and West. This final chapter brings me back to the first in reflecting the tremendous changes within the notions of culture, gender, sexuality, and ethics in modern Turkey. Ever since Turkey has become a Republic in the early twentieth century, the country has struggled to balance the traditional codes of Muslim morality with the claim of becoming a modern, Westernized nation. Focussing especially on the changing gender and sexual relations in Turkey as well as on steadfast Western stereotypical notions of what 'goes on' between and amongst the sexes in that country, it is my book's claim to pay tribute to the currency of queer Turkish culture as transnational poetics of desire.

Being queer in Turkey and trying to convey the meaning of what that means is still not easy. As Cenk Özbay, one of the leading queer Turkish scholars asserts, Turkey remains a "sex-negative culture: it is considered immoral, forbidden, despicable and sinful to talk about sexuality or the sexual/reproductive/genital parts of the body in public" (*Queering Sexualities* 4). Thus unsurprisingly, given such a sex-negative culture, Özbay finds that "homosexuality is one of the most poisonous social taboos in the twenty-first century, even among the most modern, secular and well-educated classes of Turkish society" (5). Queer people in twenty-first century Turkey, i.e. a country in which homosexuality is legal and yet subject to police harassment, experience a "double life," because on the one hand, the Turkish state and arguably large parts of the society are becoming more conservative, religious, and oppressive. "On the other hand, same-sex sexualities are performed as they are tolerated within the zones of exception, especially in certain neighbourhoods of the major metropolitan areas," which in turn leads to a "double configuration of same-sex sexual cultures, tolerance and intolerance, respect and intervention, freedom and restriction, grassroots diversity and super-imposed uniformity" (Özbay, *Queering Sexuality* 16). But Turkey's state-controlled homophobia is also part of a worldwide rise of neoliberal and conservative politics that has reached many countries such as the United States, Russia, Poland, and Hungary. Women's and LGBT organizations in these countries as well as in Turkey continue to fight against increasing governmental authoritarianism and society polarization.[7] *Queer Turkey* is meant as a contribution to that fight.

My thanks and gratitude go to my former colleagues in Turkey, many of which—like me—came when Fatih University opened its gates to include an international staff: Verena Laschinger (thanks for not only sharing an apartment with me in Istanbul but for continuous reassurance; special thanks for allowing me to use one of her marvelous Istanbul photos for the cover of this book), Martin Cyr Hicks (thanks for sharing countless nightly conversations and Efes' with me), Kevin McGinley, Terence Powers, Clyde Forsberg, Louis Mazzari, Sheenagh Pietrobruno, John Toohey, Vassil Anastassov, Jeffrey Orr, James Lambo, Jane McGettigan, Huma Ibrahim, Elizabeth Pallitto, and Joshua Parker, now my dear colleague in Salzburg, whom I still have the pleasure of sharing a professional and personal friendship with.

I was lucky and honored to have met very special people in Istanbul: Gökhan Pehlivan, Hüseyin Karagöz, David Rolland, Özgür Güler, Tayfur Düzağaç, Seval Arslan, Dilek Uner (whose yoga space was a safe haven for me). I remain grateful to Beril Erkut for introducing me to Reiki.

Without the love and deep friendship of those who supported me from afar, I could not have lasted: my parents Doris and Leo Poole, Annette Keck, Johannes Stricker, Peter Velte, Frank Völker, Sylvia Miescowski, and many more.

Special thanks to Karin Wohlgemuth, who is always there to organize and gently push me; Ioana-Mihaela Cozac and Michael Taylor, who helped me with the final stages of the manuscript.

My heart reaches out to Wolfgang Schulz, who stood by me in these Istanbul years, and still stands close.

---

7   See, for example, the queer-feminist perspectives on Turkey "Yeter! Es reicht!," a series of German and Turkish texts by Sibel Schick and Tebessüm Yılmaz instigated by the Rosa-Luxemburg-Stiftung (<www.rosalux.de>).

Works Cited

"15 Universities Shut Down in Connection with State of Emergency." Scholars at Risk Network. 26 July 2016. Web. 10 Aug 2021. <https://www.scholarsatrisk.org/2016/07/15-universities-shut-connection-state-emergency/>

"Acclaimed Turkish Actor Sued for 'Insulting President' with Twitter Posts." *Arab News.* 17 April 2021. Web. 30 Aug 2021. <https://www.arabnews.com/node/1844451/amp>

"Ahmet Metin Sekizkardeş, Türkei, in Haft seit 2016." *Wahrheitskämpfer: Portraits ermordeter und verfolgter Journalisten.* n.d. Web. 10 Aug 2021. <http://wahrheitskaempfer.de/portfolio/ahmet-metin-sekizkardes-tuerkei-in-haft-seit-2016>

"Council of Europe Leaders React to Turkey's Announced Withdrawal from the Istanbul Convention." Web. 6 Nov 2021. <https://www.coe.int/en/web/istanbul-convention/newsroom>

"cristinapitter." Web. 11 Aug 2021. <https://www.cristinapitter.com/press>

"Erdoğan Topçu Kışlasında Israrcı." *Deutsche Welle Türkçe.* 19 July 2016. Web. 10 Aug 2021. <http://www.dw.com/tr/erdo%C4%9Fan-top%C3%A7u-k%C4%B1%C5%9Flas%C4%B1nda-%C4%B1srarc%C4%B1/a-19409185>

"Fatih University Report." Academic Solidarity Initiative (ASI). Web. 10 Aug 2021. <www.academicsolidarity.com/en/fatih-university-report-2-eng/>

"Former Professor of Fatih University Sentenced to 9 Years in Prison—Still in Jail." Committee of Concerned Scientists. 1 Jan 2020. Web. 10 Aug 2021. <https://concernedscientists.org/2020/01/former-professor-of-fatih-university-sentenced-to-9-years-in-prison-still-in-jail/>

"In a Secret Document, Turkey Admitted Jailing Dozens of Journalists While Sticking to Policy of Denial in Public." Stockholm Center for Freedom. 12 May 2021. Web. 10 Aug 2021. <https://stockholmcf.org/in-a-secret-document-turkey-admitted-jailing-dozens-of-journalists-while-sticking-to-policy-of-denial-in-public/>

"More than 50 Fatih University Staff, Including Academics, Detained in Istanbul." *Hürriyet Daily News.* 27 Dec 2017. Web. 10 Aug 2021. <https://www.hurriyetdailynews.com/more-than-50-fatih-university-staff-including-academics-detained-in-istanbul-124816>

"Turkey Leaves the Istanbul Convention Despite Calls to 'Stop the Withdrawal!' by Civil Society." Web. 6 Nov 2021. <https://europeangreens.eu/news/turkey-leaves-istanbul-convention>

"Turkey to Pull Out of Istanbul Convention on Violence Against Women." Web. 6 Nov 2021. <https://www.dw.com/en/turkey-to-pull-out-of-istanbul-convention-on-violence-against-women/a-58114681>

Amnesty International. "Gezi Park Protests: Brutal Denial of the Right to Peaceful Assembly in Turkey." 2 Oct 2013. Web. 10 Aug 2021. <https://www.amnesty.org/download/Documents/12000/eur440222013en.pdf>

Atalay, Ozlem, and Petra L. Doan. "Reading the LGBT Movement through its Spatiality in Istanbul, Turkey." *Geography Research Forum* 39 (2019): 106-126.

Baba, H. Burcu. "The Construction of Heteropatriachal Family and Dissident Sexualities in Turkey." *Fe Dergi* 3.1 (2011): 56-64.

Bayramoğlu, Yener. *Queere (Un-)Sichtbarkeiten: Die Geschichte der queeren Repräsentationen in der türkischen und deutschen Boulevardpresse*. Bielefeld: transcript, 2018.

Butler, Judith. *Bodies That Matter: On the Discursive Limits of "Sex."* London: Routledge, 1993.

Çetin, Zülfukar. "The Dynamics of the Queer Movement in Turkey." 28 Sep 2015. Heinrich Böll Stiftung: The Green Political Foundation. Web. 27 June 2021. <https://www.boell.de/en/2015/09/28/die-dynamik-der-queer-bewegung-der-turkei>

Çıdam, Çiğdem. "Unruly Practices: Gezi Protests and the Politics of Friendship." *New Political Science* 39.3 (2017): 369-392.

Erol, A. E. "Queer Contestation of Neoliberal and Heteronormative Moral Geographies During #ocupygezi." *Sexualities* 21.3 (2018): 428-445.

George, Marie-Amélie. "Expanding LGBT." *Florida Law Review* 73 (2021): 243-319.

Höhler, Gerd. "Recep Tayyip Erdogan: Der beleidigte Präsident". *Salzburger Nachrichten*. 26 Aug. 2021. Web. 30 Aug 2021. <https://www.sn.at/politik/weltpolitik/recep-tayyip-erdogan-der-beleidigte-praesident-108512890>

Laschinger, Verena. "An Introduction to Turkish-American Literature." *Amerikastudien / American Studies*. "Turkish-American Literature." Ed. Verena Laschinger, 61.2 (2016). 113-119.

Lowen, Mark. "Turkey Post-Coup Purges Convulse Society." *BBC News*. 3 Oct 2016. Web. 10 Aug 2021. <https://www.bbc.com/news/world-europe-37517735>

Marzullo, Michelle A. "LGBT/Queer Sexuality, History of, North America." *The International Encyclopedia of Human Sexuality*. Ed. Patricia Whelehan et al. Malden: Wiley-Blackwell, 2015. 693-698.

Marshall, Bill. "Contextualisation, Part 1: Queer Cinema and the Global." *Image & Text* 32 (2018): 1-8. Web. 26 Oct 2021. <http://www.scielo.org.za/pdf/it/n32/02.pdf>

Massad, Joseph Andoni. "Re-Orienting Desire: The Gay International and the Arab World." *Public Culture* 14.2 (2002): 361-385.

Ordem, Eser, and Ömer Gökhan Ulum. "Gender Issues in English Language Teaching: Views from Turkey." *Acta Educationis Generalis* 10.2 (2020): 25- 39.

Özbay, Cenk. "Boğaziçi University Protests and State Homophobia in Turkey." 15 Feb 2021. Web. 26 Oct 2021. <https://cenkozbay.com/2021/02/23/bogazici-university-protests-and-state-homophobia-in-turkey/>

———. *Queering Sexualites in Turkey: Gay Men, Male Prostitutes and the City*. London and New York: I. B. Tauris, 2017.

Pultar, Gönül, Louis Mazzari, and Belma Ötüşet Baskett, eds. *The Turkish-American Conundrum: Immigrants and Expatriates between Politics and Culture*. Newcastle: Cambridge Scholars Publishing, 2019.

Sedgwick, Eve Kosofsky. "Queer and Now." *Tendencies*. Durham: Duke UP, 1993. 1-20.

Small, Zachary. "LGBTQ, Emphasis on the Q: A New Generation of Theatremakers is Ready to Blow Up the Gay Canon and Reclaim a Defiantly Queer Aesthetic." *American Theatre* 35.1 (208): 66-70.

Acknowledgments

These chapters have been published in earlier versions: "'the wonder of thy beauty:' Bayard Taylor's *Poems of the Orient* as an Intermediary Between German Poetics and American Ethics." *America and the Orient*. Ed. Heike Schäfer. Heidelberg: Winter, 2006. 73-102; "Arabesk: Nomadic Tales, Oriental Beats, and Hybrid Looks." *Dichotonies: Gender and Music*. Ed. Beate Neumeier. Heidelberg: Winter, 2009. 245-265; "Bastardized History: Elif Shafak's Transnational Poetics." *Transcultural Spaces: Challenges of Urbanity, Ecology, and the Environment in the New Millennium*. Eds. Stefan L. Brandt, Winfried Fluck and Frank Mehring. *Real: Yearbook of Research in English and American Literature* Vol. 26. Tübingen: Narr, 2010. 213-230; "Istanbul: Queer Desires Between Muslim Tradition and Global Pop." *Queer Cities, Queer Cultures: Europe Since 1945*. Eds. Matt Cook and Jennifer V. Evans. London et al.: Bloomsbury, 2014. 171-190; "Precarious Masculinities in the New Turkish Cinema." *Transnational Mediations: Negotiating Popular Culture between Europe and the United States*. Eds. Christof Decker and Astrid Böger. Heidelberg: Winter, 2015. 169-190; "'Built for Europeans who came on the Orient Express:' Queer Desires of Extravagant Strangers in Sinan Ünel's *Pera Palas*." *Amerikastudien / American Studies* 61.2 (2016): 159-180; "'One sees it better from a distance:' James Baldwin's Staging America in Turkey." *The Turkish-American Conundrum: Immigrants and Expatriates between Politics and Culture*. Eds. Gönül Pultar, Louis Mazzari and Belma Ötüşet Baskett. Newcastle: Cambridge Scholars Publishing, 2019. 153-168.

I. Queer Istanbul

1. Istanbul: Queer Desires Between Muslim Tradition and Global Pop

12 points

May 2005. It is hot, crowded and noisy. Everyone is singing, cheering, and dancing to the upbeat music from the huge screen. There is an overbearing sense of community with everybody drinking, sweating, and partying together. The atmosphere is charged with erotic energy. This is just a first impression, though. There is something strange about this picture.

I am in a bar in Istanbul—not so subtly called The Other Side[1]—surrounded mostly by men, mostly Turks, most in their early 20s. They are cheering for a song sung by a Greek performer: Helena Paparizou's "My Number One"—the 2005 winner of the Eurovision Song Contest. Greece was awarded the highest possible score of 12 points from multiple countries, including their Turkish neighbor. Why would a group of presumably exclusively gay men in a Turkish bar cheer for a Greek band, given the long-standing political animosity between the two nations and the fresh tension sparked by new controversies over Cyprus' role in Europe at the time? There is an easy answer: It is fun to be together, enjoy dance music, and flirt. But there is also a more intricate answer that needs additional explanation.

Growing up in Europe in the 1970s, it was a must for everyone to watch the Grand Prix Eurovision de la Chanson, as the annual Eurovision Song Contest (ESC) was called before its name was anglicized. Since its inception in 1956, the event has become a European institution, delineating one understanding of the European community. Originally with only seven participating countries, the contest has steadily grown, as has Europe. In 2012, 43 countries participated, making it necessary to divide the formerly one-night

---

1   The bar no longer exists.

event into two semi-finals and a final. In the course of time, the field has included most Eastern European countries as well as countries disregarded as European in other contexts: Israel and Turkey—since 1973 and 1975, respectively—among the first, and Armenia, Azerbaijan and Georgia among the later additions.² This can be seen as a means "of indicating a pro-European stance or a European affiliation" for these countries, often foreshadowing future membership in the EU (Motschenbacher 85). "Therefore," cultural historian Heiko Motschenbacher explains, "one can see the ESC as a musical test for what may lie ahead in politics. If certain countries can compete in a pop music competition, they may eventually try to cooperate on a political level." (86). For a long time, Turkey was without luck in the contest.

But a definite turning point for Turkey was the spectacular victory in May 2003, with many countries awarding it a full 12 points. After a quarter of a century of trying, and with much embarrassment, this was, as musicologist Thomas Solomon suggests, a "historical moment" (136). The failure to score points in the contest up to then has been perceived in Turkey "as an allegory of its aspirations to join the European Union and its frustratingly slow movement towards that goal, and proof of the perception, warranted or not, that Europeans do not accept Turkey as a European nation" (Solomon 136). The success of 2003 sparked new hope. Solomon makes a strong—not aesthetic, but political—claim that part of the sudden victory was due to Turkey's surprising opposition to the United States' wish for a military base in the southern region of Turkey as a point of invasion to northern Iraq. This resistance brought Turkey many sympathizers at a time of growing anti-war sentiment in continental Europe. But it was also Sertab Erener's song "Everyway that I can" with its hybrid musical aesthetics including English lyrics, Middle Eastern rhythms, and a mix of belly-dancing and hip-hop moves that "projected a Euro-friendly version of Turkey just at the time much of Europe was predisposed to be friendly with Turkey" (Solomon 145).³

So why did the gay crowd cheer for Helena Paparizou in that gay bar that evening? Certainly, there was an aesthetic point of comparison: "It seemed

---

2 For further developments of the ESC, see Poole, "Eurovision Song Contest."
3 As Matthew Gumpert states, "the ESC has *always* been a transparently political event, not only in the sense that singers are encouraged (according to the ESC rulebook) to reflect the national identity of the culture they represent, or in the way host nations use the opportunity (as they do at the Olympic Games) to export their own cultural capital, but in the voting process itself" (148).

that Greece found the right combination of a solid pop song, English lyrics, and 'ethnic' stylings in its music and performance, comparable in many ways to Sertab's 2003 performance" (Solomon 143). But this only very partially explains the hurrahs of my gay Turkish friends. More obviously, there was Helena's "highly polished" stage performance that contrasted to Sertab's fauxharem machinations (O'Connor 182). Helena was surrounded by four gorgeous, bare-chested male dancers. These boys not only looked very gay but, judging from the enthusiasm of the bar's crowd, the whole song-and-dance number exuded a distinct gay sensibility, much more so than Sertab's performance.

Both songs became immensely popular in Turkey in general and in the gay scene in particular; they highlighted the lasting appeal of the ESC for a gay male audience (Feddersen 60-65). All over Europe, the event is followed by its gay fans who often gather for celebratory parties hosted in gay bars. The contest has been called "Gay Christmas," a sort of holiday not unlike Gay Pride celebrations (Wolter 139). But the ESC does not transcend nationality; "rather, Eurovision provides a rare occasion for simultaneously celebrating both queerness and national identity" (Rehberg 60). Istanbul is no exception here, and yet it is only recently that such parties have been organized as part of a growing community and an increasingly visible queer urban scene. Istanbul, although not the political capital of the country, can clearly be considered its queer capital. The queer moments just described certainly link Istanbul to the social practices of other European queer metropoles. Yet still, between its recently resurfacing Ottoman past and the political backlash that comes with it, and the momentarily arrested precarious move towards a future membership in the EU, the largest Turkish city remains very much entangled in the nation's overall struggle to find a distinct cultural identity. Proceeding from this example of a local gay cultural practice in Istanbul's gay bar scene I will look at the way understanding and treating homosexuality have evolved in the nation in general, and in the city in particular. Three majorly radical, transitional periods in Turkish history, namely the founding of the Turkish Republic in 1923, the 1980 military coup d'état, and the Gezi protests will serve as a backdrop for a subsequent discussion of selected aspects of contemporary queer practice in Istanbul.

Turkey's Transitional Periods: Kemalist Modernization, Military Coups, Queer Activism

Speaking about homosexuality in Turkey proves to be an endeavor charged with ambiguities and paradoxes. A secular nation modelled on Western legal standards, Turkey also remains a predominantly Muslim society. Turkish homosexuality is located at the crossroads of both East and West with strict religious traditions competing against the claims of a secular nation state, and nowhere is this more obvious than in Istanbul, a city that not only in geographical terms is precariously located right on the East-West divide. For an understanding of the current situation of homosexuals in Turkey, it is necessary to acknowledge the profound change that Kemalism, that is, the project of modernization launched by the republic's founding father Mustafa Kemal Atatürk, and the ensuing concept of Turkish citizenship brought along. Since this project was conceived to oppose everything that the traditions of the Ottoman Empire entailed, its nationalist agenda can also be understood in sexual terms since "sexuality, family relations, and gender identities came to occupy a central place in discourses about modernity" (Kandiyoti, "Gendering the Modern" 114).

With women having to discard their veils and move out into the public, both radical renunciations of the Ottoman separation of genders (Poole, "Kopftuch"), the forcefully modernized man also had to adapt to a changed sexual discourse. On the upside, this meant for a woman hitherto unknown access to sites of education and work, on the downside an increased monitoring of her virtue and honor. And as for the changing concepts of masculinity, the dissolution of gendered spheres did not come along with a loosening of strictly divided sexual identities. On the contrary, masculinity was and still is "generally regarded as superior to femininity. Those who seek to live up to the former are expected to be sexually active, initiate sex and penetrate female or feminine bodies" (Szulc 17).

Whereas formerly, and by way of the division of spheres, the stronghold of homosociality may at times have included clandestinely tolerated homosexual practices, now both men and women were called upon to share all spheres making same-sex interactions more difficult and indeed unwanted. Modelled after Western conceptions of heteronormativity, the Kemalist project literally left no queer spaces. Pointing to the Turkish Constitution's Article 66 of 1982 ("Everyone bound to the Turkish state through the bond of citizenship is a Turk"), communication theorist Lukasz Szulc pointedly claims: "Every citizen of Turkey is a (straight) Turk" (11), and human rights defender Hakan Ataman adds that the "Kemalist perception of citizenship therefore excludes LGBT people in Turkey" (131).

The military has seen it as one of its prime goals to uphold the Kemalist ideology, even though acting mostly in the background. But the three coups of 1960, 1971, and 1980 prove the willingness of the military to intervene in governmental states of affairs, if the generals decide that the Kemalist ideals are in danger of being forsaken. Of the three coups, the 1980 takeover, which resulted in three years of strict military rule, had the strongest effects on the LGBT community in urban centers such as Istanbul and Ankara. There were severe restrictions for anyone not adhering to the Kemalist ideal of Turkish citizenship and especially for those deemed morally deviant and defiant. After a growing liberation and visibility of gays and lesbians during the 1960s and 1970s, nightclubs in these cities were now shut down, burgeoning gay organizations were banned, and transsexuals were imprisoned.[4]

Due to these extreme measures, however, new social movements gradually started to emerge as soon as the elected government had taken over again in 1983, among which was the founding of professional LGBT organizations. In 1993, the first Gay Pride Week was initially permitted and then banned at the very last minute, resulting in the arrest of 28 foreign delegates; the massive protest of activists that followed led to the launching of the first two Turkish LGBT organizations: Lambda Istanbul in the same year and Kaos GL in Ankara a year later (Gecim). The first Gay Pride Week then was celebrated in 2003, and in 2004 the first Gay and Lesbian Film Festival, OutIstanbul, took place in Turkey's cultural capital. It was so heavily controlled by the police that, personally present at the event, it led me to wonder whether the police were meant to protect us from—nonexistent—protesting crowds, or whether we were being threateningly monitored by the police instead. Un-

---

4   Still today, the military considers it an obligation to safeguard the nation's morals (cf. Klauda 109-110; Thumann 216-217; Sinclair-Webb 69; Altinay 78-79). In its rules, homosexuality, transsexuality, and transvestism *(eşcinsellik, transseksüellik ve travestilik)* are considered 'profound psychic disturbances,' clearly not compatible with military service involving armed combat. As proof of these, the military requires medical and psychiatric reports, as well as photographs of the individual performing passive anal intercourse. These photos often 'miraculously' show up on the internet, causing an involuntary outing for many. See also Biricik; Baba.

fortunately, the event discontinued,[5] and cineastes interested in the newest queer films again had to resort to the prestigious International Istanbul Film Festival İKSV, which for some time has included a fair share of such national and international productions. The still ongoing effort to 'cleanse' the morals of citizens led—among other things—to the effort to close Lambda Istanbul in 2008. The court decided that the existence of such an institution—in addition to not carrying a proper Turkish name—would infringe 'public morale' and the protection of family values. The Supreme Court of Appeals, however, overturned this order, and Lambda was allowed to continue operating, if under close scrutiny. On the whole, as Cenk Özbay asserts, "[g]ay life in the recent history of modern Turkey reached its peak in the early 2000s, followed by its eventual decline in terms of its visibility and diversity in social and physical spaces in the metropolitan areas" ("Same-Sex" 871). It was the period where gay—and some lesbian[6]—cafes, bars, and clubs opened, diverse media started positive coverage about queer life, and academic research was beginning to be published. Zülfukar Çetin stresses, however, that "[t]his development was only attributable to the EU accession process and did not indicate that the AKP [i.e. Justice and Development Party] had taken a tolerant policy toward queers" (6).

The 2013 Gezi protests mark a crucial hiatus in this development. The decision of Istanbul's city government to turn Taksim's Gezi Park into a shopping mall based on replica of Ottoman-era military barracks led to protests, which involved not only environmentally concerned civic activists, but also queer protesters contesting "attempts to redefine the park in neoliberal and heteronormative terms" (Erol 429). The privatization, renewal, and gentrification process of Beyoğlu, "the cosmopolitan core of not only Istanbul but also Turkey" (Atalay and Doan 113), and especially Beyoğlu's subdistricts Cihangir and Tarlabaşı, were part of the government's intrusive policies that precluded any influence of citizens over a possible restructuring of such a public urban space. This process not only disrespected basic democratic rights, but also the

---

5   In 2019, Turkey's queer film festival KuirFest, founded by trans women and sex workers in Ankara in 2011, for the first time opened in Istanbul (Hanson).

6   For the emergence of a separate lesbian social movement see Atalay and Doan, who have researched lesbian space and community building practices in Beyoğlu: "Beyogly and its subdistricts of Tarlabasi and Cihangir played a similar role for the Turkish LGBTQ community to that played by San Francisco and Greenwich Village, New York through their welcome of minorities, artists, as well as gays, lesbians, and the transgender community" (257).

choice of diverse lifestyles, since Gezi Park was one of the few remaining open spaces which also served as a popular cruising area of the LGBT community, among them gay men, rent boys and trans prostitutes, as well as transgender and gay migrants. "Hence, when the park faced the threat of demolition for reasons similar to those that had recurrently displaced gays and trans women from neighborhoods such as Ülker Sokak, Tarlabaşı, and Harbiye [...] LGBTQ people made the threat to queer livelihoods a significant site of struggle for the Gezi movement" (Zengin).

The subsequent Gezi rallies started with environmental protesters setting up tents in the park, but after the violent eviction of these activists instantly erupted into a large-scale political demonstration, one of the largest and "perhaps the most significant democratic protest of the Turkish Republic's history" (Çıdam 369). The Pride Parade, held during the Gezi protests in 2013, gathered protestors and supporters from groups as diverse as Kurds, Armenians, Kemalists, and nationalists, who all showed solidarity with the LGBT community. The Gezi Park protests, therefore, created "a critical space for increasing the visibility of the LGBT activist movement" (Atalay and Doan 120) and the Pride Parades of 2013[7] and 2014, starting at Taksim Square by Gezi Park and continuing on Istiklal Street, reached record attendance before being banned in 2015. In the meantime, the Gezi Movement reached other parts of Turkey, and all but two of Turkey's eighty-one provinces held anti-government demonstrations, leading in turn to increasing levels of police violence. "That thousands of people across the country continued to participate in demonstrations, despite intimidation tactics, such as unofficial detentions, repeated use of sexual insults, threats of sexual violence, and excessive, punitive, and abusive force used by the law-enforcement officials—constituted one of the most extraordinary aspects of the Gezi park protests" (Çıdam 370-371).[8] The momentum of the protests paved the way for various activist groups making gendered, racial, and classed claims to public space and assembly, and queers took an effective role in this diversified activism (Özbay and Savcı 517-518).

The legacy of the Gezi protests continues even beyond the failed military coup attempt in July 2016 and the ensuing state of emergency which lasted until July 2018 and gave the government the right to investigate and punish

---

7   For the 2013 Pride Parade see Pearce's "Pride in Istanbul."
8   On this excessive, abusive police violence, see Amnesty International's report "Turkey: Gezi Park Protests."

people involved in the attempted coup, although "many interpreted the ensuing crackdown as an opportunity to silence opposing views" (Zihnioğlu 15). In sum, Gezi gave rise to a shared experience, and even though the momentum of this activism may have faded, a new political discourse remained that still carries potential to "much needed acts of resistance" (Çıdam 390), given the current political climate in Turkey. The protests had a powerful impact, as one activist declares:

> [They] changed me, and thousands of others, for the better: we have got used to tear gas and are no longer afraid of water cannons, I have been reunited with friends I hadn't seen for years, met new and interesting people, given shelter to others, discovered Istanbul parks I didn't know existed, seen the inside of mysterious old buildings, learnt something about human rights, and persuaded my parents that when they hear words like "gays," "lesbians," and "transvestites" they need not be afraid. (Talay qtd. in Çıdam 391)

Sex Between Men: Ottoman Tradition and Turkish Everyday Life

Homosexuality as such is not prohibited by law in Turkey. Starting with the Ottoman Empire's adoption of the Napoleonic Code, and followed by the Turkish Penal Code of 1926—adapted from the Italian Penal Code—, homosexuality *de jure* has been decriminalized. It can be—and has been—argued, however, that the Western legal concept of decriminalization does not correspond to the Ottoman and later Turkish actual experience. "On the contrary," claims Elif Ceylan Ozsoy, "the Ottomans introduced heavier punishments for the public display of same-sex intimacy in 1858" (20).[9] The practice of accusing homosexuals as offending "public morality" has been used to harass and intimidate LGBT people until present times: "For example, the purpose of the Law on Misdemeanors (no 5326, enacted on March 30, 2005) is defined in its first article

---

9   See also Engin and Özbarlas; Akman and Tütüncü; Görkemli, "From Queer Empire;" Yılmaz. For a Foucauldian reading of the shift from the fluidity of early, premodern Ottoman homoerotic *ars erotica* to an application of the Western discourse of homosexuality see Oguzhan, who argues that the "Muslim Middle East had slowly fallen under this discourse, as sexual behaviours were now controlled and regulated through 'medical, legal and religious' methods, demonstrating a slow, albeit eventual 'discursive shift' during the eighteenth and nineteenth centuries" (133). For a similar argument see Ze'evi, *Producing Desire* 167-172; Ze'evi, "Hiding Sexuality;" Kinli.

as: 'the protection of social order, public morality, public health, environment and economic order.' Although the law has no provisions against sexual orientation or different gender identities, it is frequently invoked to stop, search, arrest, and fine LGBT people for 'indecency' or 'disturbing public order'" (Arat and Nuñez 12).[10]

Nevertheless, there is another side to this history. Cenk Özbay concedes that "[i]t is difficult to say whether 50 years ago same-sex sexualities were freer in Turkey or nowadays they are more oppressed because it is almost impossible to fully grasp the clandestine nature of queer acts in the past" ("Same-Sex" 874). But he also argues that the radical transformations that took place after the founding of the new republic in 1923 kept everyone so busy that it opened a space for queers to flourish covertly. "Same-sex sexual activities," he writes, "became a significant part of the abject, invisible yet connived urban underground culture" ("Same-Sex" 870). Thus, there are many examples to offer insights into this queer subculture throughout the twentieth century and up to the present: the novels and stories of Sait Faik Abasıyanık, Bilge Karasu, Leyla Erbil, and Tezer Özlü; Zeki Müren's and later Bülent Ersoy's queer song careers; Vat 69 as the country's 'first gay bar' to open in 1975; gay authors of the 1990s such as Murathan Mungan, Küçük İskender, and Selim İleri;[11] and from the first commercial queer films of the 1980s such as Halit Refig's *Ihtiras fırtınası* (1984) to *Two Girls* (2007) by queer director Kutluğ Ataman and adapted from Perihan Mağden's novel as the first modern lesbian film to mainstream in Turkish popular culture.[12]

(Homo)sexual practices, gender norms and queer life in Istanbul cannot be viewed without taking into account the sexual customs at large which are still heavily influenced by their Muslim heritage. Since Islam is a religion based on a legal framework, there is no morality and sin in a Western, Christian sense, but rather the abidance or violation of laws. Accordingly, to act

---

10 See also "*We Need a Law*" 64-69; Muedini 66-91; Erdem 9-21; for an outline of major discriminatory practices against LGBT individuals and their resilience, e.g. regarding labor market, public life, health services, housing, military, and media, see Yenilmez; Kiliçaslan and Işik.

11 Other Turkish writers depicting queer sexuality include Demir Özlü, Ferit Edgü, Adalet Ağaoğlu, Attilâ İlhan, Ahmet Güntan, Mehmet Bilâl, Sadık Aslankara, Niyazi Zorlu, Ahmet Tulgar, Hülya Serap Doğaner, Tijen Kino, Sibel Torunoğlu, Zeynep Aksoy, Pınar Küzeci Orhan, Ayşe Kulin, Sema Kaygusuz and Yalçın Tosun (Tiftik; Erdman).

12 See Özbay, *Queering Sexualities* 11-21; for contemporary queer Turkish films see Özmen, Parlayandemir, and Çöteli; Erdem; Hanson.

ethically for Muslims means compliance with the Sharia, which constitutes "divine law, which is, in theory, immutable—Muslim society is required to adapt to it, and not the other way around" (Sofer, 132).[13] And while the Sharia is not the directly enforceable law in Turkey, the common understanding of law and injustice is nevertheless largely associated with the older, traditionalist Islamic legal order.[14] With respect to sexuality, this implies that a sexual act can only be performed between legitimate persons. From a legal-Islamic perspective, homosexuality is fornication, *zina*, because it is defined as illegitimate and thus illegal penetration (Ghadban, "Historie" 52, 55). And yet, according to many records, 'pederasty'—the term given to male-to-male sexuality—in Muslim regions was known at least since the eighth century and almost always tolerated as a social practice. How can we account for this seeming paradox?

Muslim societies have a long tradition of erotic relations between males, which was not criminalized. Homoerotic poetry describing passionate love was common at least until the nineteenth century,[15] and pederasty or "boy-love" was acceptable because "like eunuchs, adolescent boys were also lacking

---

13   See Massad (356-371) for a scathing critique of the views on "Arab and Muslim desires" of scholars such as Jehoeda Sofer and Stephen O. Murray. However, I do not share Massad's reservations.

14   There is still dire need for research on the relation of Islam and homosexuality, and thus on, as Sabine Schmidtke puts it, one of the "least understood aspects of Islamic civilizations" (265). However, as some of the recent publications I mention here document, this "closed subject of enquiry" (Schmidtke 261) has recently begun to open up, partly through the growing interest in migrant identities in countries such as the Netherlands and Germany. Two important German publications of the early 2000s were *Homosexualität und Islam. Koran, islamische Länder, Situation in Deutschland* (Homosexuality and Islam: Quran, Islamic Countries, Situation in Germany, eds. Bochow and Marbach, 2003) and *Muslime unter dem Regenbogen. Homosexualität, Migration und Islam* (Muslims under the Rainbow: Homosexuality, Migration, and Islam, ed. LSVD Berlin-Brandenburg e. V., 2004). Both volumes evolved from the rise of queer studies and gay political activism, and include chapters on the situation of gay men in Turkey as well as on gay German-Turks. Both collections were still 'outside' accepted academic traditions at the time and published in book series predominantly addressing a queer audience, but have lost their marginal status in the meantime due to a further influx of research on related topics. On queer Turks, especially regarding migration, see also Vida Bakondy et al.'s compilation *Gook Luck! Migration Today: Vienna, Belgrade, Zagreb, Istanbul*; Yener Bayramoğlu's "Border Panic."

15   See Murray on boy-love poetry and transvestite dance traditions; see also chapter 2 on hamam practices.

in 'defining skills of males'" (Rehman and Polymenopoulou 28). The public visibility of sodomy, however, as the act of anal intercourse between two men was prohibited and severely punished. Even though the Qur'an does not specifically mention sodomy and prescribe punishment for sexual relations between men, Muslim countries such as Iran, Saudi Arabia, and Yemen even today have death penalty codified and implemented under Sharia law (Mendos 201-202).[16] The concern of human rights violations and protection against discrimination has not yet found its way into the official belief systems of these countries.[17] In many strictly traditionalist Islamic countries such as Saudi Arabia there are still strong homophilic traditions that allow premarital and sometimes even extramarital sexual activities between men due to the strict social segregation of the sexes. But this cultural practice can by no means be called homosexuality in our Western understanding. For these countries, the idea of homosexuality remains inextricably linked with that of Western decadence. And it seems that the more these countries interact with and are influenced by Western culture, the more rigid the control of Islamic law becomes in order to counteract a possible weakening of Islamic traditions. These mea-

---

16 Afghanistan's criminal code has a "possible" death penalty for same-sex intercourse (Mendos 200), but given the most recent events of August 2021 with the Taliban taking over the country and its government, this might change for the worse.

17 This could be seen, for example, in the attempt in 2003 to submit for the first time in the history of global organizations a legislative proposal to the UN Commission for Human Rights, which combines "sexual orientation and human rights" and "calls all governments to promote and protect the human rights of people, regardless of their sexual orientation" (IGLHRC 5). The proposal was drafted by Brazil and rejected by the Organization of Islamic Cooperation (OIC, formerly the Organization of Islamic Conference), an organization to which all Muslim-majority countries, including Albania and Turkey, belong. In view of the threat of economic sanctions by the OIC, a second attempt was also rejected in 2004 (cf. Klein et al. 39-40). In 2011, finally, the UN Human Rights Council passed a resolution to document "discriminatory laws and practices and acts of violence against individuals based on their sexual orientation and gender identity" (Human Rights Council 1). This counts as the first time that any United Nations body approved a resolution affirming the rights of LGBT people. The ensuing report confirmed, for instance, that "[s]eventy-six countries retain laws that are used to criminalize people on the basis of sexual orientation or gender identity" (Human Rights Council 13), and that "[i]n at least five countries the death penalty may be applied to those found guilty of offences relating to consensual, adult homosexual conduct" (Human Rights Council 15).

sures certainly only reflect a particularly drastic form and application of the Sharia, i.e. the Islamic law, as it emerges from the Qur'an and the Hadith.[18]

In Arabic and Muslim countries as well as in Turkey, active and passive sexual roles are the constituting paradigm of masculinity and femininity.[19] Homo- and heterosexuality are thus defined not so much by a concrete choice of object, but rather by sexual practices. Arno Schmitt describes this gendered logic as follows: "Men consider themselves to be stronger physically, intellectually, and morally, and be able to control instinct and emotion—unlike women, children [...] and transvestites. [...] It is the right of men to penetrate and their duty to lie on top" (2-3). A derogatory view on male homosexuality therefore relates predominantly to men who engage in receptive anal intercourse, whereas insertive anal intercourse is not considered defamatory for

---

18   According to traditional commentators, Islam's ban on homosexuality goes back to the Qur'an. In fact, however, the story of Lot only contains hints when it says: "And (remember) Lût (Lot), when he said to his people: 'Do you commit the worst sin such as none preceding you has committed in the 'Âlamîn (mankind and jinn)? Verily, you practice your lusts on men instead of women. Nay, but you are a people transgressing beyond bounds (by committing great sins).' [...] And We rained down on them a rain (of stones). Then see what was the end of the Mujrimûn (criminals, polytheists and sinners)" (The Noble Qur'an 7: 80-81, 84). More recent, less traditionalist commentators point out, in clear contradiction to their conservative colleagues, that the Qur'an does not explicitly speak of sex and certainly not of homosexuality, pederasty or even sodomy. There is also no threat of punishment. The explicit prohibition, including punitive measures, only appears in the Hadith, where the words and deeds of the Prophet Mohammed were collected centuries after his death and thus after the writing of the Qur'an. It is therefore doubtful to what extent the compilation actually goes back to Mohammed in each individual case. The Hadith, however, remains so important for Islamic law because the Qur'an itself contains few legal provisions. The relevant passage in the Hadith speaks of damnation as well as killing, stoning, throwing from a mountain, or even burning of the lutis, i.e. the sodomites (see Mohr 13-25; Ahmadi, 551-555; Rehman and Polymenopoulou 9-18; Muedini 9-28; Muslim LGBT Inclusion Project 36-38; Wafer). Sofer, furthermore, points out that the regulations of penal measures are extremely strict and codified, and there also is severe punishment for unproven accusation: "Only oral testimony by eye witnesses is admitted. Four trustworthy Muslim men must testify that they have seen 'the key entering the key hole' or the culprit must confess four times" (132).

19   Bereket and Adam write that Turkey shares this traditional sex/gender order with Mediterranean, Middle Eastern, and Latin American regions, "where male-male sexual relations are expected to embody a gendered division between an inserter partner (*aktif*) considered 'masculine' and a receptive partner (*pasif*) who is expected to show some aspect of the feminine gender in behavior, voice, or dress" (131).

the active partner (Bochow, "Junge schwule Türken" 172). 'Gay'—or Turkified as 'gey'[20]—generally defines the one who takes this role. His social depreciation relates above all to his betrayal of the masculine ideal. In contrast, the active male may even gain admiration because he has proven his masculinity without a proper external 'object of desire' (Ghadban, "Gescheiterte Integration" 223). The more recent model of the masculine, butch gay man does not qualify for this conceptualization, as his sexual identity is considered to be largely based on Western standards and thus on the customs of the urban, young, educated middle class (Tapinc 39-40). Mehmet Ümit Necef also confirms that the notion of 'homosexuality' basically is a Western import, whereas traditionally there is a distinction according to sexual roles between *kulanpara* (from Persian meaning "fucker of boys") and *ibne* (73). The practice of hate speech, for example, shows that *ibne* does not invariably signal homosexual behavior but is an appearance that lacks male sovereignty, similar to "fag," "pansy," or "pussy" in English. *Ibne* means "being fucked" in a rhetorical-symbolic way, in the sense of being unmanly and impotent, but also more generally of not being able to offer resistance (Bochow, "Junge schwule Türken" 175). This means that a colloquial threat like "I fuck you" ("Ich ficke dich" in German—where it is frequently used among young Turks), implies the willingness to fight coupled with a confidence of victory as documented in Hermann Tertilt's ethnographic study on youth gangs, *Turkish Power Boys* (1996). In general, of the 80 entries in the contemporary Turkish vocabulary that allude to same-sex sexuality, only ten refer to female homosexuality and only five to men as active partners in sexual intercourse, whereas more than 50 terms refer to men letting themselves be 'penetrated' by other men thus indicating again a cultural preoccupation with the putatively emasculated male (Günay 126).

Today, it is still difficult for young unmarried Muslim men—and thus not only for women—to live alone outside the parents' home, because this would

---

20 The coinage of 'gey' as well as 'aktif' and 'pasif' can be seen as ironic indebtment to the English language (Bereket and Adam 133), but in the case of 'gey' also as a trend to counter the derogatory words such as *ibne, eşcinsellik, homoseksüel*, or *lubunya* and thus "asserting homosexual interest ostensibly devoid of the effeminacy" (137). On the global usage of the term MSM—men who have sex with men—that starting in the 1980s—and at first predominantly in the context of the AIDS pandemic—was used "to describe the reality that many men have sex with each other without any sense of homosexual identity" (Altman et al. 443) see Mizielinska and Kulpa 103; Bereket and Adam.

violate the family's honor and the absolute authority of the father (Bochow, "Sex unter Männern" 105). Therefore, the common social practice in Muslim countries calls for heterosexual marriage as the favored way to bypass impeding marginalization. In moderate, Europeanized families, many of which live in Istanbul, it is now more common for young unwed men to live alone outside of the parental home. But still, a son's announcement of being gay nonetheless often leads to an appointment with a therapist. This practice is common across the country, but especially prevailing in a metropolis like Istanbul and supported by the Turkish psychiatry that is known to be overly conservative (Thumann 213; Oksal 514; "We Need a Law" 89-91; Günay 124; Bochow, "Junge schwule Türken"). Homosexuality thus continues to be considered a passing phase or sickness that may be overcome with professional help (Günay 124; Kiliç and Uncu 205-206).[21] The situation for lesbian women is even less encouraging. Some efforts by lesbian activists notwithstanding, who in the 1990s founded organizations such as Sappho'nun Kızları (Sappho's Girls) and Venus'un Kızkardeşleri (The Sisters of Venus), lesbianism remains almost completely invisible in public life; there is currently, for example, only one bar in Istanbul addressing a specific lesbian clientele, Bigudi Club, "the first ever exclusively lesbian venue opened in Turkey" ("Bigudi Club").[22] Transvestism and transsexuality, on the other hand, have a long tradition that differs substantially from Western understandings. The Ottoman sultans, for instance, kept young dancers (*köçekler*), who performed in woman's clothes and could

---

21   A murder case from 2009, called "the first gay honor killing in Turkey" (Bilefsky; see also Ataman 138), therefore is a case in point. Ahmet Yildiz, who lived openly as a gay man in Istanbul and was the first 'Mr. Bear' to represent Turkey at the International Bear Rendezvous in San Francisco in 2007, was shot by his father, who had urged him to return to their village to see a doctor and imam for a 'cure.' While this may or may not be a single case depending on the number of unreported cases, there were as many as 11 killings of transgender people registered in 2008-2009 alone, mostly in Istanbul and Ankara, and they must be regarded as hate crimes even though police officials claim: "A person is not killed because they [sic] are homosexual, it is because of other things" (qtd. in *Turkey: Pride and Violence*). Furthermore, while at least some of these murderers were caught, they are usually facing a lower sentence due to the claim of being 'provoked' under Article 29 of the Turkish Criminal Code.

22   See also the collegiate student association Legato, an acronym for Lezbiyen ve Gey Topluluğu (Lesbian and Gay Association), that first was launched in Ankara in the 1990s and then reached out across the country now being Turkey's largest LGBT organization and explicitly including lesbian images and stories on their webpage and print fanzine, published in Istanbul (Görkemli, "Gender Benders").

also be part of the sultan's harem (Janssen 84).[23] The term "köçek" is still being used instead of the foreign word "transseksüel" that is much more associated with a preceding, underlying male identity.

Certainly, coming out still remains an extremely painful, if not impossible act for many queer Turks and likely to lead to suffering from discrimination, disrespect, low self-esteem, internalized homophobia, paranoia, melancholia, unemployment, violence, or forced loneliness, amongst other symptoms (Özbay, *Queering Sexualities* 5; Eslen-Ziya and Koc). That was true even during the queer peak period, i.e. the early 2000s, before the ongoing backlash began. The Turkish-Kurdish human rights lawyer from Istanbul, Eren Keskin,[24] for example, reported in a Human Rights Watch interview in 2003 of increasing attacks on gays, lesbians and especially transsexuals in Turkey. She received complaints about brutal assaults and arbitrary arrests by the police, especially in Ankara, Bursa, Istanbul and Mersin. "We live in a society," says Keskin, "in which police power is very great, and militaristic. Police and military—they take homosexuality as a vice. This is why people who are homosexual face a great deal of violence" (qtd. in *"We Need a Law"* 33). At the same time, there have been openly gay Turks in Istanbul who can freely admit to their sexual orientation in both their professional and private lives. Gay bars and clubs were then and still are crowded at nights and on weekends. Pride events and marches have been held since 1993, although under continued threat of violent police measures and bans.[25] All of this means that an expanding subculture has gained greater public visibility[26] and acceptance—with a record high of 50% of the population supporting LGBT equality in 2020, according to

---

23 More on such *köçekler* in the next chapter.
24 Keskin received amongst other awards the 2001 Amnesty International Human Rights Award (German Section), the 2004 Aachen Peace Award, the 2005 Theodor Haecker Prize for Civil Courage and Political Integrity, the 2005 Hrant Dink Award, the 2018 Helsinki Civil Society Award. Most recently, she was an honorary finalist of the Martin Ennals Awards for Human Rights Defenders but could not receive the award in person due to the travel ban imposed by the Turkish authorities ("Martin Ennals Award").
25 For the ban on the 19th Pride March in Istanbul in 2021 see "Turkey: Recurrent Instances."
26 This can also be seen in the media where celebrated singers and actors for a long time may not have been 'out' but neither have they been especially closeted (cf. Kolat, "Islam" 206). More on some of these singers, especially the pop singer Tarkan, in the last chapter.

ILGA—, but is still subject to state-controlled surveillance, hate speech incidents, anti-LGBT crimes, and censorship measures (ILGA Europe). Above all, these developments towards a greater queer public visibility and acknowledgment clearly distinguishes Turkey from other countries with a predominantly Muslim population, where "homosexuality is typically perceived as forbidden, or *haram*" (Polymenopoulou) leading to homosexuals being legally suppressed, persecuted, tortured and executed to a far greater extent.[27]

Scholars such as Tarik Bereket and Barry Adam speak of globalized syncretic notions of gayness in the case of male gay Turkish men, who "are adapting, but also selecting, imported ideas of modern gay discourse and Western identity politics into their way of conceiving or re-conceiving themselves" (146). 'Traditional' and 'modern' forms of male same-sex bonding coexist, intersect, and even fuse giving credence to Turkey's geographical placement in both Europe and the Middle East and its "long tradition of cross-cultural dialogue, migration, tourism, and cultural appropriations" (Bereket and Adam 146). Accordingly, the claim to being 'gay' for many Turkish men may signify the wish to assert personal freedom and the agency to live 'beyond the closet.' For others, however, to identify as gay still is in conflict with the privileges

---

27   In 2019, there are still reported cases of gay men being hanged in Iran and tortured and beheaded in Saudi Arabia, but even in Turkey activists risk their lives and personal safety (Polymenopoulou). See for human rights violations in countries such as the Lebanon, Egypt, Iraq and Iran Gundermann and Kolb; Klein et al; Marschner and Klein. The 2018 Human Rights Watch report *Audacity in Adversity* documents LGBT activism in the Middle East and North Africa where "laws across the region are far from uniform, although in most countries, same-sex acts between consenting adults in private are treated as a criminal offense" (n.p.). On torture, specifically, see the series of Human Rights Watch reports *Dignity Debased;* "*It's Part of the Job;*" "*They Hunt Us Down for Fun;*" "*They Want Us Exterminated;*" and *In a Time of Torture*.

that a hegemonic masculinity offers in a socially stratified gender system.[28] Furthermore, the factor social class is relevant since being gay "has a certain middle and upper class connotation in the Turkish vernacular" (Özbay, "Same-Sex" 872) and entails certain ways of utilizing cultural capital and mastering symbolic codes. Özbay mentions the example of "varos" as originally negatively connoted term for masculine, straight-acting, working-class men with same-sex sexual affinities, which in Turkish gay slang has been transformed into a word that "also highlights robust virility and an authentic, uncontaminated masculinity" ("Same-Sex" 872). "Lubunya" in contrast refers to a lower-class person with a more effeminate style and is more readily acknowledged by the public as a variant of transvestite and transsexual behavior known from popular transgender singers. Accordingly, class for queers in Turkey, argues Özbay, "is deeply intertwined with desires that govern one's bodily presentations, gendered acts and the modes of interpretation that affect how homosexual subject [sic] relate to other people" (*Queering Sexualities* 19).

Emrecan Özen describes such sexual codes in a campy way. In an internet tourist guide catering to gay male patrons, he 'warns' Western tourists visiting Istanbul thus: "For some hetero men, a gay arse is the next best thing if they cannot find a woman that night! With these types, you've got nothing to do if you're looking for a long and versatile session—your only chance is to spread the legs and try and enjoy yourself till he cums." It is not easy to tell whether trendy youngsters in the gay—friendly—bars of Beyoğlu are just playing it cool—and queer—showing off their muscled-up bodies, or whether straight-looking bears drinking beer in Tekyön are later up for the transvestites of Sahra Bar, "[a] perfect example of Istanbul's underground LGBT culture" ("Sahra Club"), where it is just as likely to be ripped off by some

---

28 Massad in his critique of the liberatory project of human rights groups goes as far as to claim that the "so-called passive homosexual," who is defended by such associations as ILGA against social denigration, precisely "will fall victim to legal and police persecution as well as heightened social denigration as his sexual practice becomes a topic of public discourse that transforms it from a practice into an identity" (384-385). In contrast, Özbay and Soybakis in their account highlight the ways "Erdogan signifies the current Islamist hegemonic masculinity in Turkey" (33), and they show how Erdoğan's 'Neo-Ottoman' authoritarianism "in the political field presents at the same time a gender hegemony based on a highly masculinized public sphere, Islamized and nationalized (as anti-Western and anti-modern) cultural domain, 'conservative' family-oriented policies, and the sex-segregated social life" (33).

sleazy pimp as it is to be offered money by an eager patron. Trusting appearances may likely lead to comic misunderstandings, harsh disappointments, or more serious trouble.[29]

Istanbul at Night: Queer Literature, Arabesk Music, and Gay Bars

At night in Istanbul's party district, Beyoğlu, you can see transvestites walking on Tarlabaşı Street, as well as in Cihangir, around Taksim Square, and along the side streets of İstiklal Avenue, all of which comprise the traditional Western-Christian bohemian neighborhoods of Beyoğlu. In this area, there are most gay bars and clubs, some with darkrooms. It is also the area of prostitution, especially for men seeking transsexual partners.[30] Therefore, this group has specifically been the target of policing. Since it is very difficult for transgender people to find regular employment and even licensed bordellos are closed to them, most earn money as street workers and are thus easy prey for police harassment, blackmailing, arrests and abuse.[31] By contrast, Russell Ivy, studying gay travel patterns, finds Istanbul a particularly interesting example of a place "with a modest build-up of gay infrastructure" that serves as an "island" "surrounded by a region with little to no gay infrastructure" (353). Istanbul has been hailed as the queer capitol of Turkey and it arguably

---

29 If one looks at everyday experiences in sexual encounters, it is indeed very easy (at least as a Western man) to have sex with Turkish men, even if these men would usually not call themselves 'gay.' Lesbian sexuality, on the other hand, remains a completely invisible phenomenon in public life. Thus, while a queer community in a contemporary Western sense still does not exist in a broadly recognized social space, the practice of hidden homosexuality and the highly marginalized and stigmatized scene of transvestism and transsexuality have long persisted.

30 For a recent butching up of gay street prostitution with rent boys showing off an exaggerated masculinity, see Özbay, "Nocturnal Queers" as well as his more comprehensive study *Queering Sexualities*.

31 This state-sanctioned homophobia means gay bashers act with impunity as is documented, for instance, in the report *Human Rights Violations of LGBT Individuals in Turkey* by Kaos GL, LGBTI News Turkey, and the International Gay and Lesbian Human Rights Commission (IGLHRC), submitted to the United Nations Human Rights Council in 2014. See also Engin as well as the Human Rights Watch report on Turkey "*We Need a Law for Liberation*" (2008) and its follow-up *Turkey: Pride and Violence* (2009) as well as the newest reports of Amnesty International ("Turkey 2020") and Human Rights Watch ("Turkey: Events of 2019").

is the second most important queer location in Eastern Europe after Mykonos, Greece. Therefore, Istanbul can be perceived as the most important queer city in the Muslim world.

A pop cultural case in point reflecting such vagaries of queer Istanbul is Mehmet Murat Somer's 'Hop-Çiki-Yaya' thriller series.[32] This crime series set in contemporary Istanbul features an unnamed transvestite amateur sleuth, who, made-up as a flamboyant drag queen "with an Audrey Hepburn alter-ego" ("Mehmet Murat Somer"), manages an underground transvestite bar at night while by day—and clad in all-male attire—he runs a lucrative hacker business. Turkish author Somer explains the series' title in an interview: "Hop-Çiki-Yaya was a cheerleading chant from Turkish colleges in the early 1960s, and it came to be used in comedy shows to mean gays. If somebody was queenish, then they'd say 'Oh, he's Hop-Çiki-Yaya.' By the 1970s, it wasn't being used anymore—so I brought it back" (qtd. in Wiegand). What is most interesting is that this character, although ostensibly a transvestite and homosexual in the sense that s/he desires men and defies given gender norms, highlights the flexibility of such norms through temporal and spatial anchors. Whether on the hunt in Westernized liberal Beyoğlu, the queer hub of the city, or investigating in the visibly more Muslim Eminönü, the former center of Constantinople, s/he moves about the city effortlessly crossing the gendered East-West divide.[33]

If one compares this hero/ine to British author Barbara Nadel's Istanbul inspector Çetin İkmen, the difference becomes strikingly obvious. Similar to Somer's *The Prophet Murders*, in Nadel's ninth novel of her Çetin İkmen-detective series, *A Passion for Killing* (2007), homosexuals fall prey to a serial killer on a moral crusade. But whereas Nadel's shabby, middle-aged, chain-smoking and hard-drinking detective could be said to emblemize a variant of a (stereo)typical Turkish heterosexual male, Somer's multifaceted and flashy

---

32   There are seven novels, five of which have been translated into English so far: *The Kiss Murder* (2009, orig. *Buse Cinayetleri*, 2003), *The Prophet Murders* (2008, orig. *Peygamber Cinayetleri*, 2002), *The Gigolo Murder* (2009, orig. *Jigolo Cinayetleri*, 2003), *The Serenity Murders* (2012, orig. *Huzur Cinayetleri*, 2004), *The Wig Murders* (2014, *Peruklu Cinayetler*, 2011), *Ajda'nın Elmasları* (2013), and *Kade'in Peşinde* (2009).

33   Somer is well aware that his books may not sit well with every Turkish reader. His initial struggle to find a publisher and then being represented by the prestigious Iletisim company, which also publishes Nobel laureate Orhan Pamuk, for Sonnet are signs that he needs "Iletisim's stamp of approval" to protect his books "from a hostile reception" (qtd. in Wiegand).

hero/ine is nothing like any such stereotype. Somer names Spanish film director Pedro Almodóvar as his model and likewise spices his novels with social commentary in the form of satiric comedy, something joyous like "champagne or bubblegum" (qtd. in Wiegand). Instead of presenting transvestites in a stereotypically negative way "as either slapstick fun material or potential criminals [...], doomed to be street hookers but nothing else, with almost no moral values" ("Mehmet Murat Somer"), Somer writes against the moral grain to create a complex, contradictory, and highly likeable character and narrator with witty, yet intriguing social insights. In *The Gigolo Murder*, for example, the narrator teams up with yet another drag queen, Ponpon, in a Holmes-and-Watson-like transvestite coupling. Ruminating about the next investigatory step, the narrator stops to think over the situation: "What on earth would we do if the police, intelligence officers, Interpol, and all the others caught up to us? Either we'd be quietly locked away in an undisclosed location or our names would be released to the press. We'd be disgraced and scapegoated, and they'd be baying for our blood. My personal life, which I'd carefully kept just that all these years, would be dredged up. Society's most feverish suspicions about my dubious character would be confirmed [...]" (121). In this novel, the narrator's double life, complicated enough as it is, gets further entangled in an intricate web of homophobia, family honor, the nouveaux riches, and sexual desire. Alluding both to Turkish society's apprehensions concerning queers and to Turkey's notoriously bad reputation concerning policing tactics and prison conditions, the narrator succeeds in acknowledging and satirizing this "in-depth view of life in a transvestite community," as Jessica Moyer writes about *The Prophet Murders*. And it is modern-day—or arguably night—Istanbul which, as reviewer Kat Dawson states, "provides a fantastic playground for this humorous page-turner to unfold within" ("Galley Talk"). In this novel, the sassy amateur detective investigates cases in which the victims are all transvestites who bear the names of Islamic prophets. "The book is not as successful as a whodunit and the mystery is less than gripping," writes a blogger in his review of the novel, but maintains that "the story of these marginalized men who love to dress as women yet still know how to be men in a culture where being out and proud can lead to imprisonment and even execution is the most fascinating part of the book" (Norris). All of Somer's novels center around the world of marginalized queers and through the lens of the trans narrator many topical issues such as bigotry, fundamentalist Islamic beliefs, scapegoating people, and precarious existence are addressed.

As could be seen in Turkey's victory at the ESC that installed Sertab Erener as a national heroine who 'conquered Europe,' music has played a crucial role in the self-definition of the Turkish nation state as well as in the self-fashioning of various groups including queer audiences (Gumpert 147). Arabesk in particular is a musical style that is closely connected to Turkey's recent national and cultural history. Besides its immense and at times subversive power, which is mostly at odds with the state-regulated efforts to forge a common national identity, Arabesk also pays tribute to a questioning of how to situate an overwhelmingly popular and socially pervasive music genre within the discourse of globalized pop music. Sertab Erener's performance at the Eurovision Song Contest, for example, used elements of Arabesk and it proved to be the formula for international success. Indeed, perhaps Arabesk poses the greatest potential for thinking about how queerness functions in contemporary Istanbul, blending together gay, straight and queer elements and providing an opportunity for subversion through tradition instead of against it.

As a cultural practice, Arabesk was always quintessentially queer, blurring high and low, modern and traditional elements, and emerging on the scene from the fringes of the city during the 1950s and 1960s, where the traditional habits of immigrants from predominantly impoverished southeast Anatolian—mostly Kurdish—rural areas blended with contemporary urban lifestyles (cf. Stokes 213). From the very start, and given Turkey's Kemalist ideology, Arabesk's foreignness and alienness—its 'Arabic' style[34]—could not easily be assimilated and it posed a threat to the politics of the Turkish nation state in general and Istanbul in particular. In suggestive sexual metaphors, Alev Çınar remarks that the notion of the "provincial other" as "the alien infesting the city" has created personifying depictions of Istanbul as a beleaguered place suffering from corruption, alienation and degeneration; it is "open to penetration and destruction, a place that is defenseless in the face of the modernizing and Westernizing influences of the secular state" (386).

On the whole, Arabesk has remained in the stronghold of a masculine culture that "is strongly associated with mustaches, masculine friendship, and *rakı*-drinking, cigarette-smoking rituals" (Özbek 223). Nevertheless, the longstanding 'Othering' of Arabesk singers as well as the melodramatic lyrics of

---

34 Etymologically, the adjective 'arabesk' or 'arabesque' derives from the "French, from Italian *arabesco* Arabian in fashion, from *arabo* Arab, from Latin *Arabus*" (<www.merriam-webster.com>).

their songs have put these male performers in a somewhat ambiguous category of masculinity. The considerable popularity of transsexual performers in this genre further adds to the complexity of body politics that characterizes Arabesk in general. Despite the queerness of the practice, it could still be quite a precarious existence for performers. Following the 1980 military coup, the restrictive politics included a policing of Arabesk music and films that in turn resulted in the exile of stars like transsexual Bülent Ersoy, to pick an especially notorious and famous example.

Ersoy's cult status within the Arabesk community was the effect of various factors, amongst which her transsexuality was certainly a principal one. She had to face a fierce fight against the government's refusal to legally recognize her as a woman after the sex reassignment surgery in London in 1981—such operations were illegal in Turkey at the time—and as a consequence was forced into exile in Germany, where she successfully pursued her career for the next years. In 1988, she returned because a new Turkish Civil Code now included an amendment for male-to-female post-operative transgender people to obtain the 'pink card' to certify their new gender. Keeping to her rather male first name Bülent, Ersoy's career flourished as a female performer in Turkey.[35]

Although the change in legislation—in part the result of Ersoy's court case—seemed fairly progressive, this did not necessarily improve the situation for transgender people but brought on different problems, instead. They were now facing the pressure to eliminate any gender ambiguity, which in turn often resulted in "potential medical malpractice" (Kandiyoti, "Pink Card Blues" 279). Adhering to a hegemonically structured and strictly dichotomous gender system, a male-to-female transsexual like Ersoy was more likely to be considered an aberrant woman thus simply ignoring her former biological male sex. In consequence, 'coming out' for many queers has resulted in 'corrective' surgical procedures, as can be seen in many cases from Istanbul's transgender scene. The ambiguous fascination with transsexuals that affect the public undoubtedly has helped to solidify Ersoy's iconic stardom. Indeed, her highly visible career—particularly as Arabesk singer—says a lot of the persistence of identity issues in a society that is "strangely composite" and as such unwillingly "appropriating and incorporating into its closed circle what does

---

[35] For a renewed effort in changing and thus liberalizing the Civil and Penal Code see the publication by Women for Women's Human Rights as well as Sahika et al., "Group Psychotherapy."

not fit into the existing scheme of things" (Öncü, "Global Consumerism" 186, see also Öncü, "Istanbulites" 115).

A different, internationally even more celebrated example of how Arabesk has been queered in the last years is Tarkan. The Turkish singer, who for years has been one of country's most prominent pop exponents and exports, mixes belly-dance, rap, break-dance, Turkish classical music and Western pop. In 2006, he released his first all-English album *Come Closer*, produced in the United States, thus aiming, with his music style, dance performance, and star image, to join the global market forces. Like Sertab Erener in her ESC act, Tarkan "attempts to steer a middle course between the Scylla of Western pop music and the Charybdis of 'traditional' Turkish music" (Gumpert 151). Tarkan, a child of Turkish *Gastarbeiter* in Germany, is but one—albeit very visible—example of a booming popular culture in Turkey, centered in Istanbul's clubbing scene, but present through various media in virtually every household throughout the country. In different ways than Ersoy's migratory career, Tarkan's binational background speaks of migrant politics due to transnational economics. From a Western perspective, he can be perceived as a thoroughly Westernized and highly sexualized Orient-export. Yet his music is actually rooted in the Turkish tradition of Arabesk culture that is historically and geographically locatable as non-Western.

As I will elaborate in my last chapter, Tarkan in his videos amply alludes to Oriental belly-dancing thus precariously fashioning himself into a representation of an 'Oriental Other.' This in turn brings him in risky vicinity of feminized, exoticized and colonial notions of the Orient, which is mostly associated with sexually attractive and available women, but does not exclude men. More than other Arabesk singers, Tarkan situates himself within a cultural context of the Middle East, where belly dancing, for example, has long been both a social—or folk—practice as well as a profession performed by women *and* men alike (Shay 70, 82; Mansbridge 22). Thus, even though the dancer would be recognizable as a biological male, his gender affiliation remained questionable for the cultural outsider. From this external viewpoint, the male dance was scandalous because of his dubious sexual allure as seemingly being 'available,' yet remaining frivolously aloof.

But Tarkan in the way he styles his body and lets it move resorts to a particular Western discourse of double entendre: he covertly uses a second language that is queerly coded. For a long time, gossip has circulated within the gay community—both in Istanbul's clubbing scene as well as abroad—that enjoys to believe in the 'open secret' of Tarkan's gayness. As part of and participant in this queer discourse that covers *and* reveals simultaneously, I take it that Tarkan deliberately mixes musical genres of different cultures as well as creates hybrid body images. In this way, his body represents a terrain upon which the gender and sexual conflicts in modern Turkey play themselves out, in a highly spatialized fashion. In this way, Tarkan signifies the cultural dilemma where "gay men are forced to resort to re-appropriation, *bricolage*" (Amico 369) when attempting to imitate 'straight' society. Tarkan's local success and global appeal are markers not least of a transnational queer community that fosters a shared bond of common knowledge. This is manifest in the transnationality of the Eurovision Song Contest, but characteristic of the versatility of queer culture at large. The worldwide fandom of the ESC forges an "imagined queer community" (Rehberg 60), which also manifests itself through the very concrete and physical experience of partying together at the ESC celebration in the gay bar in Istanbul where I myself was present. "Queer culture," Michael Warner claims, "has found it necessary to develop this knowledge in mobile sites of drag, youth culture, music, dance, parades, flaunting, and cruising." These sites are mobile, not easy to recognize, and yet full of potential, and in Istanbul in particular, are as "fragile and ephemeral" (Warner 202) as ever.

This notwithstanding, with Istanbul's growing touristic appeal and global importance the gay scene is still on the rise in this megacity where, according to insider tourist guide Emrecan Özen, gay life "is probably the best way to experience Istanbul's highly cosmopolitan atmosphere and diverse cultural fabric that is stretched from East to West." In "The Gay Map of the Islamic World," published by *The Advocate* in 2007, Turkey ranked highest of all Muslim countries most likely to be visited by members of the LGBT community. While the article claims that "[d]reams of European Union membership are a liberalizing force," igniting "burgeoning gay tourism infrastructure in Istanbul" ("The Gay Map"), the fact remains that after a peak in queer visibility and freedom in the mid-2000s, an increasingly palpable conservatism of Turkey's President Erdoğan and his Justice and Development Party (AKP) have caused an Islamic backlash for the queer Turkish community. Therefore, it remains to be seen whether Istanbul can uphold the claim to being the queer metropolis of the Islamic World. However, the aim of this chapter is to demonstrate the fact that ever since Turkey's inception as a modernized, secular nation, political efforts to forge a national identity were at odds with social practices that successfully subverted such efforts. Regarding Turkey in general and Istanbul in particular, the LGBT community managed the paradoxical feat of embracing transnational notions of queerness while staking out sites of resistance, here exemplified in the vagaries of the histories of Istanbulite queer (night) life. This blending and interlacing of subversion alongside tradition instead of against it has led to a highly flourishing, if greatly contradictory queer capital where the modern and traditional, the rural and the urban, the margin and the center, and above all gay and straight merge into a hotbed of contemporary queerness at the crossroads of East and West.

Works Cited

"Bigudi Club." Web. 31 July 2021. <https://www.istanbulgay.com/bars/bigudi.html>

"Martin Ennals Award Finalist Eren Keskin Honoured." *Scoop World*. 11 May 2019. Web. 27 July 2021. <https://www.scoop.co.nz/stories/WO1905/S00085/martin-ennals-award-finalist-eren-keskin-honoured.htm>

"Mehmet Murat Somer—the Euro Crime Interview." *Euro Crime*. 8 May 2008. Web. 28 July 2021. <http://eurocrime.blogspot.com/2008/05/mehmet-murat-somer-euro-crime-interview.html>

"Sahra Club." Web. 31 July 2021. <https://www.istanbulgay.com/bars/sahra.html>

"The Gay Map of the Islamic World." *The Advocate* 990. Web. 17 Nov 2011. <http://questia.com>

"Turkey 2020." *Amnesty International Report 2020/21*. Web. 31 July 2021. <https://www.amnesty.org/en/countries/europe-and-central-asia/turkey/report-turkey/>

"Turkey: Events of 2019." *Human Rights Watch World Report 2020*. Web. 31 July 2021. <https://www.hrw.org/world-report/2020/country-chapters/turkey>

"Turkey: Gezi Park Protests: Brutal Denial of the Right to Peaceful Assembly in Turkey." *Amnesty International* 2 Oct 2013. Web. 11 Nov 2021. <https://www.amnesty.org/en/documents/eur44/022/2013/en/>

"Turkey: Recurrent Instances of Violence Against LGBTQI+ and Women's Rights Defenders." fidh: International Federation for Human Rights. 6 July 2021. Web. 27 July 2021. <https://www.fidh.org/en/region/europe-central-asia/turkey/turkey-recurrent-instances-of-violence-against-lgbtqi-and-women-s>

Ahmadi, Shafiqa. "Islam and Homosexuality: Religious Dogma, Colonial Rule, and the Quest for Belonging." *Journal of Civil Rights and Economic Development* 3.26 (2012): 537-563.

Akman, Canan Aslan, and Fatma Tütüncü. "Gender and Citizenship in Turkey at the Crossroads of the Patriarchal State, Women, and Transnational Pressures." *Societal Peace and Ideal Citizenship for Turkey.* Eds. Rasim Özgür Dönmez and Pınar Enneli. Landham et al.: Lexington, 2011. 179-205.

Altinay, Ayşe Gül. *The Myth of the Military Nation: Militarism, Gender, and Education in Turkey.* New York: Palgrave Macmillan, 2004.

Altman, Dennis et al. "Men Who Have Sex With Men: Stigma and Discrimination." *Lancet* 380 (2012): 439-445.

Amico, Stephen. "'I Want Muscles:' House Music, Homosexuality and Masculine Signification." *Popular Music* 20.3 (2001): 359-378.

Arat, Zehra F. Kabasakal, and Caryl Nuñez. "Advancing LGBT Rights in Turkey: Tolerance or Protection?" *Human Rights Review* 18 (2017): 1-19.

Atalay, Ozlem, and Petra L. Doan. "Making Lesbian Space at the Edge of Europe: Queer Spaces in Istanbul." *Journal of Lesbian Studies* 24.3 (2020): 255-271.

Ataman, Hakan. "Less than Citizens: The Lesbian, Gay, Bisexual, and Transgender Question in Turkey." *Societal Peace and Ideal Citizenship for Turkey.* Eds. Rasim Ö. Dönmez and Pinar Enneli. Lanham: Lexington, 2011. 125-157.

Audacity in Adversity: LGBT Activism in the Middle East and North Africa. Human Rights Watch. 16 April 2018. Web. 27 July 2021. <https://www.hrw.org/report/2018/04/16/audacity-adversity/lgbt-activism-middle-east-and-north-africa>

Baba, H. Burcu. "The Construction of Heteropatriachal Family and Dissident Sexualities in Turkey." *Fe Dergi* 3.1 (2011): 56-64.

Bakondy, Vida et al. / Initiative Minderheiten. *Viel Glück! Migration Heute: Wien, Belgrad, Zagreb, Istanbul / Good Luck! Migration Today: Vienna, Belgrade, Zagreb, Istanbul.* Wien: Mandelbaum, 2010.

Bayramoğlu, Yener. "Border Panic Over the Pandemic: Mediated Anxieties About Migrant Sex Workers and Queers During the AIDS Crises in Turkey." *Ethnic and Racial Studies* 44.9 (2021): 1589-1606.

Bereket, Tarik, and Barry Adam. "The Emergence of Gay Identities in Contemporary Turkey." *Sexualities* 9.2 (2006): 131-151.

Bilefsky, Dan. "Soul-Searching in Turkey After a Gay Man is Killed." *New York Times.* 25 Nov 2009. Web. 28 July 2021. <https://www.nytimes.com/2009/11/26/world/europe/26turkey.html>

Biricik, Alp. "Rotten Report and Reconstructing Hegemonic Masculinity in Turkey." *Conscientious Objection: Resisting Militarized Society.* Eds. Özgür

Heval Çınar and Coşkun Üsterci. London and New York: Zed, 2009. 112-117.

Bochow, Michael. "Junge schwule Türken in Deutschland: Biographische Brüche und Bewältigungsstrategien." *Muslime unter dem Regenbogen. Homosexualität, Migration und Islam*. Ed. LSVD Berlin-Brandenburg e.V. Berlin: Querverlag, 2004. 168-188.

———. "Sex unter Männern oder schwuler Sex: Zur sozialen Konstruktion von Männlichkeit unter türkisch-, kurdisch- und arabischstämmigen Migranten in Deutschland." *Homosexualität und Islam. Koran, Islamische Länder, Situation in Deutschland*. Eds. Michael Bochow and Rainer Marbach. Hamburg: MännerschwarmSkript, 2003. 99-115.

Çetin, Zülfukar. "The Dynamics of the Queer Movement in Turkey." 28 Sep 2015. Heinrich Böll Stiftung: The Green Political Foundation. Web. 27 June 2021. <https://www.boell.de/en/2015/09/28/die-dynamik-der-queer-bewegung-der-turkei>

Çıdam, Çiğdem. "Unruly Practices: Gezi Protests and the Politics of Friendship." *New Political Science* 39.3 (2017): 369-392.

Çınar, Alev. "National History as a Contested Site: The Conquest of Istanbul and Islamist Negotiations of the Nation." *Comparative Studies in Society and History* 43.2 (2001): 364-391.

Dawson, Kat. "Galley Talk." *Publishers Weekly*. 17 Nov 2008. Web. 11 Aug 2021. <https://www.publishersweekly.com/pw/by-topic/new-titles/galley-talk/article/9360-galley-talk.html>

Dignity Debased: Forced Anal Examinations in Homosexuality Prosecutions. Human Rights Watch. 12 July 2016. Web. 27 July 2021. <https://www.hrw.org/report/2016/07/12/dignity-debased/forced-anal-examinations-homosexuality-prosecutions>

Engin, Ceylan, and Zeynep Özbarlas. "Tracing the Reverse History of Homosexuality from the Ottoman Empire to Contemporary Turkey: From Tolerance to Discrimination." *The Routledge Handbook on Contemporary Turkey*. Ed. Joost Jongerden. London and New York: Routledge, 2021. 201-229.

———. "LGBT in Turkey: Policies and Experiences." *Social Sciences* 4 (2015): 838-858.

Erdem, Azmi Mert. "İbne, Gey, Lubunya: A Queer Critique of LGBTI+ Discourses in the New Cinema of Turkey." MA Thesis. CUNY 2019.

Erdman, Michael. "A Rainbow in Stormy Skies: LGBT Writing in the Northern Middle East." Asian and African Studies Blog. 26 June 2017. Web. 5

Aug 2021. <https://blogs.bl.uk/asian-and-african/2017/06/a-rainbow-in-stormy-skies-lgbt-writing-in-the-northern-middle-east.html>

Erol, Ali. E. "Queer Contestation of Neoliberal and Heteronormative Moral Geographies During #OccupyGezi." *Sexualities* 21.3 (2018): 428-445.

Eslen-Ziya, Hande, and Yasin Koc. "Being a Gay Man in Turkey: Internalised Sexual Prejudice as a Function of Prevalent Hegemonic Masculinity Perceptions." *Culture, Health & Sexuality* (2016). Web. 9 Nov 2021. <http://dx.doi.org/10.1080/13691058.2015.1133846>

Feddersen, Jan. *Wunder gibt es immer wieder: Das große Buch zum Eurovision Song Contest*. Berlin: Aufbau, 2010.

Gecim, Hakan. "A Brief History of the LGBT Movement in Turkey." *ILGA* 1 Oct 2009. Web. 8 Feb 2013. <http://ilga.org/ilga/en/article/420>

Ghadban, Ralph. "Gescheiterte Integration? Antihomosexuelle Einstellungen türkei- und arabischstämmiger MigrantInnen in Deutschland." *Muslime unter dem Regenbogen: Homosexualität, Migration und Islam*. Ed. LSVD Berlin-Brandenburg e.V. Berlin: Querverlag, 2004. 217-225.

———. "Historie, Gegenwart und Zukunft der Einstellung zur Homosexualität und Pädophilie in islamischen Ländern." *Muslime unter dem Regenbogen: Homosexualität, Migration und Islam*. Ed. LSVD Berlin-Brandenburg e.V. Berlin: Querverlag, 2004. 39-63.

Görkemli, Serkan. "'Gender Benders, Gay Icons and Media: Lesbian and Gay Visual Rhetoric in Turkey." *Enculturation: A Journal of Rhetoric, Writing, and Culture*. 13 Jan. 2011. Web. 31 July 2021. <http://enculturation.net/gender-benders>

———. "From Queer Empire to Heterosexual Republic: Modernity, Homosexuality, and Media." *Grassroots Literacies: Lesbian and Gay Activism and the Internet in Turkey*. Albany: SUNY Press, 2014. 23-69.

Gumpert, Matthew. "'Everyway that I can:' Auto-Orientalism at Eurovision 2003." *A Song for Europe: Popular Music and Politics in the Eurovision Song Contest*. Eds. Ivan Raykoff and Robert Deam Tobin. Aldershot: Ashgate, 2007. 117-157.

Günay, Koray Ali. "Homosexualität in der Türkei und unter Türkeistämmigen in Deutschland: Gemeinsamkeiten und Unterschiede." *Homosexualität und Islam: Koran, Islamische Länder, Situation in Deutschland*. Eds. Michael Bochow and Rainer Marbach. Hamburg: MännerschwarmSkript, 2003. 116-139.

Gundermann, Eva, and Thomas Kolb. "Menschenrechtsverletzungen auf Grund sexueller Identität am Beispiel von Libanon und Ägypten." *Mus-*

lime unter dem Regenbogen. Homosexualität, Migration und Islam. Ed. LSVD Berlin-Brandenburg e. V. Berlin: Querverlag, 2004. 81-97.

Hanson, Matt. "Queer Film Fest Touring Turkey. Talking to Director Esza Özban." *Mashallah News*. 27 March 2019. Web. 5 Aug 2021. <https://www.mashallahnews.com/queer-film-fest-touring-turkey/>

Human Rights Council. "Annual Report of the United Nations High Commissioner for Human Rights: Discriminatory Laws and Practices and Acts of Violence Against Individuals Based on Their Sexual Orientation and Gender Identity." A/HRC/19/41. 11 Nov 2011. Web. 27 July 2021. <https://www.ohchr.org/Documents/Issues/Discrimination/A.HRC.19.41_English.pdf>

IGLHRC United Nations Human Rights Commission. "Resolution on Sexual Orientation and Human Rights." 24 April 2003. Web. 27 July 2021. <https://outrightinternational.org/sites/default/files/213-1.pdf>

ILGA Europe. *Annual Review of the Human Rights Situation of Lesbian, Gay, Bisexual, Trans and Intersex People in Europe and Central Asia 2021*. Web 28 July 2021. <https://www.ilga-europe.org/sites/default/files/2021/turkey.pdf>

In a Time of Torture: The Assault on Justice In Egypt's Crackdown on Homosexual Conduct. Human Rights Watch. 29 Feb 2004. Web. 27 July 2021. <https://www.hrw.org/report/2004/02/29/time-torture/assault-justice-egypts-crackdown-homosexual-conduct>

"It's Part of the Job:" Ill-treatment and Torture of Vulnerable Groups in Lebanese Police Stations. Human Rights Watch. 26 June 2013. Web. 27 July 2021. <https://www.hrw.org/report/2013/06/26/its-part-job/ill-treatment-and-torture-vulnerable-groups-lebanese-police-stations>

Ivy, Russell L. "Geographical Variation in Alternative Tourism and Recreation Establishments." *Tourism Geographies: An International Journal of Tourism Space, Place and Environment* 3.3 (2001): 338-355.

Janssen, Thijs. "Transvestites and Transsexuals in Turkey." *Sexuality and Eroticism Among Males in Moslem Societies*. Eds. Arno Schmitt and Jehoeda Sofer. New York: Harrington Park, 1992. 83-91.

Kandiyoti, Deniz. "Gendering the Modern: On Missing Dimensions in the Study of Turkish Modernity." *Rethinking Modernity and National Identity in Turkey*. Eds. Sibel Bozdoğan and Raşat Kasaba. Seattle and London: U of Washington P, 1997.

———. "Pink Card Blues: Trouble and Strife at the Crossroads of Gender." *Fragments of Culture: The Everyday of Modern Turkey*. Eds. Deniz Kandioyti and Ayşe Saktanber. London: I. B. Tauris, 2002. 277-293.

Kaos, GL, IGLHRC, and LGBTI News Turkey. *Human Rights Violations of LGBT Individuals in Turkey.* Nov 2014. Web. 31 July 2021. <https://ilga.org/wp-content/uploads/2016/02/Shadow-report-16.pdf>

Kiliç, Deniz, and Gaye Uncu. "Turkey." *Unspoken Rules: Sexual Orientation and Women's Human Rights.* Ed. Rachel Rosenbloom. London: Cassell, 1996. 203-214.

Kiliçaslan, Seher Cesur, and Toprak Işik. "Being LGBTI in Turkey: Views of Society, Rights and Violations." *Journal of Strategic Research in Social Science* 3.1 (2017): 1-20.

Kinli, Irem Özgören. "Reconfiguring Ottoman Gender Boundaries and Sexual Categories by the Mid-19th Century." *Política y Sociedad* 50.2 (2013): 381-395.

Klauda, Georg. *Die Vertreibung aus dem Serail: Europa und die Heteronormalisierung der islamischen Welt.* Hamburg: Männerschwarm, 2008.

Klein, Dennis, Queercom, and Jürgen Bieniek. "Zwischen Standesamt und Steinigung." *männer aktuell* 1 (2005): 39-42.

Kolat, Kenan. "Islam, Islamismus, Religiosität." *Muslime unter dem Regenbogen. Homosexualität, Migration und Islam.* Ed. LSVD Berlin-Brandenburg e. V. Berlin: Querverlag, 2004. 204-216.

Mansbridge, Joanna. "The *Zenne*: Male Belly Dancers and Queer Modernity in Contemporary Turkey." *Theatre Research International* 42.1 (2017): 20-36.

Marschner, Andreas, and Dennis Klein. "Barbarei im Iran." *männer aktuell* 9 (2005): 36.

Massad, Joseph Andoni. "Re-Orienting Desire: The Gay International and the Arab World." *Public Culture* 14.2 (2002): 361-385.

Mendos, Lucas Ramón. *State-Sponsored Homophobia.* 13th ed. 2019. Web. 28 July 2021. <https://ilga.org/downloads/ILGA_State_Sponsored_Homophobia_2019.pdf>

Mizielinska, Joanna, and Robert Kulpa. Guest Editors. Special Issue "'In Transition:' Central / Eastern European Sexualities." *Lambda Nordica* 4 (2012).

Mohr, Andreas Ismail. "Wie steht der Koran zur Homosexualität?" *Muslime unter dem Regenbogen. Homosexualität, Migration und Islam.* Ed. LSVD Berlin-Brandenburg e.V. Berlin: Querverlag, 2004. 9-38.

Motschenbacher, Heiko. "The Discursive Interface of National, European and Sexual Identities: Preliminary Evidence from the Eurovision Song Contest." *Intercultural Europe: Arenas of Difference, Communication and Mediation.* Eds. Barbara Lewandowska-Tomasczcyk and Hanna Pulaczewska. Stuttgart: ibidem, 2010. 85-103.

Moyer, Jessica. "The Prophet Murders." *Booklist* 15 Sept 2008. 30.

Muedini, Fait. *LGBTI Rights in Turkey: Sexuality and the State in the Middle East.* Cambridge et al: Cambridge UP, 2018.

Murray, Stephen O. "Corporealizing Medieval Persian and Turkish Tropes." *Islamic Homosexualities: Culture, History, and Literature.* Eds. Stephen O. Murray and Will Roscoe. New York and London: New York UP, 1997. 132-141.

Muslim LGBT Inclusion Project. New York: Intersections International, 2011.

Necef, Mehmet Ümit. "Turkey on the Brink of Modernity: A Guide for Scandinavian Gays." *Sexuality and Eroticism Among Males in Moslem Societies.* Eds. Arno Schmitt and Jehoeda Sofer. New York: Harrington Park, 1992. 71-71.

Norris, J. F. "Crime Fiction on a EuroPass: Mehmet Murat Somer." Web. 9 Nov 2021. <https://prettysinister.blogspot.com/2011/10/crime-fiction-on-europass-mehmet-murat.html>

O'Connor, John Kennedy. *The Eurovision Song Contest: The Official History.* London: Carlton, 2007.

Oguzhan, Fatih. "Foucault Observes the Ottomans: Ars Erotica, Construction of the Homosexual, and the Paradox of Homoeroticism." *The Melbourne Arts Journal* 2 (2019): 126-137.

Oksal, Aynur. "Turkish Family Members' Attitudes Toward Lesbians and Gay Men." *Sex Roles* 58 (2008): 514-525.

Öncü, Ayşe. "Global Consumerism, Sexuality as Public Spectacle, and the Cultural Remapping of Istanbul in the 1990s." *Fragments of Culture: The Everyday of Modern Turkey.* Eds. Deniz Kandioyti and Ayşe Saktanber. London: I. B. Tauris, 2002. 171-190.

———. "Istanbulites and Others: The Cultural Cosmology of Being Middle Class in the Era of Globalism." *Istanbul: Between the Global and the Local.* Ed. Çağlar Keyder. Lanham et al.: Rowman & Littlefield, 1999. 95-119.

Özbay, Cenk. "Nocturnal Queers: Rent Boys' Masculinity in Istanbul." *Sexualities* 13.5 (2010): 645-663.

———. "Same-Sex Sexualities in Turkey." *International Encyclopedia of the Social & Behavioral Sciences.* 2nd ed. Vol. 20. Oxford: Elsevier, 2015. 870-874.

———. *Queering Sexualites in Turkey: Gay Men, Male Prostitutes and the City.* London and New York: I. B. Tauris, 2017.

———, and Evren Savcı. "Queering Commons in Turkey." *GLQ: A Journal of Lesbian and Gay Studies* 24.4 (2018: 526-521).

———, and Ozan Soybakis. "Political Masculinities: Gender, Power, and Change in Turkey." *Social Politics* 27.1 (2020): 27-50.

Özbek, Meral. "Arabesk Culture: A Case of Modernization and Popular History." *Rethinking Modernity and National Identity in Turkey.* Eds. Sibel Bozdoğan and Reşat Kasaba. Seattle and London: U of Washington P, 1997. 211-232.

Özen, Emrecan. "Tourist Guide to Istanbul Gay Nightlife." Web. 9 Feb 2021. <http://www.nighttours.com/istanbul/gayguide/>

Özmen, Seçkin, Gizem Parlayandemir, and Sami Çöteli. "Construction of Queer Characters in the New Turkish Cinema." *International Journal of Arts & Sciences* 10.2 (2017): 475-484.

Ozsoy, Elif Ceylan. "Decolonizing Decriminalization Analyses: Did the Ottomans Decriminalize Homosexuality in 1858?" *Journal of Homosexuality* (2020): 1-24. Web. 8 July 2021. <https://doi.org/10.1080/00918369.2020.1715142>

Pearce, Susan C. "Pride in Istanbul. Notes from the Field: Summer 2013." *Societies Without Borders* 9.1 (2014): 111-128.

Polymenopoulou, Eleni. "Same-Sex Narratives and LGBTI Activism in the Muslim World." *SFS: Georgetown Journal of International Affairs* 18 May 2020. Web. 28 July 2021. <https://gjia.georgetown.edu/2020/05/18/same-sex-narratives-and-lgbti-activism-in-muslim-world/>

Poole, Ralph J. "Eurovision Song Contest." *Global Encyclopedia of Lesbian, Gay, Bisexual, Transgender and Queer History*. Eds. Howard Chiang et al. Farmington Hills: Charles Scribner's Sons / Gale / Cengage Company, 2019. 522-525.

———. "Kopftuch unter der Perücke oder der Aufstand der islamischen Töchter gegen den türkischen Kemalismus". *Kopf- und andere Tücher*. Eds. Gisela Engel and Susanne Scholz. Berlin: trafo, 2006. 9-29.

Rehberg, Peter. "Winning Failure: Queer Nationality at the Eurovision Song Contest." *SQS: Journal of Queer Studies in Finland* 2.2 (2007): 60-65.

Rehman, Javaid, and Eleni Polymenopoulou. "Is Green a Part of the Rainbow? Sharia, Homosexuality and LGBT Rights in the Muslim World." *Fordham International Law Journal* 37.1 (2013): 1-52.

Sahika, Yuksel et al. "Group Psychotherapy with Female-to-Male Transsexuals in Turkey." *Archives of Sexual Behavior* 29.3 (2000): 279-290.

Schmidtke, Sabine. "Homoeroticism and Homosexuality in Islam: A Review Article." *Bulletin of the School of Oriental and African Studies* 62.2 (1999): 260-266.

Schmitt, Arno. "Different Approaches to Male-Male Sexuality/Eroticism from Morocco to Usbekistān." *Sexuality and Eroticism Among Males in Moslem Societies*. Eds. Arno Schmitt and Jehoeda Sofer. New York: Harrington Park, 1992. 1-24.

Shay, Anthony. "The Male Dancer in the Middle East and Central Asia." *Belly Dance: Orientalism, Transnationalism, and Harem Fantasy*. Eds. Anthony Shay and Barbara Sellers-Young. Costa Mesa: Mazda, 2005. 51-84.

Sinclair-Webb, Emma. "Military Service and Manhood in Turkey." *Imagined Masculinities: Male Identity and Culture in the Modern Middle East*. Eds. Mai Ghoussoub and Emma Sinclair-Webb. London: Saqi, 2006. 65-92.

Sofer, Jehoeda. "Sodomy in the Law of Muslim States." *Sexuality and Eroticism Among Males in Moslem Societies*. Eds. Arno Schmitt and Jehoeda Sofer. New York et al.: Harrington Park, 1992. 131-149.

Solomon, Thomas. "Articulating the Historical Moment: Turkey, Europe, and Eurovision 2003." *A Song for Europe: Popular Music and Politics in the Eurovision Song Contest*. Eds. Ivan Raykoff and Robert Deam Tobin. Aldershot: Ashgate, 2007. 135-145.

Somer, Mehmet Murat. *The Gigolo Murder: A Hop-Çiki Yaya Thriller*. Trans. Kenneth James Dakan. London: Serpent's Tail, 2009.

———. *The Prophet Murders: A Hop-Çiki Yaya Thriller*. Trans. Kenneth James Dakan. London: Serpent's Tail, 2008.

Stokes, Martin. "Islam, the Turkish State and Arabesk." *Popular Music* 11.2 *A Changing Europe* (1992): 213-227.

Szulc, Lukasz. "Contemporary Discourses on Non-Heterosexual and Gender Non-Conforming Citizens." *International Review of Turkish Studies* 1.2 (2011): 10-31.

Talay, Zeynep, "The Ongoing Turkish Protests Have Left Us Enlightened and Emboldened." *The Guardian* 20 July 2013. Web. 3 Sept 2015. <http://www.theguardian.com/commentisfree/2013/jul/20/turkish-protests-enlightened-emboldened>

Tapinc, Huseyin. "Masculinity, Femininity, and Turkish Male Homosexuality." *Modern Homosexualities: Fragments of Lesbian and Gay Experiences*. Ed. Ken Plummer. London: Routledge, 1992. 39-49.

Tertilt, Hermann. *Turkish Power Boys: Ethnographie einer Jagendbande*. Frankfurt a.M.: Suhrkamp, 1996.

The Noble Qur'an in the English Language. Transl. Muhammad Taqî-ud-Dîn Al-Hilâlî and Muhammad Muhsin Khân. Madinah: King Fahd Complex, n.d.

"They Hunt us Down for Fun:" Discrimination and Police Violence Against Transgender Women in Kuwait. Human Rights Watch. 15 Jan 2012. Web. 27 July 2021. <https://www.hrw.org/report/2012/01/15/they-hunt-us-down-fun/discrimination-and-police-violence-against-transgender-women>

"They Want Us Exterminated:" Murder, Torture, Sexual Orientation and Gender in Iraq. Human Rights Watch. 17 Aug 2009. Web. 27 July 2021. <https://www.hrw.org/report/2009/08/17/they-want-us-exterminated/murder-torture-sexual-orientation-and-gender-iraq>

Thumann, Michael. Der Islam-Irrtum: Europas Angst vor der muslimischen Welt. Frankfurt/M.: Eichborn, 2011.

Tiftik, Sevcan. "LGBTI Identities in Turkish Literature." The Global Literature in Libraries Initiative. 19 Aug 2017. Web. 5 Aug 2021. <https://glli-us.org/2017/08/19/lgbti-identities-in-turkish-literature/>

Turkey: Pride and Violence. Human Rights Watch. 22 June 2009. Web. 31 July 2021. <https://www.hrw.org/news/2009/06/22/turkey-pride-and-violence>

Wafer, Jim. "Muhammad and Male Homosexuality." Islamic Homosexualities: Culture, History, and Literature. Eds. Stephen O. Murray and Will Roscoe. New York and London: New York UP, 1997. 87-96.

Warner, Michael. Publics and Counterpublics. New York: Zone Books, 2005.

"We Need a Law for Liberation:" Gender, Sexuality, and Human Rights in a Changing Turkey. Human Rights Watch. 21 May 2008. Web. 31 July 2021. <https://www.hrw.org/sites/default/files/reports/turkey0508webwcover.pdf>

Wiegand, Chis. "Different Beats." The Guardian (London). 14 May 2008. Web. 28 July 2021. <https://www.theguardian.com/books/2008/may/14/crimebooks.chriswiegand>

Wolter, Irving. Kampf der Kulturen. Der Eurovision Song Contest als Mittel national-kultureller Repräsentation. Würzburg: Königshausen & Neumann, 2006.

Women for Women's Human Rights / NEW WAYS. Turkish Civil and Penal Code Reforms from a Gender Perspective: The Success of Two Nationwide Campaigns. Istanbul: WWHR / NEW WAYS 2005.

Yenilmez, Meltem Ince. "LGBTQIs in Turkey: The Challenges and Resilience of This Marginalized Group." Sexuality Research and Social Policy 18 (2021): 440-449.

Yılmaz, Volkan. "The New Constitution of Turkey: A Blessing or a Curse for LGBT Citizens?" Turkish Policy Quarterly 11.4 (2013): 131-140.

Ze'evi, Dror. "Hiding Sexuality: The Disappearance of Sexual Discourse in the Late Ottoman Middle East." Social Analysis 49.2 (2005): 34-53.

———. Producing Desire: Changing Sexual Discourse in the Ottoman Middle East, 1500-1900. Berkeley et al.: U of California P, 2006.

Zengin, Aslı. "What Is Queer about Gezi?" Hot Spots. Fieldsights. 31 Oct 2013. Web. 4 Oct 2021. <https://culanth.org/fieldsights/what-is-queer-about-gezi>

Zihnioğlu, Özge. "The Legacy of the Gezi Protests in Turkey." *After Protest: Pathways Beyond Mass Mobilization*. Ed. Richard Youngs. Washington, DC: Carnegie Endowment for International Peace, 2019. 11-17.

2. Architecture of Seduction, or: What (Really) Goes On in the Hamam?

> At the Turkish Bath
> his chest, hairy as a gorilla's,
> his penis, puckered
> under its ruddy dome,
> squat as a fireplug.
> My father and I sat
> ass to ass in the steam.
> (Richard J. Fein, 34)

The Turkish bath—or hamam—has attained the status of a modern myth having "always held enormous fascination for the West" (Vanzan 1), and it continues to be celebrated for its "sublime" and "transformative" pleasures ("Mystery & Wonder"). Doubtlessly, visiting a Turkish bath while being in Istanbul seems both obligatory and challenging for dedicated tourists. It can be a relaxing and sensual experience—to be immersed in musky steam and subdued darkness. The Ottoman hamams are gorgeous in their architectural design, though some of them unfortunately are not kept to a standard everyone feels comfortable with. A dear friend of mine, whom I dragged into one of the oldest existing hamams in Istanbul—the Kılıç Ali Paşa Hamamı, now reopened after seven years of restoration[1]—dreaded getting all kinds of infections due to the lack of appropriate hygiene. He complained about reused towels, bath shoes 'alive' with bacteria, and the soap sponge used for massages having seen too many generations of dead skin follicles. And yet, by now even he has stored away this anxiety-ridden experience as a fond memory of experiencing Istanbul as a tourist, which now always serves as a laughter-inducing anecdote.

---

1   See <http://kilicalipasahamami.com/about/>.

Having myself paid repeated visits to most of the hamams in Istanbul, I can attest to some of my friend's concerns. I, however, particularly struggled with haggling about massage fees and tips, and sometimes with the overzealous, blood-drawing efforts of the masseurs, and yet, I returned again and again. The drowsy atmosphere of this all-male space can have an intoxicating, addictive effect—the all-female counterpart of a women's hamam must have a similar result from what I have been told, but of course, I would not know and therefore cannot share this experience myself.[2] What goes on in a hamam—what *really* goes on—is something that certainly differs depending on the selected hamam, on one's biological sex, on whether one is a local or a foreigner, and on one's openness to experiment if the chance is given. My own range of experience has been surprisingly broad, given my habitual shyness and usual reluctance to unknown experimentation. But no doubt, I did perceive the hamam as an alluring—and queer—space, prone to promises of pleasure and seduction. With this admission, I am aware of inscribing myself into the myth-laden tradition of exoticizing and eroticizing a space that is not part of my own cultural background and that has led to the abundant production of Orientalist fantasies surrounding the hamam experience, ranging from travel accounts such as Flaubert's and Lady Montagu's to gay pornography such as Jean-Daniel Cadinot's luscious *Hammam* (2004).[3]

---

2   See Hahn (464-465) for a discussion of a documentary on historical hamams in Istanbul that includes descriptions of the treatments and interactions in the female section between the service personnel and the clients.

3   See Boone, who calls Cadinot's *Harem: Sex Bazaar* (1984) and *Hammam* (2004) "modern avatars" of the hamam with their wild mix of authentic location shots "with Orientalist porn-props" (*Homoerotics* 90). Boone also includes, in his selection of such "modern avatars," Özpetek's *Hamam* as well as Salah Abu Seif's *Hammam al-Malatily* (1973; *The Malatili Baths*), the latter "a rare instance of homosexuality handled with relative non-judgment in Egyptian film" (*Homoerotics* 90). These examples show that the trope of the bath "has remained such a consistently productive site for homoerotic imaginings and for Orientalist projections over the past four hundred years" (*Homoerotics* 90).

Travelers' Hamam Fantasies

"Es ist die Sünde, die durch den Blick geboren wird. Der Sehsinn ist der Verführung besonders leicht ausgesetzt" (Groschner 26).[4] With this résumé, Gabriele Groschner closes her synopsis of the secret pleasure of looking while bathing. In what follows, I wish to offer a few and selected 'insights' into the history and practice of the hamam, but above all about the myths it has triggered. Indeed, the 'peculiarity' of the pleasure that Groschner attests to undoubtedly is heightened by the exotic allure—for foreigners—of the place. It is almost impossible for a Western visitor and observer to break away from the sultry-erotic fantasies about the hamam that are so strongly embedded in our culture. But I want to counteract the dominance of a straight male voyeuristic gaze that attests to a long-standing tradition of privileged, hegemonic politics and economics of gazing. There are definitely different, less hierarchical constellations than that of a man who lustfully and secretly looks at a naked woman while bathing. Exchanging gazes in the context of bathing can follow completely different erotic rules and seductive skills, especially when this exchange entails a male-only setting.

First, however, I would like to look at precisely those depictions of the Turkish bath that are dedicated to that dominant, gender-coded economics of gazing, and thus first at the most famous male-Orientalist representation of the hamam: Jean August Dominique Ingres's *Le Bain turc* from 1862. The painting shows naked harem ladies bathing. Ingres painted this picture at the age of 82. He wrote his age on the canvas and according to Walter Pach, this painting was "a kind of résumé of all Ingres's work on similar themes" (132). In fact, he 'recycled' various bathing and odalisque figures for this picture, such as *La Grande odalisque* (1814) and above all *Baigneuse de Valpinçon* (1808). When Pach describes the painting as a "technical triumph of European painting" (132) and, moreover, as Ingres's "most emphatic statement of his feeling for women" (133), this does not hide the fact that it is also a major work of the Orientalist art wave of the nineteenth century.

The ladies in the painting do not seem particularly animated, but rather are, as one critic notes, exhibited like classic statues in a gallery full of antiques (Danto). This may be because Ingres created this painting as an assemblage, as a collection of different women and motifs that he borrowed from his own

---

4   "It is sin that is born by looking. The sense of sight is particularly easily exposed to seduction" (transl. R. P.).

and other sources of inspiration and brought together here. But it is also true that Ingres did not paint based on living models, and certainly not based on living Turkish models. The fact that his bathing ladies look so European is not least because he had never been to an authentic hamam, be it in Turkey or elsewhere, for example in Egypt or Algeria. Rather, he took his inspiration for the Turkish bath from the descriptions of Lady Mary Wortley Montagu's *Turkish Embassy Letters* from 1716 to 1718, to which I will return shortly. Arthur Danto compares Ingres's Orientalism with that of Delacroix's *Femmes d'Alger dans leur appartement* (1834) contrasting Delacroix's "unmatched visual excitement" to Ingres's "almost incomprehensibly inanimate painting" (Danto). Danto interprets Ingres's neoclassical use of antiquity as a conscious maneuver "to exclude himself, as if he were obeying the sanctions of the harem."[5] Ingres herewith contributes to the craze of 'classical' French Orientalism,

> [which] was centred on erotic images of unveiling or what might be termed the 'Scheherezade syndrome.' This fiction, a projection of European masculine fantasies, which claimed to uncover and expose to the public gaze the inner secrets of the forbidden and sacred, the harem and the Turkish baths (hammam), reflected French colonial hegemony, an invasion and sexual conquest of the space that Muslim society held to be most forbidden (haram). (Macmaster and Lewis 148)

I do not deny that the authors are right to interpret Ingres's pictorial composition in such an Orientalist manner, according to which "the 'eye' of the viewer is positioned as that of somebody peering in upon naked women, who are oblivious of the intrusion" (Macmaster and Lewis 149). I want to point out two aspects, however, that I find missing in this reading and that will be important to me in the following: the homoerotic allusions on the one hand, because some of the women unmistakably touch each other with relish; and the question of testimony, on the other: who is the viewer of this scene, and who guarantees authenticity?

Ingres was able to fall back on an established tradition for his Oriental inspiration, according to which European travelers had discovered, praised, and copied the Ottoman bathing culture at least since the eighteenth century. The term "Turkish bath" comes from these records, although geographically at that time a hamam did not necessarily have to be in Turkey or the Ottoman

---

[5] Danto also comments: "By contrast, Delacroix gained entry to the women's quarters in Algiers."

Empire, but could be found in every other Oriental country with Islamic religion. Descriptions of visits to such baths were meant to arouse the interest of the European public in the exotic Orient. As with the paintings, it was mostly male travelers who provided the best possible evocative and detailed descriptions of bathing practices in letters and reports. In contrast to the paintings, however, the problem arose here that, due to the sexually separated bathing culture, men could only ever have access to the men's hamam, but not to the women's hamam. While descriptions of the women's hamam were thus left to the readers' erotic imagination, descriptions of visiting a men's hamam, if painted in erotic colors, could easily become unintentionally—or in some cases deliberately—homoerotic.

According to Ulrich Müller, Salomon Schweigger was the first to describe a Turkish bath in the German language in 1608. Schweigger was sent to Constantinople in 1577 as an embassy preacher in the service of Emperor Rudolf II. In his travel diary with the original title *Ein newe Reyssbeschreibung auss Teutschland nach Konstantinopel und Jerusalem* (A New Description of a Voyage from Germany to Constantinople and Jerusalem), the Protestant clergyman from Nuremberg describes one such hamam in Constantinople. He begins by explaining the architecture, which he compares with European church buildings, and then delves into the bathing practices:

> Sobald einer hineinkompt, setzt er sich auf diesen Herd. Da kompt ein Badknecht, der umbfahet ihn, renkt ihm den Leib hin und her, als wollt er ihm den Leib ineinanderrichten, desgleichen dehnet er ihm auch die Glieder, Arm, Händ und die Schenkel, als wollt er mit ihm ringen. Darnach legt er ihn nach der Läng auf den Herd, steht ihm auf den Leib, doch sänftiglich; daher unter unserm Gesind diese Schimpfred entstanden ist: "Ich will gehen und mich für die Langeweil lassen mit Füßen treten," das ist: "Ich will ins Bad gehen." (118)[6]

What is striking, in contrast to later descriptions of Western travelers, is the absence of that 'peculiar pleasure' in secret looking, despite all the compar-

---

6   "As soon as one comes in, he sits on this stove. Then a bath servant, who knocks him around, turns his body back and forth as if he wanted to straighten his body, at the same time he also stretches his limbs, arm, hands, and thighs, as if he wanted to wrestle with him. Then he lays him down on the stove, stands on his body, but gently; therefore, among our servants, this insult has arisen: 'I want to go and let myself be trampled for boredom,' that is: 'I want to go to the bathhouse.'" (Transl. R. P.)

ative cultural perspectives. It may be due to Schweigger's priesthood or his status as a diplomat, given the delicate political relations between the Habsburgs and Ottomans, that he lacks this desire—also and especially when referring to female bathing practices. On the contrary, he emphasizes the lack of chastity of the Germans in comparison to the 'barbaric' Turks:

> Die Männer haben besondere Bäder und die Weiber auch besondere. Sie bedecken sich im Baden fein züchtig und ehrbarlich und nicht so schimpflich wie die Teutschen, da es das Ansehen hat, als wollt einer die Scham mit Fleiß zeigen, oder— wie ich zu Venedig gesehen hab—daß die Männer allerdings bloß und unbedeckt ins Bad gehen. Sie knüpfen aber ein blauleinen Tuch umb die Hüft, das geht zweimal herum und geht bis auf den Boden hinab; also daß wir Christen in diesem Fall sollten Zucht und Ehrbarkeit von diesen Barbaris lernen. (119)[7]

Although Müller describes Schweigger's description as the "beginning of the fascination that the Turkish baths and bathing customs increasingly exerted on (Western) Europeans" (291, transl. R. P.), the report remains remarkable in contrast to many of the following because of its attention to detail and precisely because of the lack of voyeuristic desires. In another testimonial, written by the Prussian lieutenant Helmuth Karl Bernhard Graf von Moltke, the comparative cultural perception of the Turkish bath is mixed with another, namely emotional component: astonishment and horror. Von Moltke initially started on an educational trip to Southeastern Europe, but then served as an instructor for the Turkish troops from 1836 to 1839 at the request of the Ottoman Sultan and traveled to Constantinople and the desert of Mesopotamia, among other places. He experienced his first visit to the hamam after a long ride, which not only left him exhausted but also completely hypothermic. Before he is led into the center of the bathroom, he is frightened by the chill in the anteroom:

---

[7] "Men have special baths and women have special baths, too. In bathing, they cover themselves decently and respectably and not as disgracefully as the Germans, because it looks as if someone wants to show their private parts with diligence, or—as I saw in Venice—that the men go into the bathroom indeed bare and uncovered. But they tie a blue linen cloth around the waist, it goes around twice and goes down to the floor; so that in this case we Christians should learn discipline and respectability from these barbarians." (Transl. R. P.)

Mit Erstaunen erblickte ich auf der hölzernen Estrade, welche rings das Gemach umgab, mehrere Männer auf Teppichen und Matratzen liegen, bloß mit einem dünnen Leintuch zugedeckt, behaglich die Pfeife rauchend und sich wie an einem schwülen Sommertage an der Kühle labend, die mir in diesem Augenblick so entsetzlich schien.

Der Badewärter, der in unseren bedenklichen Mienen las, führte uns in ein zweites Gewölbe, in welchem schon eine ganz anständige Hitze war. Hier bedeutete man uns durch Zeichen, daß wir uns entkleiden möchten; man wickelt sich ein halbseidenes blaues Tuch um die Hüften [...]. Nach dieser Einkleidung schob man uns in eine dritte gewölbte Halle hinein, deren marmorner Fußboden so stark geheizt war, daß man ihn nur auf hölzernen Pantinen (Galendschi) betreten konnte. Der Telektschi (Tellak) oder Badewärter schreitet nun zu einer ganz eigentümlichen Prozedur. (59-60)[8]

This description of the rooms as well as what the text subsequently describes as a "procedure" on the "patient," to which von Moltke now confidently surrenders, may be regarded as the massage and washing application that is more or less still valid today:

Der ganze Körper wird gerieben und alle Muskeln gereckt und gedrückt. Der Mann kniet einem auf die Brust oder fährt mit dem Knöchel des Daumens den Rückgrat herab; alle Glieder, die Finger und selbst das Genick bringt er durch eine leichte Manipulation zum Knacken. [...] Der Patient wird nun demselben Verfahren unterworfen wie die türkischen Pferde beim Striegeln, indem nämlich Wärter einen kleinen Sack aus Ziegenhaar (Gebrek) über die rechte Hand zieht und damit den ganzen Körper anhaltend überfährt. Dies ist allerdings eine gründliche Reinigung, und man möchte

---

8   "With astonishment, I saw several men lying on carpets and mattresses on the wooden dais that surrounded the room, covered only with a thin sheet, comfortably smoking their pipe and refreshing themselves as if on a sultry summer day on the coolness that I had in this moment found so appalling. The bath attendant, who read our worried expressions, led us into a second vault, in which there was already a decent heat. Here we were indicated by signs that we should undress; you wrap a half-silk blue cloth around your hips [...]. After this cladding, we were pushed into a third vaulted hall, the marble floor of which was so heated that you could only enter on wooden slippers (Galendschi). The Telektschi (Tellak) or bath attendant now proceeds to a very peculiar procedure." (Transl. R. P.)

sagen, daß man noch nie gewaschen gewesen ist, bevor man nicht ein türkisches Bad genommen. Der Telektschi erscheint nun aufs neue mit einer großen Schüssel mit wohlriechendem Seifenschaum. Mittels eines großen Quastes aus den Fasern der Palmrinde seift er seinen Mann vom Scheitel bis zur Fußsohle, Haare, Gesicht, alles ein, und mit wahrem Vergnügen gießt man dann das kalte Wasser über Kopf, Brust und Leib.

Jetzt ist man fertig: statt der durchnäßten Tücher erhält man trockene, über dem Feuer erwärmte, umgewickelt, einen Turban auf dem Kopf und ein Laken über die Schultern, denn die größte Dezenz wird beobachtet. (60-61)[9]

Having returned to the cool entrance hall, von Moltke now feels a great sense of comfort while enjoying coffee and a pipe: "It is impossible to describe how refreshing and beneficial such a bath is when you are very tired," he enthuses in conclusion (61, transl. R. P.). Other authors, however, emphasize less the slack relaxation, and more the erotic excitement of the hamam experience. The praised eroticism of the Orient, often referred to as a heterosexual male fantasy that focuses on a feminized Other, also features homoerotic fantasies. Nevertheless, even Edward Said's *Orientalism* has a blind spot here. Joseph Boone, in contrast, points to the proliferation of implicit heterosexist metaphors in the West appropriating the East and thus names "Said's failure to account for homoerotic elements in Orientalist pursuits" ("Vacation Cruises" 92). Boone concludes that not everything that appears seductively feminine has to be female. He takes Said's description of Gustave Flaubert's trip to Egypt in 1849/50 as an example of such a heteronormative discourse regarding Orientalism. Said interprets Flaubert's affair with the professional

---

9   "The whole body is rubbed and all muscles are stretched and pressed. The man kneels on your chest or runs the knuckle of the thumb down the spine; all limbs, fingers, and even the neck crack with his delicate handling. [...] The patient is now subjected to the same procedure as the Turkish horses when grooming, namely by the attendant pulling a small sack of goat hair (Gebrek) over the right hand and driving it over the whole body. This is a thorough cleansing, however, and one would like to say that one has never been washed before having taken a Turkish bath. The Telektschi now appears again with a large bowl of fragrant soap foam. Using a large tassel made from the fibers of the palm bark, he soaps his man from head to toe, hair, face, everything, and with real pleasure the cold water is then poured over head, chest, and body. Now you are done: instead of the soaked sheets you get wrapped in dry ones, heated over the fire, a turban on your head, and a sheet over your shoulders, because the greatest decency is observed." (Transl. R. P.)

female dancer Kuchuk Hanem as a paradigmatic example of the mechanism of a male, penetrating Orientalism:

> She was surely the prototype of several of his novels' female characters in her learned sensuality, delicacy, and (according to Flaubert) mindless coarseness. [...] The Oriental woman is an occasion and an opportunity for Flaubert's musings; he is entranced by her self-sufficiency, by her emotional carelessness, and also by what, lying next to him, she allows him to think. Less a woman than a display of impressive but verbally inexpressive femininity, Kuchuk is the prototype of Flaubert's Salammbô and Salomé [...]. (Said 186-187)

Said sees Flaubert here as a prototypical representative of the Western bourgeois traveler of the nineteenth century, who made an indiscriminate association between the Orient and—female—sexual availability, "although Flaubert's genius may have done more than anyone else's could have to give it artistic dignity" (188). Boone, in contrast, refers to the fact that Flaubert's first erotic encounter was not with Kuchuk but with a male dancer named Hasan. In a letter to Louis Bouilhet, dated 16 December 1849, Flaubert indulged in detailed descriptions of Hasan's erotic body play and his seductive dance skills:

> After our lunch on that same day we had dancers in—the famous Hasan el-Belbeissi and one other, with musicians; the second would have been noticed even without Hasan. They both wore the same costume—baggy trousers and embroidered jacket, their eyes painted with antimony (*kohl*). The jacket goes down to the abdomen, whereas the trousers, held by an enormous cashmere belt folded over several times, begin approximately at the pubis, so that the stomach, the small of the back and the beginning of the buttocks are naked, seen through a bit of black gauze held in place by the upper and lower garments. The gauze ripples on the hips like a transparent wave with every movement they make. [...] The effect comes from the gravity of the face contrasted with the lascivious movements of the body; occasionally, one or the other lies down flat on his back like a woman about to offer herself [...]. Now and again, during the dance, their impressario makes jokes and kisses Hasan on the belly. Hasan never for a moment stops watching himself in the mirror. (*Flaubert* 69-70)

A month later, in a letter of 15 January 1850, he again wrote to his best friend and confidant Bouilhet: "We have not yet seen any dancing girls [...]. But we have seen male dancers. Oh! Oh! Oh!" (*Flaubert* 83). He goes on, however, to deliver an extended and much cruder version of this last description:

> From time to time, during the dance, the impresario, or pimp, who brought them plays around them kissing them on the belly, the arse, and the small of the back, and making obscene remarks in an effort to put additional spice into a thing that is already quite clear in itself. It is too beautiful to be exciting. I doubt whether we shall find the women as good as the men; the ugliness of the latter adds greatly to the thing as art. I had a headache for the rest of the day, and I had to go and pee two or three times during the performance—a nervous reaction that I attribute particularly to the music.—I'll have this marvelous Hasan el-Belbeissi come again. He'll dance the Bee for me, in particular. Done by such a bardash as he, it can scarcely be a thing for babes. (*Flaubert* 84)

So far, Flaubert does not name the "thing that is already quite clear in itself." He chooses to remain ambiguous and resorts to sexual allusions such as "dance the Bee for me," instead. Also, referring to Hasan as bardash opens the space for further implications that are "quite clear" for knowledgeable insiders.[10] Only later, in the same letter and right after praising Hasan's dancing skills, does Flaubert explicitly confess to a same-sex experience. Significantly, this takes place in the hamam where his adventure ends with the admission of engaging in what he now names "sodomy." Flaubert writes: "Speaking of bardashes, this is what I know about them. Here it is quite accepted. One admits one's sodomy, and it is spoken of at table in the hotel. Sometimes you do a bit of denying, and then everybody teases you and you end up confessing. Traveling as we are for educational purposes, and charged with a mission by the government, we have considered it our duty to indulge in this form of ejaculation" (84). Taking his 'educational mission' seriously—and one can sense the

---

10 Murray explains that Flaubert uses *bardash* as a term for a cross-dressing dancing boy known in Ottoman culture: "Transvestitic homosexuality has occurred and continues to occur in addition to (and mixed with) pederasty. After all, *berdache*, the word European colonists applied to sexual and gender variances around the world, derives from the Persian *bardash* through Arabic" (24). He adds that the word in Persian originally refers to slaves of ambiguous gender, yet whereas Mediterranean (including Islamic) societies use slaves sexually, for them "the sense of effeminacy and sexual receptivity does not seem to have been primary originally. Although clearly a term for a homosexual role used by French observers of Arab (and other) societies, its status as a native term for a homosexual role is uncertain" (Murray 45).

self-irony in this admission—Flaubert seeks and finds the opportunity in the hamam: "It's at the baths that such things take place. You reserve the bath for yourself (five francs including masseurs, pipe, coffee, sheet and towel) and you skewer your lad in one of the rooms" (84). Afterwards, a masseur takes over "when all the rest is done" (84), and while Flaubert was hoping for one of the "nice young boys," his masseur was "a man in his fifties, ignoble, disgusting," nevertheless devoted to providing the pleasure Flaubert was seeking. The ensuing scene is rendered in a comic tone, wavering between bawdy pleasure, economic obligation, and brazen admission:

> my *kellaa* was rubbing me gently, and when he came to the noble parts he lifted up my *boules d'amour* to clean them, then continuing to rub my chest with his left hand he began to pull with his right on my prick, and as he drew it up and down he leaned over my shoulder and said "*baksheesh, baksheesh.*" [...] I pushed him away a little, saying "*làh, làh*" ("no, no")—he thought I was angry and took on a craven look—then I gave him a few pats on the shoulder, saying "*làh, làh*" again but more gently—he smiled a smile that meant, "You're not fooling me—you like it as much as anybody, but today you've decided against it for some reason." As for me, I laughed aloud like a dirty old man, and the shadowy vault of the bath echoed with the sound. (85)

Ultimately, in yet another letter (2 June 1850), he answers Bouilhet's question regarding sex with any of these young men in the affirmative: "By the way, you ask me if I consummate that business at the baths. Yes—and on a pockmarked young rascal wearing a white turban. It made me laugh, that's all. But I'll be at it again. To be done well, an experiment must be repeated" (*Flaubert* 203-204).[11]

---

11   The editor includes a footnote here—as I do here as well—to mention that Sartre in his study on the young Flaubert, *L'Idiot de la Famille*, has doubts about Flaubert's consummation of "that business in the baths." According to Sartre, the "pederastic talk in his letters to Louis Bouilhet is merely a form of joking [...] and all the references to bardashes in the baths were the swank of a traveler wanting to impress a stay-at-home with his exotic experiences" (204). Bleys (112-113) and Murray (24) are among those—like myself—who differ from Sartre on this question.

Lady Montagu Visits the Hamam

Besides all the male travelers and reporters, there were also some women who were interested in the baths, visited them, and told their compatriots about them. No one did this as successfully as Lady Mary Wortley Montagu, not least through her influence on visual artists like Ingres. In contrast to her male colleagues in the writing guild, her *Turkish Embassy Letters* from 1716/18 explicitly emphasize female nudity and she does so, which is crucial here, as an eyewitness: "The emphasis on nakedness in Lady Mary's 'letter,' which was composed specifically for publication, runs counter to all other accounts, which state that only slaves or 'women of the lower orders' went naked in the women's baths" (Conner 39). However, she does not measure herself against other writers, but rather against visual artists. It should, therefore, be emphasized that Montagu strangely takes on a male gaze position—she calls it "wickedness"—when she asks her readers to imagine that she is an invisible male painter who casts forbidden glances on the bathing scenario: "I had wickedness enough to wish secretly, that Mr. Gervase [i.e., Charles Jervas, a popular Irish portrait painter, R. P.] could have been there invisible. I fancy it would have very much improved his art to see so many fine women naked" (Montagu 59). With this ethnomasquerade[12] she achieves two things: while she strengthens her narrative authority as a travel reporter, this strategy also prevents accusations of lesbian desire. She not only testifies to not having attended any indecent acts but also assures her readers that she herself was always dressed. The very thing that Montagu did not see or want to describe, namely eroticism among women, is what Ingres extracted from her lines and brought to the canvas. Lady Montagu's letters had eight editions alone in France at the time of Ingres and they were an important part of the Orientalist mania. Ingres copied the following passage from Montagu and it would serve as inspiration for his erotic painting:

> I believe, in the whole, there were two hundred women [...], all being in the state of nature, that is, in plain English, stark naked, without any beauty or defect concealed. [...] so many fine women naked, in different postures, some in conversation, some working, others drinking coffee or sherbet, and

---

12 Kader Konuk uses this term to describe Montagu's participation in Ottoman culture: "Ethnomasquerade is defined here as the performance of an ethnic identity through the mimicking of clothes, gestures, appearance, language, cultural codes, or other components of identity formation" (393).

2. Architecture of Seduction, or: What (Really) Goes On in the Hamam?

many negligently lying on their cushions while their slaves (generally pretty girls of seventeen or eighteen) were employed in braiding their hair in several pretty manners. (Montagu 59)

Not only had Ingres never visited a hamam—and certainly not a women's hamam—in this text he decidedly asks his viewers to envision an image of the erotic customs of Muslim women. And he does so in a way that differs from Lady Montagu: she also wanted her readers to get a picture of the female Oriental, but this picture was far more complex than the one Ingres painted. Scholars are divided on whether she used cultural difference as a distinguishing feature in her description of the Turkish bath or as a means of dialogic collaboration. Her supposedly male artist gaze in particular becomes the target of different readings here. Joseph Lew draws attention to the various frames of the description and interprets them as Montagu's skillful maneuver to shield herself from accusations of erotic projections, which she must have anticipated since the tableau of herself amid two hundred naked women undoubtedly builds up an erotic connotation. But Lew also notes how she explicitly draws attention to the frame, namely the artist, in whose place she steps:

> The reader of the letter sees not merely the spectacle of the two hundred and one women (Lady Mary as the "one") but also the fantasized male artist watching the spectacle, learning from it, and later reproducing it—as Ingres actually did. [...] By placing herself inside the central frame with the Oriental women, yet also insistently remaining outside the larger frame as artist, producer, and letter writer, she foregrounds her solidarity with the Turkish women as subject / subjected: all women become *objects d'art* for the Western male. (Lew 443)

Although it withdraws the interest from the woman (herself) or the (other) women and redirects it to the frame, she actually gives herself freedom of agency: "she escapes being framed by framing the framer (Mr. Jervas). [...] Lady Mary's victory, however, remains purely personal: the one may escape representation by presenting herself; the two hundred cannot" (Lew 443). Srinivas Aravamudan also recognizes a partial identification of Montagu with the Turkish women but sees this as a utopian Levantization that reaches its climax in the bath.[13] It is of particular importance here on the one hand that of all identifiable addressees the decisive hamam letter is intended for an anonymous lady and thus becomes a metafictional reference by fusing the author and the reader and turning the text into a masquerade: "The subject, Montagu, addresses her object, womanliness, through a *mise en abîme* that reduces womanliness to masquerade. [...] anonymity, fictionality, and realism concerning female interiority coincide" (Aravamudan 78). On the other hand, the letter becomes political just at the moment when the bathhouse serves as an equivalent to the coffee house for English ladies. Montagu invokes a social institution as a comparative model that did not even exist: "'tis the women's coffee house, where all the news of the town is told, scandal invented etc." (Montagu 59).

Inge Boer notes the transgressive aspect of this comparison, namely that in this exclusive feminine place, the hamam, women can meet and exchange ideas undisturbed, regardless of social hierarchies (Boer 57). But the coffee house was a masculine monopoly in the English sociopolitical sphere, and therefore this is not just a comparison that should make it easier for the domestic audience to make a cultural transfer.[14] On the contrary, it implies, as Lew affirms, a deep disturbance of the male English reader and a directive to the female English reader: "we must first remember that Lady Mary's true median term, a women's coffee house, did not exist. English coffee-houses were male enclaves; this suggests a 'haremization' of English men. Second, Lady Mary believes her median concept *should* exist" (Lew 441). Ahmed Al-Rawi also emphasizes the lack of homosocial spaces for English women implied by Montagu and refers to the opening of the first Turkish bath in London in the

---

13   Aravamudan notes that Montagu's perception reflects the increasing loss of a ritual-symbolic significance and in turn the rising modernization and "cross-cultural levantinization:" "Montagu's own gesture converts the liminal communitarianism of the *hammam* into what Victor Turner characterizes as the 'liminoid' genre of free tropological appropriation typical of modern commodity culture" (87).

14   Said considers such comparisons as part of an Orientalist discourse: "Something patently foreign and distant acquires, for one reason or another, the status more rather than less familiar. One tends to stop judging things either as completely novel or as completely well-known: a new median category emerges, a category that allows one to see new things, things seen for the first time as versions of a previously known thing" (58). The argument of the well-known falls short in Montagu's example, however, since both the hamam and the coffeehouse are unknown to the female English readership.

1860s.[15] While the Turkish women in hamams formed a tight social network that could take on cathartic functions in the exchange of joys and sorrows, there was nothing like this for the English women:

> By 1739, there were 551 coffeehouses in England but women were forbidden to enter them. As a matter of fact, Montagu satirized England and its society for limiting the freedom of British women, because they did not take part in these important social gatherings where different intellectual and political topics were discussed. (Al-Rawi 26)

In addition to Montagu's controversial artist's perspective, her clothing—or rather her insistence on such within the hamam—triggered a debate among critics. First of all, in contrast to the considerable number of naked women, Montagu prefers to be mostly—but not entirely, as many inadvertently note[16]—clothed. She writes: "I was in my traveling habit, which is a riding dress, and certainly appeared very extraordinary to them. Yet there was not one of them that showed the least surprise or impertinent curiosity, but received me with all the obliging civility possible" (58). While Lew admits Montagu's subtle etiquette here ("she refrains from 'going Turkish'" [442]), Mary Jo Kietzman admits that the reference to the riding costume could symbolize the authority of her national identity, but then reads the description as a conscious and ironic self-presentation:

> By calling attention to her costume, Montagu paints an ironic self-portrait that emphasizes the tentative essays of a foreigner who is willing to interrogate her positionality and to assume the relatively limited role of participant in the *creation* of culture rather than that of a detached cultural analyst. (540, original emphasis)

---

15 John Potvin describes the inauguration of the male hamam by the ex-diplomat David Urquhart in London's West End in 1862 as a temple of health, distinct from the city's polluted streets but also as an ambiguous space of homoerotic potential: "Here, masculinity's integrity and gender performance are at once challenged and maintained in the very embodiment precipitated by how the senses are enlivened, that is, the touching, the sensuality—things not allowed for in the outside world. [...] It stands to reason, therefore, that these baths, particularly those charged with a heightened sense of the exotic, were spaces in which masculinity and sexuality were as slippery as the soapy passageways of the baths themselves" (330).

16 See, for example, Lew 441; Boer 57; Aravamudan 83.

Such a view emphasizes the extraordinariness of the situation in such a way that Montagu, as an outsider, takes on the culturally restrictive role of the English woman. Nothing embodies this restriction more vividly than the vestmental element of the corset:

> The lady that seemed the most considerable amongst them entreated me to sit by her and would fain have undressed me for the bath: I excused myself with some difficulty, they being however all so earnest in persuading me, I was at last forced to open my shirt, and show them my stays, which satisfied them very well, for I saw they believed I was so locked up in that machine, that it was not in my own power to open it, which contrivance they attributed to my husband. (Montagu 59-60)

It is not the Ottoman woman who has to suffer under her husband's rule here, but the English woman whose husband strangles her in such a way that she is "locked up in that machine." Even though Montagu presents this as a presumption on the part of the Turkish women, the image of her 'locked up' body remains a gesture that thwarts the usual binary of veiled/unveiled and suppressed/free in many descriptions of the Orient. In doing so, she prevents the Orientalist desire to free the woman of the East from the fetters of her unjust patriarchy from being continued. But she also demonstrates, as Teresa Heffernan states, "her cognizance of the gender inequity that underlies the very articulation of freedom in the social contract, a document that, although supposed to protect individual freedom assumes, as Locke does, the 'natural' right of the husband over his wife" (211).[17] Montagu's game of veiling and revealing goes as far as ascribing protective anonymity to the veil of Turkish women as well as to the nudity in the hamam, which liberates women from the compulsion to distinction. She writes about the equality of nakedness: "I was here convinced of the truth of a reflection I had often made, that if it was the fashion to go naked, the face would be hardly observed" (59). And in view of her allusion to the control of her own husband, it is particularly piquant

---

17   Heffernan goes on to quote from John Locke's *An Essay Concerning Human Understanding*: "But the husband and wife, though they have but one common concern, yet having different understandings, will unavoidably sometimes have different wills too; it therefore being necessary that the last determination, i.e. *the rule*, should be placed somewhere; it *naturally* falls to the *man's share*" (qtd. in Heffernan 211-212, emphasis added).

how in another letter she fantasizes wearing a veil not only as a democratizing piece of clothing but also as a license to transgression:

> 'Tis very easy to see they have more liberty than we have, no woman, of what rank so ever being permitted to go in the streets without two muslins, one that covers her face all but her eyes and another that hides the whole dress of her head [...]. You may guess then how effectually this disguises them, that there is no distinguishing the great lady from her slave and 'tis impossible for the most jealous husband to know his wife when he meets her, and no man dare either touch or follow a woman in the street. (71)

These and other passages in Montagu's *Letters* remain ambiguous, trapped in a "fictional double bind" (83), as Aravamudan puts it: she affirms her own English modesty through the 'false' modesty of the Turkish women. For the English readership, her allusion to the prison of the corset is most likely "a fictional by-product of the steamy bathhouse atmosphere, [...] readily associated with the English pornographic fantasy concerning the oversexed Turkish milieu that confuses harem with *hammam*" (84). Even if Montagu affirms, "there was not the least wanton smile or immodest gesture amongst them" (59), there is still the possibility for the reader to fantasize an alternate scenario: "In this description of naked interiors, 'Sapphism' will suggest itself, but in a very different way from the salacious discussion by previous male writers with overheated imaginations. [...] The bathhouse letter conceals a challenge to its addressees even as it delivers it" (Aravamudan 85).

Harem Suare: Fictions within Fictions

Linking the hamam and the harem is still a veritable motif even in our time,[18] particularly suitable for the representation of Oriental practices. The Turkish-Italian film director Ferzan Özpetek used this connection to make it a central location in his film *Harem Suare* (1999). The film takes place on two spatiotemporal levels, the older of which shows the last harem of the Ottoman Sultan Abdülhamit II in 1908 before his empire goes to pieces and the harem is dissolved. The second plot takes place in 1953 in a train station café in Parma, Italy, where an older woman tells a younger one about her past, with verbal

---

18 See Macmaster and Lewis (148), who note that both the hamam and the harem are spaces of the sacred as well as of the forbidden in Muslim society.

and visual allusions making it clear that this is the protagonist of the main narrative, the harem lady Safiye. Winner of a number of awards, this historical film thus tells, as the English poster promises, "An Erotic Tale of Sexual Freedom" and, significantly, uses a hamam scene in the film as the poster motif.

For me, the film serves as a bridge between Ingres's French-Orientalist neoclassicism and a nostalgic, indigenous introspection. Like Ingres, Özpetek uses the secret male gaze and shows women on erotic display. Yet the situation here is more complicated by the fact that Özpetek deals with his own culture; accusing him of Orientalization thus becomes problematic. The film follows the impossible love between Safiye, the sultan's favorite harem lady, and the sultan's servant and guardian of the harem, the eunuch Nadir.[19] While the revolution, and with it the dissolution of the sultanate, is already forming in front of the gates of the Yıldız Palace, the interior of the palace and especially the harem still seem a place of absolute seclusion and exclusivity. And yet here, too, signs of 'decay' hint at the intrusion of 'foreign' influences: a young concubine drowns herself 'outside' in the river, the sultan has Safiye translate and rewrite European operas—he would like *La Traviata* performed with a happy ending—, and Safiye, herself an outsider in the harem who comes from Italy and was sold as a slave in Cairo, falls in love with the black servant Nadir.

Just as Sultan Abdülhamit adapted the opera for his escapist purposes while simultaneously preparing the opening of the future Turkish nation to the West, the figure of Safiye also testifies to a historical turning point. Her Western education, her emancipated spirit, and her will to transgress mark her as a mediator between cultures. Especially if you take into account her narrative role in the spatiotemporally suspending space of the waiting room of the train station, the Italian Safiye, who lives in exile in Turkey, can be interpreted as the stand-in for the director, who was born in Istanbul and took Italian citizenship, and who says about the film: "With a Westerner's eye I'm trying to unravel one of the most crucial knots of my original culture:

---

19 Nadir therefore is a "Kızlar Agha," "the third highest-ranking officer of the empire, after the Sultan and the Grand Vizier (Chief Minister). [...] He was the most important link between the Sultan and the Valide Sultan (mother of the Sultan). The Kizlar [sic] Agha led the new odalisque to the Sultan' bedchamber, and was the only 'man' who could enter the harem should there have been any nocturnal emergencies. His duties were to protect the women, to provide and purchase the necessary odalisques for the harem, to observe the promotion of the women (usually after the death of a higher-ranking Kadin [sic]) and eunuchs" (Sansal).

the end of the Ottoman Empire, portrayed in one of the places dearest to the imagination—the harem" (qtd. in "Harem Suare Reviews").

Özpetek certainly serves most Western fantasies of the harem as an exotic place of excessive sexuality, where willing beauties give themselves to their potent master. The submissive, lascivious harem ladies—called odalisques (Turkish for slave and thus de facto at the lower end of the harem hierarchy) and at the time a popular subject of Western painters—live in this purely female space, completely cut off from the outside world. After all, harem comes from the Arabic *arām*, meaning "forbidden." But Özpetek also shows this place as a porous space of diverse ambiguities, in which women of different generations—by no means only odalisques and concubines—tell each other stories, in which the Sultan's family lives, men—albeit eunuchs—also socialize and, ultimately, solid politics are negotiated. Historically there was even a so-called "Sultanate of Women," which shows that in the sixteenth and seventeenth centuries the women of the royal Ottoman harem exercised extraordinary political influence on state affairs. Thus, it was mainly the mothers of the heir to the throne and the later sultans (*valide sultan*, royal mother) who often took on important diplomatic and economic functions. Leslie Peirce emphasizes that "[t]he Western stereotype of harems as stables of sex objects for male masters misses some important features of élite social structures in Muslim societies. Among them is the important fact that women controlled their own property and therefore had business dealings" (n.p.).[20]

Özpetek's film shows, in addition to all the pomposity, this unknown side of the harem, above all the resulting struggles among women for rank and power, as well as in the closing sequences the great bond and loyalty that has developed between the women. In the brutal process of the harem's dissolution, the formerly sacrosanct place is forcibly opened by the military, and the women are sent into 'freedom,' where they are left to their own devices completely unprotected. And Safiye, formerly the favorite (*ikbal*) and informal wife (*kadın*) of the Sultan with the birth of a son, says goodbye to Nadir and hires herself out as a dancing harem lady in an Italian cabaret, Harem Soiré.

Due to the encroachment of historical reality into the harem's sheltered space, the Italian film title turns out to be only partially a nostalgic-Orientalist portrayal of customs of a past era, while also referring self-referentially and self-ironically to the act of staging a night in the harem and the legends that

---

20   See also Peirce's *The Imperial Harem*.

come to encircle such a night. Just as Safiye glosses over her story to the strange woman at the train station (for example, by converting Nadir's suicide into a happy ending) thus continuing the sultan's practice of escaping reality, the last look at and into the historical harem can no longer match the voyeuristically enjoyed "strange lust" that Groschner describes above. At the end of the film, this look is not innocent anymore. The film about the harem turns into a film about storytelling.

And so, in retrospect, the insight that the film gives into the women's hamam also changes, because part of the daily routine in the harem consists of visiting the hamam. Initially, Özpetek uses standardized clichés here too: naked women have their lavish bodies oiled and massaged; they lie lasciviously by the pool and adorn themselves for the powerful ruler, whose status symbol they are considered to be. The first hamam scene in the film shows exactly such a scenario, only to be rewritten subversively by the second scene. While in the first scene Safiye is being prepared for her aptitude test as a concubine and is being observed by Nadir, who is carrying out this test, the second scene shows a completely different scenario. Again, Safiye is massaged by a black female slave and observed by Nadir, but she first reverses the roles and massages the irritated slave in a strikingly erotic manner only to finally acknowledge her awareness of Nadir's presence by addressing him directly. Here, too, Safiye turns out to be a clever strategist, just like before when she misled Nadir during the aptitude test. She stages an erotic performance in the hamam in front of Nadir—and in extension for the cinema audience—only to question any lesbian desire by exposing her cognizance. In addition, a playful, erotic ménage à trois is created, which places her as a white woman between two black partners. Although all three actors are slaves in the legal sense, a quasi-colonial situation is played out, which grants Safiye sole power in the constellation. The hamam room, shrouded in myth, proves once again to be the scene of forbidden eroticism, and yet the scene is metatextually charged due to its performative character. Like the film about the harem as a whole, this special incident in the hamam turns out to be self-reflective fiction within fiction.[21]

---

21 See chapter 4 for Sinan Ünel's portrayal of a female harem experience in his play *Pera Palas*.

Hamam: The Official Tour Guide Version

Harem Suare was not Özpetek's first film to deal with Turkish erotic cultural history. Rather, the director became known through an earlier film that is central to the recent reception of the Turkish bath and shows that the myths surrounding a visit to a hamam are still circulating today. In every travel guide of Istanbul or Turkey, there is a chapter on the hamam with explicit instructions on 'correct' tourist behavior. One should respect the rules of modesty of the locals, Manfred Ferner admonishes, for example, in his *KulturSchock Türkei* (CultureShock Turkey), a guide addressed to German tourists. Even if there are "establishments" (152) spiced up with fitness studios and saunas that accept mixed audiences, this is an offer specifically catering to tourists. Ferner thus refers to the traditional hamam's gender segregation and emphasizes that no Turkish man ever shows himself completely naked. It is in this context that he mentions the film by Ferzan Özpetek, *Hamam—Il bagno turco* (1997), which, with its homoerotic theme, revived an image of Turkish bathing culture that infuriated the Turkish hamam guild. The film offers a false, distorted fantasy that has nothing in common with everyday reality, according to Ferner. Under the rubric "The intercultural encounter in everyday life: cleanliness and purity," he concludes his description of the standard cleaning and massage procedure as follows:

> Während der ganzen Prozedur bleibt das nasse Badetuch lose zwischen den Beinen und um die Hüfte gewickelt; kein türkischer Mann pflegt sich nach seiner Beschneidung jemals nackt zu zeigen. Als vor wenigen Jahren der Film "Hamam," eine italienisch-türkisch-spanische Koproduktion unter der Regie von Ferhan [sic] Özpetek, das Thema der Homosexualität aufnahm—seit osmanischer Zeit kursieren Gerüchte, dass die Badeanstalt mehr als nur der körperlichen Entspannung dienten—, verwahrte sich der türkische Bäderverein wütend gegen derartige Lästerungen und wies darauf hin, dass gerade Männer abends das Hamam gezielt und kurz als Badeanstalt zu nutzen pflegen. (153)[22]

---

22 "During the entire procedure, the wet bath towel remains loosely wrapped between the legs and around the waist; no Turkish man ever shows himself naked after his circumcision. When the film "Hamam," an Italian-Turkish-Spanish coproduction directed by Ferhan Özpetek, took up the subject of homosexuality a few years ago—rumors have been circulating since Ottoman times that the baths were used for more than just physical relaxation—the Turkish bathing association angrily protested against such

This passage has curious gaps and allusions. On the one hand, the information that no circumcised, i.e. adult Turkish man ever shows himself naked here implies the added, but unspoken qualifier 'naked in front of another man.' Furthermore, homosexuality seems connected to the mutual presentation of male nakedness as well as to an activity that is "more than just bodily relaxation." The anger of the Turkish officials against such "blasphemies" resorts to the assertion that men visit the bathhouse only briefly and in the evenings. This not only implies that there is no time for anything like naked sex (but what about the relaxation? doesn't that take some time?); it also, and again without saying so directly, entails the reasoning that this applies to men only. So, what about the women and their own hamam tradition?

Ferner's skirting the question of what possibly was and still is going on in the hamam leads to the somewhat lame conclusion that all "this is certainly true because, in contrast to women, who always come in groups and often spend the whole day in the hamam, men only visit the bath for a relatively short time after work. They also often come alone, want to be silent and relax from the day's troubles" (153, transl. R. P.).[23] The same quality that makes the visit to the bath a "social happening" (153) for women is a solitary experience for the male visitor. So it seems.

This author can personally testify that a visit to a hamam does not have to be as chaste and modest as the Turkish bathing association would like us to believe.[24] Yet he is not the only such source: the 'rumors' revolving around

---

      blasphemies and pointed out that men in particular use the hamam as a bathing establishment in the evenings for a short time." (Transl. R. P.)

23 "Das stimmt sicherlich, denn im Gegensatz zu den Frauen, die stets in Gruppen kommen und oft den ganzen Tag im Hamam verbringen, besuchen Männer nach der Arbeit das Bad nur für eine relative kurze Zeit. Auch kommen sie häufig allein, wollen schweigen und sich von den Mühen des Tages entspannen."

24 A case in point is the Çukurcuma Hamamı, a historical hamam built in the 1830s that closed in 2007 allegedly because of its decrepit condition, though it was openly rumored that the real reason was too much men-on-men activity going on. Indeed, gay travel brochures at the time advertised this highly popular bathhouse as particularly welcome to gay tourists who want to meet Turkish men of all ages for sex, and having seen the rampant (and mostly unsafe) sexual activity there, I find it most likely that policing actions caused the shutdown. This bath is noteworthy also for having been Constantinos Kavafis's favorite haunt while he lived in Istanbul between 1880 and 1885, and it served as setting for Özpetek's *Hamam*. Both references signify a gay history and are listed on the official homepage. After renovation, the hamam reopened in 2018 as a "boutique Turkish Hammam," now being advertised as a mixed hamam for male and

what goes on in hamams can also be confirmed insofar as there are sufficient historical pictorial and textual sources in this regard. Klaus Kreiser (64) mentions, for example, the literary genre of the "hamam praise" (*Hammâmîye* or *Hammâm-nâme*), in which Ottoman poets sang in classic poetry forms such as *ghazals* about the steam bath as a place where bath attendants were adolescents of adorable beauty, whose sexual services were also available.[25] The 'moral history' of the hamams is also documented in some texts by bath attendants themselves:

> A text from the late 17th century called "Book of the Heart-Opening Bath Servants" offers a dramatic panorama of the city's pederast scene. The author, a certain Dervîş İsmâ'îl, the chairman of the guild of bathing tenants and a connoisseur, moved within the circles of the Janissaries of the 59th Regiment and the sailors of the Golden Horn. His slender document presents the physical qualities and professional habits of eleven adolescents who were employed as bath attendants (*tellâk*) in various hammams of the city, but not only working with soap and bathing gloves but also fulfilling the sexual desires of certain visitors. […] The boys took at least 70 *akçe* for intercourse. The particularly popular Yemenici Balcı asked for 300 for a whole night on the shared mattress. Of course, the operators of these baths were instructed and knew in which side rooms "a henna-colored lamb" was waiting for customers who "pounced like donkey bees on a bowl of honey." Obviously, certain baths at night were reserved exclusively for the pleasure of those "curly hyacinths." […] During the day, the pleasure boys called *tokmakçı* (from *tokmak* "club, mallet") attracted attention in the coffee houses. Dervîş İsmâ'îl describes a so-called Sipâhî Mustafâ Bey, who was so attractive that a very rich customs tenant became interested in him and a high-ranking kadi (after all, the Molla of Galata) brought him home from the bathhouse, "dressed him in the finest of clothes, buried himself in his jewelry and appointed the darling pipe keeper (*çubukdâr*, which could also be translated as 'holder of the rod')." (65, transl. R. P.)[26]

---

female customers ("Çukurcuma Hamamı 1831"). For contemporary tourists' anecdotal accounts of hamam visits, including gay sexual encounters, see, for example, "Hammam – Paul's Travel Blog."

25 See chapter 5 for more on *ghazals*.
26 "Ein 'Buch der herzöffnenden Badediener' genannter Text aus dem späten 17. Jahrhundert bildet ein drastisches Panorama der Päderastenszene der Stadt. Der Verfasser, ein gewisser Dervîş İsmâ'îl, seines Zeichens Zunftvorstand der Badepächter und Con-

Besides providing an annotated list of historical bathhouses in Istanbul, a Turkish hamam guide by Orhan Yılmazkaya (translated into English) also includes a section on "The Baths and Sex," which confirms that Ottoman literature often refers to same-sex encounters in the bathhouses. This literature celebrates the legendary dancing boys, whose reputation was based not least on the fact that women in the Ottoman Empire were forbidden to dance in public, and therefore young men were hired to do so.[27] Such a *köçek* could also be rented for sexual services, as well as the aforementioned *tellak* (bath attendant), who did more than dance for his customers. "Oğlancılık," literally "using a boy," was the common word for sexual activity with these young men. Yılmazkaya also refers to the already mentioned bath attendant Dervish İsmail, who published a book in 1685 under the title *Dellakname-i Dilkuşa (The Pleasure-Giving Tellak)*. It recounts the legendary life stories of eleven famous bath attendants vividly and in great detail, including their price lists for corresponding sexual services to customers. The dedication and the intention to

---

naisseur, bewegte sich im Milieu der Janitscharen des 59. Regiments und der Schiffsleute vom Goldenen Horn. Seine kleine Schrift stellt die körperlichen Vorzüge und professionellen Gewohnheiten von elf Jünglingen vor, die als Badediener (*tellâk*) in verschiedenen Hammams der Stadt beschäftigt waren, dort aber nicht allein mit Seife und Badehandschuh arbeiteten, sondern auch die sexuellen Wünschen [sic] bestimmter Besucher erfüllten. [...] Die Knaben nahmen für einen Verkehr mindestens 70 *Akçe*. Ein besonders gefragter Yemenici Balcı verlangte für eine ganze Nacht auf der gemeinsamen Matratze 300. Selbstverständlich waren die Betreiber dieser Bäder eingeweiht und wussten, in welchen Seitenräumen 'ein hennafarbenes Lämmlein' auf eine Kundschaft wartete, die sich 'wie Eselbienen auf eine Schale Honig' stürzte. Offensichtlich waren bestimmte Bäder nachts ausschließlich dem Vergnügen mit jenen 'Hyazinthenlockigen' reserviert. [...] Tagsüber machten die *Tokmakçı* (von *tokmak* 'Keule, Schwengel') genannten Lustknaben in den Kaffeehäusern auf sich aufmerksam. Dervîş İsmâ'îl beschreibt einen sogenannten Sipâhî Mustafâ Bey, der so attraktiv war, dass sich ein steinreicher Zollpächter für ihn interessierte und ein hochrangiger Kadi (immerhin der Molla von Galata) ihn vom Bad nach Haus holte, 'mit den edelsten Gewändern bekleidete, sich in seine Schmucksachen vergrub und den Liebling zum Pfeifenwärter (*çubukdâr*, was man auch mit 'Halter der Stange' übersetzen könnte) ernannte.'"

27 See the miniature painting from the eighteenth century showing these dancing boys in women's clothes, from the collection of the Topkapı Palace museum in Istanbul <www.newworldencyclopedia.org/entry/Prostitution>. See Boone (*Homoerotics* 77-90) for more historical and contemporary illustrations of homoeroticism in hamam settings.

write are based on the praise of male beauty and eroticism by the aforementioned young *tellak* Yemenici Bali:

> I wrote this book upon the enticement and teasing of an attractive lover, a lover whose beauty is wondrous and unique. The most honorable name of that young man is Yemenici Bali, a personage whose beauty is the jewel in his crown, a lad whose sable eyebrows are the very object of his sinner's desire. [...] One day Yemenici Bali told me, "Master, each day is followed by a night. What if the work we do pleasuring others could be described in a little book? And what if—after we are long gone—his book were to remain as a memory of who we were and what we did?" And thus did he entice me and so I began to write. (qtd. in Yılmazkaya 54)

In poetic diction he describes the career of the young bath attendant: "Bali was once an apprentice to a scarf maker in Tophane, but now the dainty boy struts around the garden like a peacock in his clogs" (qtd. in Yılmazkaya 54). And of another *tellak*, Hamleci İbrahim, Dervish İsmail writes:

> He's the light of our eyes, tall as a sapling, with the traits of an angel; the locks on his cheeks are golden threads; he has a narrow waist, and dainty hands and feet; his lips are a perfect rose; his tummy is a flower, a hyacinth. He's a sip of cool water. When he reclines on the turquoise mattress he has spread on the white marble floor of a private cubicle he imparts new life into another life. He only works with the most elite and gets 200 kurush each time he does. He gets 1000 kurush for a night on the mattress, and 250 kurush for providing extra services. (qtd. in Yılmazkaya 55)

In addition to other evidence from later centuries, Yılmazkaya also mentions kidnappings of *tellaks* by Janissaries as well as newspaper reports of jealousy dramas about these young, desired men. In 1908 (i.e. the year that *Harem Suare* also took as the starting point of its narrative), as a result of constitutional reform, any sexual activity by these bath attendants was forbidden. And yet, Yılmazkaya somewhat surprisingly—given the explicit evidence just provided regarding same-sex practices in baths—ends this informative section with the warning to the tourist that such sexual practices in the hamam largely correspond to Orientalized Western ideas of Turkish baths:

> The history of sex in the Ottoman bath differs greatly from the general western impression of the Turkish bath as representing the "mystique of the harem." And while there was some sex at the bath (*usually same sex*),

this was the exception and far from the rule. Some mistakenly believe that the Turkish bath was a place for group sex and that people of both sexes bathed together. Some "tourist" baths [...] support the myth by providing tourists with "mixed baths." This is unfortunate as it does great injustice to *the essence of the Turkish bath* and may be a ploy to humiliate women. Be forewarned and use your common sense! (Yılmazkaya 56-57, emphasis added)

Here too, just like in Ferner's admonition, there are breaks and omissions, albeit differently positioned. On the one hand, a richly documented literary history of same-sex bathing is charted for pages, only to end up with the conclusion that this was by no means a matter of regular behavior. The violation of the rules, previously documented as a literary topos, is on the other hand linked to the accusation of Orientalization and the assurance that the hamam can neither serve the myth of the harem nor fantastic ideas of group sex. With a double negation, the previously described and documented tradition of same-sex practice is eradicated and converted into a warning to the tourist that he should not denigrate the "essence of the Turkish bath" with 'dirty fantasies.'

After Sex Is before Sex: The Hamam as Sacred Space of Transition

Beyond erotic allusions and practices, there are many Turkish or Arabic sources in which the hamam is understood from a historical perspective as both a sacred space of transition and a decaying phenomenon. With the decline of the Ottoman Empire and the founding of the republic at the beginning of the twentieth century as having an avowedly Western orientation, Turkey sought to abandon 'unfashionable' customs, and this included the use of the hamam. At the same time, a change in understanding of existing same-sex erotic practices took place, which was reflected in the linguistic usage: "The word 'homosexual' entered Turkish by translations from European languages: first as *homoseksüel*. During the turkification of the language after the foundation of the republic in 1923 the word *eşcinsel* (equal-sex-ual) was coined, but this did not fit the roles and identities in Turkey and confusion arose" (Necef 73). With the adoption of European legal norms, boy love (pederasty)—still common in the Ottoman Empire[28]—gave way to a strict rejection of 'homosexual' men: "One component of [the founding father Kemal] Atatürk's criticism of the Ottoman Empire was the polemic against homosexual practices, which was taken as a reason for its decadence and its decline" (Bochow 108, transl. R. P.). Atatürk's resistance to the supposedly ailing morality of the Ottomans was also expressed in the criticism of the institution of the Turkish bathhouse.

The architectural, habitual, and literary history of the Turkish bath therefore not only provides information about the history of the decline of the Ottoman Empire but also about the related changes of sexual practices, because the hamam as a social phenomenon gives manifest insights into the connection between everyday life and larger historical contexts. Following Arjun Appadurai, one can also say that local phenomena are to be considered within a larger, global economic, social, and cultural network, because "locality is itself a historical product [...] subject to the dynamics of the global" (18). Viewed this way, the hamam, too, is no monolithic institution that remained unchanged over centuries in its pure form. On the contrary, the history of the hamam traces the moral history of Turkey.

The oldest baths in Turkey are of Roman origin and testify to the expansion of the Roman Empire to England, North Africa, Anatolia, and the Middle East. The Roman model still combined a visit to the bath with physical exercise and was also a space frequented by both sexes. From the fifth century AD, the importance of the baths initially declined, especially because they were increasingly viewed as concealed brothels. With the rise of the Byzantine and later the Ottoman Empire, however, their popularity increased again. After the conquest of Istanbul in 1453 by Sultan Mehmet the Conqueror, a bathing culture flourished, which was also to be considered an expression of a powerful Ottoman Empire. At the height of the bathing boom, there were 237

---

28 According to records, pederasty, euphemistically called 'boy love,' was practiced from at least the eighth century and has become habitualized as a social practice due to the gender segregation prevailing in Islam, although it is explicitly condemned as a homoerotic danger in the hadiths. Hadith scholar Ibn al-Jawzī wrote in *The Devil's Deception* that a boy in the hamam is a devilish temptation: "Abdullāh Ibn al-Mubārak said: Once when Sufyān al-Thawrī had entered the bath there entered after him a handsome boy. Sufyān bade them remove him, saying: I see one devil accompanying each woman, but see a dozen or so accompanying each young boy" (395). A multitude of classical Islamic literary examples, in which the veneration of boys and young men is sung about as literary topos, testify to the flourishing of boy love (see also Mohr 29).

baths in Istanbul alone, and many more in other parts of the empire as far as Hungary (Yılmazkaya 15). The hamam—"the word means something like 'heat source'" (Gouvion 87, transl. R. P.)—was now in the service of religion and therefore transformed into a sexually segregated space. In addition to religious purposes, the hamam also served medical-therapeutic and hygienic interests, which is why there were barbers and doctors on-site in addition to the masseur. The income from hamam visits in the Ottoman period was also administered by the sultan's family and used for religious charitable purposes. The Ottoman hamam not only separated the sexes but also Muslims from non-Muslims due to the Muslim purity law. The changing rooms or the devices for cleaning the body, for instance, could not be used by Muslims and people of different faiths at the same time (Yılmazkaya 21). For the Muslim woman, on the other hand, the extremely high level of social control to which she was subject made visiting the hamam the one exception where she was allowed to leave the home without a father or spouse. For women, the bathhouse therefore not only became a place of religious cleansing and elaborate body care but above all a center of social life:

> For over 1000 years, Arab women have had a fitness center, including a cosmetic institute, which, since it is affordable for all budgets, including its countless beauty products, is also deeply democratic. While the men spend an hour or two at most in the hamam, the women stay there for half a day. The body care procedure is interrupted by other pleasant rituals: the women rest, chat, drink mint tea, and nibble on pastries. (Gouvion 103-104, transl. R. P.)

The Turkish bath can therefore to be understood as a social space where the secular meets the religious. For the devout Muslim, the body practices performed in the hamam bring body and mind, sexuality and sacredness into harmony. The hamam thus figures as a concrete and symbolic place, and hence fulfills a significant function as a space of transition between the organization of sexual experience in everyday life and the perception of religious prayers. According to Muslim belief, purity is an integral part of the faith: "The men who devoted themselves to cleansing their bodies in the hamam in order to obey the prophet's purity law—'Purity is half of faith. The key to prayer is purity'—were increasingly discovering sensual wellbeing" (Gouvion 95, transl. R. P.).

Devout Muslims are supposed to wash themselves after any form of physical activity and before every prayer. That is why a hamam is traditionally always in the immediate vicinity of a mosque. Since impurity in Islam is seen in close connection with the devil, ritual cleansing is also understood as a security technique with which one protects oneself against the devilish temptation that emanates from wicked spirits: "Djinns are supposed to live in dirty places so bathhouses make perfect djinn houses" (Yılmazkaya 27). Body secretions such as blood, urine, or excrements are considered to be minor impurities that only require local, limited washing, while those secretions resulting from a sexual act, masturbation, childbirth, or menstruation require extensive body cleansing: "On a religious level, *hamams* allowed Muslims to perform the full-body ablution (*gusül*) which is necessary to restore ritual purity (*taharet*) after defilement through sexual activity, menstruation, childbirth or touching a dead body" (Cichocki 99). Bouhdiba, therefore, understands the cleansing process in a ritualist sense not only as cleaning of the body, which has been polluted especially by sex, but also in its now restored purity as a preparation for the sexual act: "The hammam is the epilogue of the flesh and the prologue of prayer. The practices of the hammam are pre- and post-sexual practices" (165).

The hamam is thus a transitional place in a state of emergency: entry into the hamam and exit from it form a preparative framing concerning the following religious act. And it is crucial for an understanding of this framing that the Qur'an may not be quoted within the rooms of the hamam. The topographical and ritual tabooing of God's word results in a temporary suspension of the moral constraints this word imposes. And to the extent that purification and sexuality are intertwined in Islam, the hamam is the place that provides the necessary connection between sexual pleasure and religious devotion. The practices of the hamam are therefore to be understood as a series of adaptations toward the spiritual and toward relieving physical and psychological tension. This is why Bouhdiba speaks of a "hammam complex" (169) governing the way in which a whole field of sexual life is organized around the hamam visit:

> The hammam has been the way that has enabled Muslim society sufficient leeway. If Muslim society has been able to preserve itself for so many centuries, it may be because of the hammam, which has been able to function as a powerful release of all the tensions of which the Muslim is necessarily subject. In using the hammam Muslim society has forged a valuable instrument for itself to channel the sexual drives liberated by religion, but repressed by the misogynist Puritanism that grew up over the centuries and

by a strict, universal separation of the sexes that might have proved fatal to it. (173-174)[29]

Thus, Bouhdiba maintains that the hamam is a social space par excellence as it can harmonize the sexual and the sacred for the Muslim (173). That may sound illogical and paradoxical, but it leads to the crux of my argument. Since a traditional understanding of gender has continued to be predominant in Turkey, heterosexual marriage as a common social practice remains the most common way to escape threatening marginalization through homosexuality. Because marriage remains one of the basic institutions of Turkish society, bachelordom continues to be perceived as abnormal. Accordingly, Koray Ali Günay claims the behavior based on firmly anchored gender roles to be responsible for a same-sex eroticism in Turkey that can only occur in firmly outlined patterns and in very specific spaces: "The patriarchal order with the overshadowing imperative of reproduction not only rigorously excludes a deviating sexual orientation, but everything that questions the dichotomous gender system which unequivocally defines femaleness and maleness" (Günay 131, trans. R. P.). As a result of both sexes having clearly assigned roles "whose spaces, freedoms, and limits are clearly defined" (Günay 130, trans. R. P.), the borders of separating private and public established for Western countries are also delineated in different ways. Due to this clear segregation,

---

[29] For the male Muslim in particular, the visit of a hamam turns out to be an initiation rite, because only when he reaches puberty does he gain access to the male hamam. Before that, he is still with his mother or his sisters in the women's hamam until it is determined that it is now time for him to join the adult men. With this transferal, the boy ritually enters the world of men and from then on moves almost exclusively in this homosocial environment. Bouhdiba describes this process of ritualist transition in a very drastic way: "Indeed one must now enter another social sphere, that of monosexual promiscuity. Spiritual actions, but also political, economic, aesthetic and even biological actions are performed in common. The body is now literally snatched up by the male world. Purification is performed collectively in the *midhas* or hammams and prayer in the mosques. Everywhere [...] the youth belongs to an all-male community. More seriously still, this is accompanied by the de-realization of the female world. The world of women is a 'sub-world,' devoid of seriousness and all too easily treated with the contempt that boosts the male's confidence in himself, in his knowledge, in his wishes and in his power" (169). With the entry into such a 'monosexual' world, the male adolescent not only loses his previous point of reference to the world of the feminine—Bouhdiba calls this the de-realization of the female world; from now on he also generates his complete understanding of himself and his environment from his interactions with other men.

spaces that are considered public in our understanding can have a much more 'private' meaning in Turkey, because they are strictly homosocial spaces. And these spaces, in turn, often allow for dealing with members of one's own sex in a way that blurs the boundaries between private and public as well as between social and sexual. The hamam traditionally is such a space where according to Günay—and in contrast to the 'official' version outlined above—the "main events" take place, "where men often have sex with men:" "In the hamams, family fathers can have sex with other men; when they step outside on the street again, they are again all married and honorable men" (Günay 130, trans. R. P.).

Through the privatization of the baths in Turkey at the end of the nineteenth century, the hamams no longer primarily served the general welfare. And yet at the same time, the social-religious practices in the baths themselves changed. In the context of a reorganization or, better still, reregulation of the gender order, this process reflected the gradual Europeanization and urban modernization of the young Turkish republic. With the weakening of the Ottoman Empire and, in return, growing cultural and political contact with Europe, it was not only a privatization of the baths that took place in the nineteenth century, contributing to the decline of the esteemed bath culture. New public spaces such as avenues, parks, theaters, and cinemas moreover emerged in the urban cartography, intended—based on the French model—to have a 'de-Orientalizing' effect, and gradually softened Ottoman society's rigid gender segregation and its associated social, religious, and sexual practices. Even if this was primarily an elite phenomenon at first, unveiled women and mixed-sex couples could increasingly be seen in public, at least in urban centers. This disruption of gender segregation as well as the changed city architecture with now increasingly private bathrooms in one's own house meant that it was simply no longer 'chic' to go to the hamam. The public bathhouse now symbolized an Islamic traditionalism and thus stood in the way of a modernization desired by the elite. Atatürk's reforms in the twentieth century targeted a reformist, republican nation, and the bathhouses as quasi-religious institutions of daily life opposed this secular and nationalist idea (see Cichocki 102-106).

This only changed again with the emergence of modern tourism in the second half of the twentieth century, which now praised the exoticism and eroticism of pre-modern Turkey in a decidedly nostalgic revival. The Turkish baths were recognized as a newly strengthened source of money, and in the wake of restoration efforts, which were now taking place again, the public attitude towards the Ottoman cultural heritage shifted. This produced that double effect of destructive nostalgia as well as emancipatory reconsideration, which Özpetek's film *Hamam* in particular captures and with which I conclude my reflections.

Hamam: Architecture of Seduction

The hamam—and what happens in it—stands in the midst of the interplay of local denial and foreign interest that characterizes the treatment of homosexuality in and around Turkey in general. The real scandal of the film *Hamam* lies not so much in the portrayal of male nudity and intimacy per se—the film shows almost nothing in this regard—but rather in the public display, the exposure, of a strictly regulated and long-established tradition of homosocial and in part thoroughly homo*sexual* practice.[30]

Özpetek's film *Hamam* follows a codified visitor routine that goes back a long way and thus nostalgically ties in with a lost Ottoman bathing culture. Francesco, the protagonist of the film, inherits a house in Istanbul from his aunt. From his perspective of both an Italian tourist in Istanbul and a professional interior designer, we follow Francesco on a physical and psychological journey of discovery through a city in a radical upheaval between decay and modernization. Since Francesco's aunt had settled in the city long before the events of the film, he did not even know her. The beginning of the film shows him as a man who is annoyed with and bored by his life with Martha, his dominant wife and business partner, and who is now going to Turkey to sell his aunt's house as quickly as possible and take the burden off himself to get rid of the inheritance. However, when it turns out that the house is an old hamam, to everyone's surprise he decides to renovate and reopen it. The host family with whom the aunt had been living welcomes him with open arms, and while the daughter immediately falls in love with him, the son Mehmet also shows interest. Francesco initially flirts with the daughter, but then increasingly responds to Mehmet's advances. As Francesco's return to Italy comes to be delayed longer and longer, Martha finally loses her patience and travels after her husband to set things straight. She confesses to Francesco that for many years she has had an affair with a mutual friend and colleague and now wants to get a divorce. Against her will, she also succumbs to the charm of the

---

30   See chapter 1 for more general reflections on male homosexual practices in Turkey.

city. The film ends in an extremely dramatic climax: Francesco is murdered and Martha now seems to take over the hamam instead.

The film is framed by two sets of correspondence. In the beginning, we listen to and read with Francesco long-ago letters from his deceased aunt to her Italian sister (Francesco's mother), and at the end, it is Martha, who in turn begins an exchange of letters with Mehmet, thus continuing the tradition of women reporting on the hamam and the changing urban life. The film uses these letters from two travelers to express the 'magical' attraction a visit to a historic hamam entails. Francesco, too, begins to be interested in the institution of the hamam after reading his aunt's letters. This incentive, already evident in Lady Montagu, is here transferred to the modern tourist and exemplified by the two women, but especially by the character of Francesco. Before he even knows that he has inherited a hamam himself, he feels drawn to another old hamam in an almost mystical way. The visit that takes place there leads to significant eye contact with a young man, which is to be understood as a proleptic preview of his later homoerotic relationship with Mehmet. Francesco is shown here in the role of a tourist who is unfamiliar with the place and who is magically lured by its exoticism, only to fatally succumb to its Oriental charms.

This is a critical reading of the film, which acknowledges it mainly as a vehicle for a revitalized and at the same time nostalgic-morbid Orientalism. Elisabetta Girelli, for instance, sees the film as depicting an "image of Turkishness [that] is a textbook Orientalist representation, resting on Western notions of Oriental difference, antiquity, seduction, and alternative lifestyle; [...] it depends on an original distance between the Self and the Oriental Other" (23-24). Cichocki draws a connection from the film to the Orientalist travel accounts and paintings of the nineteenth century: "the *hamam* has come to symbolize the epitome of the sensual Orient that many tourists wish to experience and has thus entered the codified visiting routine, or moral structure, of sightseeing in Istanbul" (107). For as soon as Francesco gets involved in the magical eroticism of the strange place, he embarks on a process of transformation that frees him from an unhappy and also sexually unsatisfactory marriage and carries him into the arms of Mehmet. The hamam, the place where this homoerotic desire is realized, is once again the setting of a sensual Orient, where the promise of an authentic encounter with Turkish culture is literally fulfilled in the climactic encounter of physical intimacy with a pretty young Turk. However, Francesco's violent death at the end of the film does not grant the male relationship any future. He is stabbed to death on the threshold of his hamam on behalf of a scheming real estate speculator who wants to buy the property on which the old building stands and plans to erect a modern urban business park instead. Francesco's plan to restore his inherited bathhouse in the old style and memory of his aunt had thwarted this plan.

This scenario reflects the problematic modernization process of a city like Istanbul, where magnificent buildings from Ottoman times are now being restored and 'refurbished,' while the sunken underground architecture of the baths prevents them from serving such an externally visible representative purpose. Francesco, who as an anticapitalist troublemaker heroically and single-handedly wants to stop this process, is removed and symbolically transformed into a martyr. The simultaneous elimination of the burgeoning homoerotic desire reinforces a negative effect, which is absorbed and postponed by the suggestion at the end that instead of getting divorced as planned, Francesco's widowed wife will now take over the hamam in his place, thus continue the unusual legacy of his aunt as a female hamam owner. This nostalgic recourse to a female desire that is not based on sexual pleasure but cultural fascination not only puts Martha on the level of the film's plot in the tradition of the exiled and extravagant aunt but also links her to travelers to the Orient from earlier times in their search for experiences beyond those of one's own familiar occidental world.

Yet the film allows another, covert reading based on the second effect that the film produces. The fact that, despite all adversities, the old, closed hamam is restored to its former glory with laborious, collective manual labor, is a consequence of the aforementioned newer trend of the hamam revival, especially in Istanbul. In the course of growing tourism and the resulting increased interest in the 'authentic' hamam experience, many bathhouses that have long been closed have reopened their doors in recent years. This revival stands in the larger context of a rediscovery of the Ottoman past and culminates in urban redevelopment projects, which serve less for their own—Turkish—cultural memory and more for the purpose of tourism-oriented consumption. And yet this revival has a secondary effect on the modern, young, urban middle class of the locals because they are now participating in the renaissance of a culture that they believed to have been lost. Nina Cichocki speaks of an "internal tourism," according to which Turks walk in the footsteps of foreign tourists in autoethnographic fashion and rediscover their own culture from an ethnographic perspective: "the otherized Ottoman past becomes a foreign country—within their own home country—where Turks like to travel as tourists, follow tips given by guide books and visit such sites as the *hamams*" (108). Although Cichocki explicitly eclipses Özpetek's film from her semiotic analysis of tourism as much as she implicitly excludes a remembering of queer desire from the hamam revival, I believe that Özpetek calls up such a scenario of culturally reminiscent reexperiencing in this film as well as in his other films.

It is not insignificant at this point that Özpetek himself is an openly gay Turkish director who lives and works mainly in Italy, but often takes up Turkish themes in his films. He does this explicitly in *Hamam* and *Harem suaré*, the historical film about the harem of the last Ottoman sultan that I mentioned earlier. But in other films with a predominantly Italian setting such as *Le fate ignoranti* (2001), *La finestra di fronte* (2003), *Saturno contro* (2007), *Magnifica presenza* (2012), *İstanbul Kırmızısı* (2017), and *La dea fortuna* (2019) Turkish characters (above all those played by Serra Yılmaz) also appear who, like himself, take on a culturally hybrid position in society through their experience of emigration and exiled existence.[31] His 'transnational Orientalist' view from Italy on Istanbul's bathhouse culture may be nostalgically romanticized and only covertly denounce the homophobic and misogynic gender order of his homeland.[32] There is only one scene in *Hamam* that openly discusses homosexuality, which occurs in the course of the marital dispute after Martha discovers Francesco's relationship with Mehmet. But Özpetek's film also offers insights and outlooks that take new cultural developments into account. The decisive factor here is the economy of the gaze, which often runs counter

---

31 See Serena Anderlini-D'Onofrio, who recognizes *Hamam*'s and *Le fate ignoranti*'s complexity within Özpetek's transnational, diasporic context as process of becoming, which "destabilizes discrete categories like homosexual and heterosexual, inasmuch as it foregrounds bisexual behaviour and the process of becoming a queer, namely a person aware of how one's non-normative sexual and erotic practices define one's sexual identity as non-normative too" (164).

32 See Girelli for such a reading, which argues that "Özpetek's use of an Orientalist code relates dynamically to the experience of dislocation, serving the director's mnemonic strategy by framing and conserving a specific national image" (23). While for Girelli "'transnational' may well denote a double bind, a double cultural weight to negotiate" (25), Elena Boschi proposes considering Özpetek's films in terms of a critical transnationalism "without erasing the national as the dominant backdrop against which differences are defined, while incorporating a consideration of popular music in the national imaginary" (247). Boschi thus aims to complicate Özpetek's making visible queer identities by showing how such identities are spatially and musically contained and 'othered' within the landscape of Italian mainstream cinema.

to the diegetic action. From the moment Francesco sets foot on Turkish soil, his homoerotic desire manifests itself. But this desire is never directly articulated verbally, but primarily through looks.[33] His first visit to an old hamam is marked by a clear division along the axis of age. The older Turks go about their bathing routine very traditionally, unimpressed by the foreigner. It is the young Turks, among whom Mehmet will then also belong, who express their erotic interest in Francesco through looks, which Francesco then increasingly reciprocates.

This eye contact, guided for the viewer through Francesco's perspective, is due to a modern cultural practice that can be described as cruising. As the Viennese architect Helge Mooshammer writes in his study on the connection between architecture, psychoanalysis, and queer cultures, cruising is about an experience of architectural spaces that lies beyond traditional practices and is based in particular on the playfully performative interface of visibility and invisibility. Cruising describes "a way of approaching," which, as Mooshammer notes, "can lead us to a different notion of architecture: its locations do not necessarily require visual-materialized representation, they are often dark, blurred, and 'in-visible.' They unfold in the physical performance of the desires and imaginations of those involved" (7, transl. R. P.). Not only has the practice of cruising, i.e. the search for anonymous sexual adventures in public space, proven to be an "often targeted field of cultural studies and queer studies in recent years" (Mooshammer 8, transl. R. P.). The theorization that follows this practice, in turn, makes it possible to describe certain paradoxical phenomena that have arisen in the course of urban modernization processes.

The recoding of a same-sex sexual practice like that of Islamic cultures, which is based on a traditionalist segregated gender order and does not understand sex between men as homosexuality, to a nontraditionally coded, genuinely homoerotic desire can be grasped with the changed architectural script of cruising in the hamam. According to the psychoanalytically shaped idea of a homophobic society—and I would claim that Özpetek follows such an

---

33   It should be noted that Francesco spends his first night at the Pera Palas Hotel (more about the history of this hotel in chapter 4), where a zealous young bellboy leads him, gossiping about the history of famous visitors of the hotel, to his room, the "Trotskiy Room," named after 'one of those former' celebrities, the Russian revolutionist Leon Trotsky. The bellboy's tongue-in-cheek comment "Good night, Signor Trotsky" might well be taken as a foreshadowing of Francesco's 'revolutionary' personal change.

idea—this homophobia is characterized by the separation of being and doing, existence from action. In her study on *Space, Time, and Perversion*, Elizabeth Grosz describes this as a form of oppression that "reduces homosexuality to a legible category [...] and in a certain way minimises the threat that the idea of a labile, indeterminable sexuality, a sexuality based on the contingency of undertaking certain activities and subscribing to certain ideas, has on the very self-constitution of the heterosexual norm" (226). Grosz's interest, however, lies "in the ways in which homosexual relations and lifestyles, expelled from and often ignored by the norms of heterosexuality, nonetheless, seep into, infiltrate the very self-conceptions of what it is to be heterosexual, or at least straight" (227). The reopening of the hamam in Özpetek's film is situated on the threshold of the rediscovery of such an erotic potential, now under the auspices of coherence of existence and action. The two men, Francesco and Mehmet, no longer belong to the homophobic generation of Mehmet's father, and they can therefore meet in this space of possibilities for pleasure, seduction, and subversion. In this sense, the film is dedicated to an analytical-archaeological technique of unearthing hidden layers and exploring a spatial practice of sexual desire as a process of mutual transformation.[34]

The two cultures from East and West, which meet here in this space of possibilities, encounter one another both symbolically and spatially, and precisely on the threshold of a historical turning point: with the appearance of Francesco, not only is Mehmet's queer desire set free, the women in the host family also increasingly begin to oppose the *nom du père*, the law of the father, and develop their own structures of desire. The father, still completely relying on the traditional model of a homosocial male society, is gradually losing his authority as the head of the family. The son moves abroad after Francesco's death and presumably continues on his way as a young urban *gay* man, the daughter does *not* marry the chosen candidate, and the mother allies with the emancipated foreigner, Francesco's Italian widow Martha, who is now the new hamam owner.

---

34 In his description of cruising, Mooshammer employs the archaeological metaphor that Freud used as a model of psychoanalysis. He sees the peculiarity of this metaphor "not in offering a straightforward explanation of what is buried under other layers, but rather in exploring the resistance that a spatial practice has to deal with (in particular its dynamics of discovering, uncovering, reading and understanding material, and thus also the cultural handling of locations and their architectural designs)" (40, transl. R. P.).

Archives of Feeling: *Hamam*'s Queer Temporality

Francesco's death was supposed to restore the established temporal and spatial order according to which the outdated bathhouse was to give way to a modernized and lucrative business. But Martha's claim of ownership interrupts this scheme, ultimately breaking apart the utilitarian forward movement into a more profitable future. Instead, she concludes her late husband's plan of rekindling a past tradition, thus actively resisting the pressure of capitalist corporate policymaking. But her interference has even more consequences upsetting social orders and gender customs.[35] Queer scholars such as Elizabeth Freeman call such forms of interruptions "queer temporalities" as points of resistance to a given spatiotemporal order "that, in turn, propose other possibilities for living in relation to indeterminately past, present, and future others: that is, of living historically" (xxii). Besides intervening in 'male' economic affairs, a "hiccup in sequential time," as Martha has produced in her act of defiance and restoration, has "the capacity to connect a group of people beyond monogamous, enduring couplehood" (3). Her decision to stay in Istanbul as self-chosen exile in the state of widowhood and as hamam owner is a queer act of dissidence, I claim, that both commemorates her queer husband and the queer history of the hamam without, however, discounting her own presence and autonomy. On the contrary, as her letter writing suggests, she is very much engaged with current affairs.

The last moments of the film, after Francesco's violent death, are dedicated to Martha, who sincerely mourns her estranged husband after all—she puts on his wedding ring on her own finger—and wanders through the halls of the hamam, caressing the newly restored ornaments. Her voiceover can be heard as she reads from her letter to Mehmet. She tells him about family news, her enthusiasm to take over the hamam, and ensures him of her devotion to him. The letter points to the future ("Since you left, the neighborhood has rapidly changed," she writes), but it can also be related to the past through her admission of lingering melancholy: "Sometimes at sunset, I am overwhelmed by melancholy. But then suddenly this cool breeze comes and carries it away. It's a strange wind that I haven't felt anywhere else. Almost flattering. And he loves me." With these last words of the films and while she stands on top of a roof in the breeze looking out onto the Bosphorus, her voice blends into a hypnotic

---

35 I want to thank Michael Taylor for urging me to give Martha's character more space and attention.

song, "Istanbul Uyurken" ("While Istanbul Sleeps"), which then concludes the film. The song includes lyrics that like Martha's feelings oscillate between loss, despair, and hope such as "Köhneyi anlat / Seni çok sevdiğimi / Düğümlü yolları / Çıkmaz sokakları / Yarın yarın diyerek / Geçen zamanı" ("Tell me about the old / I love you so much / Knotted paths / Dead end streets / Saying tomorrow tomorrow / Elapsed time").[36] Emphasizing the film's archival agenda, the trance music blends past and present through its fusion of traditional Middle Eastern sounds and percussion, and modern ethno-ambient electronics. Also, Martha's melancholic feeling can be related to the traditional Turkish notion of *hüzün*, a feeling of loss, of pain over the death of loved ones, which in a Sufi understanding also denotes a feeling of personal insufficiency caused by not getting close enough to God. In his autobiography, Orhan Pamuk interprets this Turkish variant of melancholia in a modern sense. For him, it represents a failure in life, a lack of initiative, evoked by the humiliation of the fall of the Ottoman Empire and 'ruling over' a ruined Istanbul ever since. Crucially, however, for Pamuk this feeling of melancholia is a transmitted affect derived from, among others, Flaubert's foreign travel writings and his exoticized images of Istanbul. *Hüzün* in Pamuk's understanding is a symptom of the Turkish "love-hate relationship with the Western gaze" (212), since it reveals the way "we see ourselves reflected [...]. To feel this *hüzün* is to see the scenes, evoke memories, in which the city itself becomes the very illustration, the very essence, of *hüzün*" (Pamuk 84). *Hüzün* still today allows Istanbulites to perceive their metropolis through the eyes of outsiders, as a formerly splendid treasure of the Ottoman Empire that has deteriorated into a city of ruins, and therefore Pamuk gets a sense of communally shared pride from this foreign gaze: "But being unable to depend on tradition alone as my text, I am grateful to the outsider who can offer me a complementary version—whether a piece of writing, a painting, a film" (260). As contradictory or even masochistic as this may seem, *hüzün* in this interpretation allows contemporary Istanbulites to longingly commemorate former splendor through Western exoticized images but at the same time generate a sense of identity as survivors in a ruined, but cherished city (Laschinger 113). And just as for Pamuk artworks give *hüzün* an aesthetic expression, making it culturally productive by integrating

---

36   Özpetek contributed to the lyrics of the song by Transcendental, a duo comprised of Aldo De Scalzi and Pivio, two Genoese composers, who aim for a fusion of Mediterranean/Middle Eastern musical traditions, Sufi spiritual ceremonies, and modern electronics ("Transcendental").

the contradictory perspectives of outsiders and insiders, Özpetek's film can be said to embrace *hüzün* on multiple levels: as an homage to the director's homeland, as an archival commemoration of the living history of the hamam, and as a narrative that questions and transcends traditional norms of gender and sexuality. Martha's melancholia cannot be identical to that of native Istanbulites, since *hüzün* is "not a feeling that belongs to the outside observer [...]. Westerners coming to the city often fail to notice it" (Pamuk 93). But precicelsy because she senses *hüzün*, as the film's final images and sounds in their archival thrust of blending past and present suggest, Martha is transitioning from an outsider to an Istanbulite who starts to feel like one, too.

Although the intercultural gay love story leads nowhere, other doors have opened and paths have branched out. Martha is not victimized and silenced by the apparent gender asymmetry that seems to favor male queer desire. On the contrary, she moves out of the binary male/female model, frees herself from the strictures of heteronormativity, and ultimately steps into a queer position herself. The film's last images show her as powerful, independent woman, and even though she is and will remain a foreigner for others, she is shown to have found her equilibrium, being in harmony with her situation and surroundings, specifically the hamam and Mehmet's family, and also significantly Istanbul at large. Through Martha, the film's ending links the past—the Ottoman legacy of the hamam customs as well as, more personally, the legacy of Francesco's aunt as hamam owner—to the present and the future in ways that supersedes conventional, normative forms of association, belonging, and identification. Jack Halberstam thinks of such eccentric economic practices, visionary life schemes, and strange temporalities as "queer uses of time and space [that] develop, at least in part, in opposition to the institutions of family, heterosexuality, and reproduction" (1). This notion of queerness is detached from sexual identity and therefore from the tendency to focus on gay men, as I myself have partly done when tracing the 'gayness' of hamam practices throughout history and especially in Özpetek's film *Hamam*. As my discussion of his other film, *Harem Suare*, has shown, a queer archival project needs to pay particular attention to female queer desire and identity, precisely because it is less visible as well as less fixed. While in many ways the hamam is more discernibly a space of male desire for men, it also and more clandestinely can be a space of female desire for women. Özpetek's portrayal of female characters and desires offers queer possibilities in rewriting the past and imagining future memories outside a dominant temporal and spatial organization. Through inviting us to look to partially negated and forgotten, partially recovered and revived histories, Özpetek's films bring the past into play with the present in ways that counteract a temporality which is based on linearity and that José Esteban Muñoz has called the autonaturalizing temporality of "straight time." For him, straight time "tells us that there is no future but the here and now of our everyday life. The only futurity promised is that of reproductive majoritarian heterosexuality, the spectacle of the state refurbishing its ranks through overt and subsidized acts of reproduction" (22). In contrast, queerness's time means stepping out of the linearity of straight time and imagining another collective belonging, reaching from a depressive position of failure to a queer futurity. Within the confines of straight time, the queer can only fail (Muñoz 173), and in the case of *Hamam*, Francesco's futile attempt to stop the spatiotemporal norms of straight time undoubtedly counts as failure. But his project in the end does not. Martha's continuation and completion of Francesco's project shows her as a queer agent in her own right, giving credence to the film's ultimate purpose of demarcating heteronormativity's bias against a queer aesthetics of desire.

Francesco's hamam project has made a symbolic—and for Mehmet and Martha real—return to the traditional family system based on gender segregation and reproductive heterosexuality impossible. And this paves the way for an increasing queering of gendered and cultural orders, from the desiring female gaze on a male as an erotic object, to the intercultural love of two men and an emancipated female foreigner establishing herself as a Turkish hamam owner. In this sense, the film dedicates itself to an archeological technique of excavating hidden layers of desire. The hamam figures in all this as a space of various potentials of seduction and thus as a spatial practice of sexual and cultural transformations. Throughout history, the hamam has reinvented itself as a truly transnational site, "a living cultural heritage spanning time, geography, religion and ethnicity. [...] one of the rare remaining multicultural utopian spaces: a space of hope" (Sibley and Fadli 117). In both his films but especially in *Hamam*, Özpetek pries open the archives of a queer past, provides a glimpse of ephemeral traces from other times and places that may appear nostalgic but that nonetheless "assist those of us who wish to follow queerness's promise, its still unrealized potential, to see something else," a surplus that is both cultural and affective and, in the words of Muñoz, "a queer feeling of hope" (28). Likewise speaking of the affective power that archives—and especially archives of sexuality and queer lives—can evoke, Ann Cvetkovich emphasizes that the preservation must include not only knowledge but feeling. And precisely because it is difficult to document and chronicle intimacy, sexuality, and love through the materials of a traditional archive, it is even more important that archives of feelings "address the traumatic loss of history that has accompanied sexual life and the formation of sexual publics, and [] assert the role of memory and affect in compensating for institutional neglect" (110). Borrowing the term from Toni Morrison, Cvetkovich calls this "emotional memory," remembering "details of experience that are affective, sensory, often highly specific, and personal" (110). These unusual, idiosyncratic, incoherent, fragmented, and ostensibly arbitrary archives record and preserve what has been contested and invisible. Earlier histories of homoeroticism and same-sex relations—"different forms of sexual public cultures" (Cvetkovich 111) that I have been tracing in this chapter—remain a historiographic challenge that nevertheless can be conjured and preserved through the affective power of artworks such as films: "Popular culture has much to teach us about this archive because it is so vulnerable to dismissal as trivia or waste or low culture and because it is also kept alive through personal history, nostalgia, and other queer investments" (Cvetkovich 137). A film like *Hamam* is, to my understanding, emotionally invested in archiving stereotypes and myths about the hamam and at the same time in reinventing this past for a different, resignified future. The pain of loss is not discarded, the cultural mourning of a lost hamam tradition and the personal mourning of a lost beloved are both conjured and intricately intertwined. Even though this is a film of the 1990s, predating the peak in queer visibility and freedom in the next decade, it still today figures as a counternarrative, as a powerful critique of the political backlash of the present. With its call to feel beyond its ending, *Hamam* urges to open up queer spaces for affecting otherwise.

Works Cited

"Çukurcuma Hamamı 1831." Web. 3 July 2021. <http://www.cukurcumahama mi.com/en#gallery>

"Hammam – Paul's Travel Blog." Web. 12 April 2022. <https://paulstravelblog .com/?p=174>

"Harem Suare (1999): User Reviews." Web. 1 July 2021. <https://www.imdb.co m/title/tt0179841/reviews>

"Mystery & Wonder of Hammam." *World Travel Magazine*. 14 Aug 2015. Web. 19 Aug 2021. <https://www.wtravelmagazine.com/the-mystery-wonder-o f-hammam-2/>

"Transcendental—Steam (Hamam: The Turkish Bath) Original Motion Picture Soundtrack." *Valley Entertainment*. Web. 30 Nov 2021. <https://www.valley-entertainment.com/products/transcendental-steam-hamam-the-turkish-bath-original-motion-picture-soundtrack>

al-Jawzī, al-Hāfiz Abū'l-Faraj Ibn. *The Devil's Deceptions: Being a Translation of His Masterpiece 'Talbīs iblīs.'* Transl. Haitham Hamdan. Birmingham: Dār as-Sunnah Publishers, 2014.

Al-Rawi, Ahmed. "The Portrayal of the East vs. West in Lady Mary Montagu's *Letters* and Emily Ruete's *Memoirs*." *Arab Studies Quarterly* 30.1 (2008): 15-30.

Anderlini-D'Onofrio, Serena. "Bisexual Games and Emotional Sustainability in Ferzan Özpetek's Queer Films." *New Cinemas: Journal of Contemporary Film* 2.3 (2004): 163-174.

Appadurai, Arjun. *Modernity at Large. Cultural Dimensions of Globalization*, Minneapolis: U of Minnesota P, 1996.

Aravamudan, Srinivas. "Lady Mary Wortley Montagu in the Hammam. Masquerade, Womanliness, and Levantinization." *ELH* 62:1 (1995): 69-104.

Bleys, Rudi C. *The Geography of Perversion: Male-to-Male Sexual Behavior Outside the West and the Ethnographic Imagination, 1750-1918*. New York: New York UP, 1995.

Bochow, Michael. "Sex unter Männern oder schwuler Sex: Zur sozialen Konstruktion von Männlichkeit unter türkisch, kurdisch- und arabischstämmigen Migranten in Deutschland." *Homosexualität und Islam. Koran, Islamische Länder, Situation in Deutschland*. Eds. Michael Bochow and Rainer Marbach. Hamburg: MännerschwarmSkript, 2003. 99-115.

Boer, Inge E. "Despotism from under the Veil: Masculine and Feminine Readings of the Despot and the Harem." *Cultural Critique* 32 (1995-1996): 43-73.

Boone, Joseph A. *The Homoerotics of Orientalism*. New York: Columbia UP, 2014.

———. "Vacation Cruises: Or, the Homoerotics of Orientalism." *PMLA* 110.1 (1995): 89-107.

Boschi, Elena. "Loose Cannons Unloaded: Popular Music, Space, and Queer Identities in the Films of Ferzan Özpetek." *Studies in European Cinema* 12.3 (2015): 246-260.

Bouhdiba, Abdelwahab. *Sexuality in Islam*. Transl. Alan Sheridan. Orig. 1975. London: Saqi, 2004.

Cichocki, Nina. "Continuity and Change in Turkish Bathing Culture in Istanbul: The Life Story of the Çemberlitaş Hamam." *Turkish Studies* 6.1 (2005): 93-112.

Cvetkovich, Ann. "In the Archives of Lesbian Feelings: Documentary and Popular Culture." *Camera Obscura* 49, 17.1 (2002): 107-147.

Conner, Patrick. "On the Bath: Western Experience of the Hammam." *Renaissance and Modern Studies* 31 (1987): 34-42.

Danto, Arthur Coleman. "The Late Works of Delacroix." *The Nation*. 9 Nov 1998. Web. 8 Dec 2020. <https://www.questia.com/magazine/1G1-21280072/the-late-works-of-delacroix>

Fein, Richard J. *At the Turkish Bath*. Towson: Chestnut Hills, 1994.

Fernández Carbajal, Alberto. "Queering Orientalism, Ottoman Homoeroticism, and Turkishness in Ferzanj Özpetek's *Hamam: The Turkish Bath* (1997)." *Queer Muslim Diasporas in Contemporary Literature and Film*. Manchester: Manchester UP, 2019. Web. 21 Aug 2021. <https://www.manchesterhive.com/view/9781526128119/9781526128119.00010.xml>

Ferner, Manfred. *KulturSchock Türkei*. Bielefeld: Peter Rump, 2001.

Flaubert, Gustave. *Flaubert in Egypt: A Sensibility on Tour*. Transl. and ed. Francis Steegmuller. New York et al.: Penguin, 1996.

Freeman, Elizabeth. *Time Binds: Queer Temporalities, Queer Histories*. Durham and London: Duke UP, 2010.

Girelli, Elisabetta. "Transnational Orientalism: Ferzan Özpetek's Turkish Dream in *Hamam* (1997)." *New Cinemas: Journal of Contemporary Film* 5.1 (2007): 23-38.

Gouvion, Colette. *Spa: Vom arabischen Hamam bis zur Modernen Wellness-Oase*. Transl. Christa Trautner-Suder. München: Knesebeck, 2007.

Groschner, Gabriele. "Badeszenen: Die absonderliche Lust und das heimliche Schauen." *Badeszenen: Ritual, Entrüstung und Verführung*. Ed. Gabriele Groschner. Salzburg: Residenzgalerie Salzburg, 2009. 9-27.

Grosz, Elizabeth. *Space, Time, and Perversion. Essays on the Politics of Bodies*. New York and London: Routledge, 1995.

Günay, Koray Ali. "Homosexualität in der Türkei und unter Türkeistämmigen in Deutschland. Gemeinsamkeiten und Unterschiede." Eds. Michael Bochow and Rainer Marbach. *Homosexualität und Islam: Koran, Islamische Länder, Situation in Deutschland*. Hamburg: MännerschwarmSkript, 2003. 116-139.

Hahn, Kornelia. "*Kese* and *Tellak*: Cultural Framings of Body Treatments in the 'Turkish Bath.'" *European Review* 24.3 (2016): 462-469.

Halberstam, Jack J. *In a Queer Time and Place: Transgender Bodies, Subcultural Lives*. New York and London: New York UP, 2005.

Hamam / Il bagno turco. Dir. Ferzan Özpetek. Perf. Alessandro Gassmann, Francesca d'Aloja, Carlo Cecchi, and Halil Ergün. Sorpasso Film, 1997.

Harem Suare. Dir. Ferzan Özpetek. Perf. Marie Gillain, Alex Descas, and Lucia Bosè. R&C Produzioni, 1999.

Heffernan, Teresa. "Feminism Against the East/West Divide: Lady Mary's *Turkish Embassy Letters*." *Eighteenth-Century Studies* 33.2 (2000): 201-215.

Kietzman, Mary Jo. "Montagu's *Turkish Embassy Letters* and Cultural Dislocation." *Studies in English Literature, 1500-1900*, 38.3 (1998): 537-551.

Konuk, Kader. "Ethnomasquerade in Ottoman-European Encounters: Reenacting Lady Mary Wortley Montagu." *Criticism* 46.3 (2004): 393-414.

Kreiser, Klaus. *Istanbul: Ein historisch-literarischer Stadtführer*. München: Beck, 2001.

Laschinger, Verena. "Das Ende der *hüzün*. Orhan Pamuks *Istanbul: Memories of a City* und der Traum von Europa." *Grenzgänge. Beiträge zu einer modernen Romanistik* 13.26 (2006): 107-117.

Lew, Joseph W. "Lady Mary's Portable Seraglio." *Eighteenth-Century Studies* 24.4 (1991): 432-450.

Locke, John. *An Essay Concerning Human Understanding*. Ed. Peter H. Nidditch. Oxford: Clarendon, 1979.

Macmaster, Neil, and Toni Lewis. "Orientalism: From Unveiling to Hyperveiling." *Women and Islam: Critical Concepts in Sociology*. Vol 1.: *Images and Realities*. Ed. Haideh Moghissi. London and New York: Routledge, 2005. 147-161.

Mohr, Andreas Ismail. "Wie steht der Koran zur Homosexualität?" *Muslime unter dem Regenbogen. Homosexualität, Migration und Islam*. Ed. LSVD Berlin-Brandenburg e. V. Berlin: Querverlag, 2004. 9-38.

Montagu, Lady Mary Wortley. *The Turkish Embassy Letters*. London: Virago, 1994.

Mooshammer, Helge. *Cruising. Architektur, Psychoanalyse und Queer Cultures*. Wien: Böhlau, 2005.

Müller, Ulrich. "'Mich lustet vil sêre daz wir in das bat gân:' Die erste Beschreibung eines türkischen Bades (Hamam) in deutscher Sprache: Salomon Schweigger 1608." "*Er ist ein wol gevruinder man:*" *Essays in Honor of Ernst S. Dick on the Occasion of His Eightieth Birthday*. Eds. Karen McConnell and Winder McConnell. Hildestheim et al.: Georg Olms, 2009. 275-293.

Muñoz, José Esteban. *Cruising Utopia: The Then and There of Queer Futurity*. New York and London: New York UP, 2009.

Murray, Stephen O. "The Will Not to Know: Islamic Accommodations of Male Homosexuality." *Islamic Homosexualities: Culture, History, and Literature*. Eds. Stephen O. Murray and Will Roscoe. New York: New York UP, 1997. 14-54.

Necef, Mehmet Ümit. "Turkey on the Brink of Modernity: A Guide for Scandinavian Gays." *Sexuality and Eroticism Among Males in Moslem Societies*. Eds. Arno Schmitt and Jehoeda Sofer. New York and London: Haworth, 1992. 71-75.

Pach, Walter. *Ingres*. New York: Harper & Brothers, 1939.

Pamuk, Orhan. *Istanbul: Memories of a City*. Trans. Maureen Freely. London: Faber and Faber, 2005.

Peirce, Leslie. *The Imperial Harem: Women and Sovereignty in the Ottoman Empire*. New York: OUP, 1993.

———. "The Sultanate of Women." Web. 1 July 2021. <http://www.channel4.com/history/microsites/H/history/e-h/harem.html>

Potvin, John. "Vapour and Steam: The Victorian Turkish Bath, Homosocial Health, and Male Bodies on Display." *Journal of Design History* 18.4 (2005): 319-333.

Said, Edward W. *Orientalism: Western Conceptions of the Orient*. London: Penguin, 1995.

Sansal, Burak. "The Ottoman Harem." Web. 1 July 2021. <https://www.allaboutturkey.com/harem.html>

Schweiger, Salomon. *Zum Hofe des türkischen Sultans*. Ed. Heidi Stein. Leipzig: VEB F. A. Brockhaus, 1986.

Sibley, Magda, and Fodil Fadli. "The Utopian Space of the Islamic Bathhouse or *hammām*." *Muslim Spaces of Hope: Geographies of Possibility in Britain and the West*. Ed. Richard Philips. London and New York: Zed Books, 2009. 104-119.

Vanzan, Anna. "Turkish Hamman and the West: Myth and Reality." *Acta Turcica* II.2 (2010): 1-12.

von Moltke, Helmut. *Unter dem Halbmond: Erlebnisse in der alten Türkei 1835-1839*. Tübingen and Basel: Horst Erdmann, 1979.

Yılmazkaya, Orhan. *Turkish Baths: A Guide to the Historic Turkish Baths of Istanbul. A Light onto a Tradition and Culture*. Transl. Nancy F. Öztürk and Judith Ülgen. Istanbul: Çitlembik, 2003.

II. Istanbul and the Queer Stage

3. "But we are all androgynous:" James Baldwin's Staging America in Turkey

Speaking from Another Place

In a film, shot towards the end of black American author James Baldwin's (1924-1987) on-and-off stay in Istanbul, that encompassed most of the 1960s,[1] Turkish director Sedat Pakay (1945-2016) positions Baldwin within an unmistakably Turkish setting. The short film, aptly titled *James Baldwin: From Another Place* (1973), starts with a shot that briefly lingers on Baldwin's hands playing with Turkish worry beads, *tespih*, markedly linking him to a cultural habit that must be alien to him. This discrepancy between foreignness and familiarity continues throughout the film, both in word and image. The *tespih*-shot, taken in a public ambiance, switches to an interior scene with Baldwin lying in bed. The film's black-and-white visual aesthetics highlights the play of Baldwin's black body first while in bed partially covered by starkly white sheets and then mostly uncovered, clad only in white briefs.[2] Baldwin then gets up, walks to

---

[1] Baldwin's first entry into Istanbul was in October 1961. He then stayed at Engin Cezzar's apartment near Taksim, in the area where, towards the end of his Istanbul period, he had his own apartment. Biographer David Leeming chronicles Baldwin's various lodgings, especially highlighting the residency at the Pasha's Library near Bebek, where Baldwin worked on *Tell Me How Long the Train's Been Gone* and *The Welcome Table*. Leeming describes the "house, known by everyone as 'the Pasha's Library,'" as "a red wooden and stucco structure" located "in Rumeli Hisar[ı], a few miles from downtown Istanbul. The house had once been a library belonging to the nineteenth-century intellectual Ahmet Vefik Pasha. […] A central room with a decorated vaulted ceiling and a marble fireplace was surrounded by a glassed-in gallery offering views of the Bosphorus and the hills of Asia across the straits" (263, 274).

[2] Pakay also took photographs of Baldwin with the same setting which even more strikingly stress the black-and-white play with Baldwin's body (see, for example, "Ja-

the window, looks out, and we can see over his shoulder a glimpse of the outside—an Istanbulite street view. He then turns, walks towards the camera, and gets into a robe (see fig. 3.1 and 3.2).

fig. 3.1: James Baldwin: From Another Place. James Baldwin with tespih
fig. 3.2: James Baldwin: From Another Place. James Baldwin at window

This is a very intimate and private scene, culminating in a close-up with Baldwin looking directly into the camera, before the film shifts to scenes where we see him in assorted public spaces, clearly standing out as the only black person amongst a crowd consisting mostly of male Turks. While we first watch his nearly naked body silently moving around this most private sphere, the bedroom, we also hear his voice-over articulating what amounts to Baldwin's overall creed during this period of his life, if not his entire life:

> I suppose that many people do blame me for being out of the States as often as I am. But one can't afford to worry about that. [...] And [...] perhaps only someone who is outside of the States realizes that it's impossible to get out. The American power follows one everywhere. [...] One sees it better from a distance [...] from another place, from another country. (*James Baldwin: From Another Place*)

These opening remarks of the short film stake out two interrelated points I want to make here. First of all, even though Baldwin from early on chose to live predominantly outside the United States, he nevertheless felt very much

---

mes Baldwin in bed, Istanbul, 1970," reprinted in Zaborowska's study on *Baldwin's Turkish Decade* [90], where she repeatedly refers to Pakay's film).

connected to his native country. He even claimed to have a better understanding from afar. While many black activists—especially of the 1960s—asserted Baldwin's political ineffectiveness, I argue that Baldwin *was* highly effective and lastingly so until today—but operating from a transatlantic post. And secondly, the quote alludes to one of Baldwin's most celebrated novels, *Another Country* (1962). He famously 'signed' this transatlantic work with "Istanbul, Dec. 19, 1961," thus linking the conclusion of this novel, which depicts the arrival of Eric's French lover Yves in New York, to his own arrival in Turkey. Through this hyper-textual bio-reference interfacing his French protagonist's experience of exile with his own, he implicitly acknowledges a Turkish influence on the text.

Besides finishing this particular novel, Baldwin wrote and published a whole series of texts during his "Turkish Decade," as biographer Magdalena Zaborowska entitles her study on that period of Baldwin's life, such as *The Fire Next Time* (1963), *Blues for Mister Charlie* (1964), *Nothing Personal* (with Richard Avedon, 1964), *Going to Meet the Man* (1965), *A Rap on Race* (with Margaret Mead, 1971), and *No Name in the Street* (1972).[3] The question invariably arises as to whether and how his presence in Istanbul adds another layer of meaning to his discussions of American racial and sexual affairs that he deals with in these texts in various degrees of explicitness. I want to look at another set of works, however, which links Baldwin to Istanbul *and* the trope of the "stage." With sensational success, Baldwin staged John Herbert's (1926-2001) prison drama *Fortune and Man's Eyes* (1967), wrote the novel *Tell Me How Long the Train's Been Gone* (1968) about an aging and ailing bisexual black actor, and conceived his third, as of now still unpublished, play *The Welcome Table*, which he did not finish until twenty years later in southern France just before his death in 1987. These works all revolve around staging, performing and play-acting. Baldwin in turn engages with them both from a theatrical perspective and with a notion of sexuality in mind that cuts across borders of race, class, nation, and gender.

---

3   *The Fire Next Time* and *No Name in the Street* are essay collections; *Blues for Mister Charlie* is Baldwin's second play and is based on the murder of fourteen-year-old Emmett Till, who was lynched in Mississippi in 1955; *Nothing Personal* is an essay on race relations with photographs by Richard Avedon (1923-2004); *Going to Meet the Man* is a short story collection; and *A Rap on Race* contains conversations between Baldwin and the anthropologist Margaret Mead (1901-1978).

Approaching the works with Baldwin's Turkish abode in mind, Istanbul comes to serve as transatlantic queer space where such border-crossing sexualities may be tested and lived in stark contrast to Baldwin's own American experiences. And yet, his trajectory remains American, and therefore these works deal with American matters although being written and/or performed—staged—in Turkey.

I discuss below first the intersection of race, sexuality and nationality in Baldwin, the "reluctant queer;" then, the significance of his staging the above-mentioned play in Istanbul, a city where he was a "stranger;" and finally, the way he, as a "freak" at the "welcome table," brought his exceptional American experience to the staging of the play.

The Reluctant Queer

Baldwin's Turkish years coincide with his demise as public spokesperson in the United States. Famously Eldridge Cleaver regarded Baldwin critically, but so did Martin Luther King before Cleaver, and later Ishmael Reed and Amiri Baraka.[4] At first, Baldwin was accused of being misinformed; later, with the rise of the Black Power Movement, Baldwin allegedly lacked youth and radicalism. Behind these claims, however, as became increasingly clear during those years, were doubts about Baldwin's suitability as a racial spokesperson due to his sexuality, thus his emerging nickname at the time "Martin Luther Queen." This epithet came with the implication, as Douglas Field suggests, "that a 'queen' could not participate in the violent and manly battle for civil rights" (461). According to Morris Dickstein,

> [t]he crucial charges against Baldwin had little to do with his politics, or his literary craftsmanship, or even, for that matter, his precise position on the race questions. The argument was that Baldwin's homosexuality, his unconfident masculinity, is the hidden root of all his writing and completely disqualifies him as a representative spokesman. (168)

While actually there never was any doubt about Baldwin's homosexuality, he himself remained extremely reluctant to use the terms "gay," "homosexual," or

---

4   On the Cleaver debate, see, for example, Reid-Pharr; and Taylor; on Baldwin's homophobic reception by Cold War liberals, see Corber; and for Baldwin's "Letter from Istanbul" on the Nation of Islam, see Fortuny.

"bisexual" in his non-fictional statements, being, however, more outspoken in his novels.[5] It was as late as 1985, i.e. long after the turbulent 1960s and even longer after his 1956 novel *Giovanni's Room*, now being considered a gay classic, that Baldwin in his essay "Freaks and the American Ideal of Manhood" (1985)[6] more explicitly spoke about his sexuality.[7] As Field claims—and as we can witness in Pakay's film when Baldwin is asked about his sex life—Baldwin "experienced deep anxieties about his roles both as writer and as revolutionary from the mid-1960s" (469). In his long essay *No Name in the Street*, Baldwin writes that the "conflict was simply between my life as a writer and my life—not spokesman exactly, but as public witness to the situation of black people. I had to play both roles" (122). Similarly, in his novel *Tell Me How Long*, the narrator states that "I was one of the speakers at this [political] rally. [...] Our common situation, the fact of my color, had brought us together here [...]. Our differences were reducible to one: I was an artist" (108-109). Baldwin's use of role acting in *No Name in the Street* can therefore be linked to his novel *Tell Me How Long* about a middle-aged bisexual actor, Leo Proudhammer, who, very much like Baldwin himself in the mid-1960s, ruminates about juggling different social, political, and sexual roles. In *No Name in the Street*, Baldwin writes: "what in the world was I by now but an aging, lonely, sexually dubious, politically outrageous, unspeakably erratic freak?" (18), while Leo, who calls himself a "dirty old man," states: "Some people considered me a fagot [sic.], for some I was a hero, for some I was a whore, for some I was a devious cocks-man, for some I was an Uncle Tom" (Baldwin, *Tell Me How Long* 454).

---

5   The "seismic shift in Baldwin studies" (Ross 633) demanding increasing attention to his sexual orientation has brought forth studies such as Guy Mark Foster's essay "African American Literature and Queer Studies: The Conundrum of James Baldwin" (2010); the collections edited by McBride; and by Kaplan and Schwarz; Brim's recent monograph; and Kenan's young adult biography.

6   The essay was originally published in *Playboy*, in January 1985, and then included in the collection *The Price of the Ticket* (1985) under the title "Here Be Dragons."

7   Baldwin's response to the question of his gayness in a 1984 interview with Richard Goldstein is often cited for its equivocation: "The word 'gay' has always rubbed me the wrong way, I never understood exactly what is meant by it. [...] Even in my early years in the Village, what I saw of that world absolutely frightened me, bewildered me. I didn't understand the necessity of all the role playing. [...] I didn't have a word for it [i.e. being gay]. The only one I had was homosexual and that didn't quite cover whatever it was I was beginning to feel. Even when I began to realize things about myself, began to suspect who I was and what I was likely to become, it was still very personal, absolutely personal" (174-175).

What strikes me with *Tell Me How Long* is that this is the first time Baldwin depicted a sexual relationship between two black men in one of his novels, and it is one of his most American novels in that its setting is solely in the United States. And yet, this is the only novel that he predominantly wrote while in Turkey; and although his least successful novel, it is brutally honest in the way it negotiates revolutionary public and sexually private roles, articulated through the lens of a middle-aged actor. Field, more lenient than most other critics in assessing this novel, concedes that this is "Baldwin's attempt to reconcile his sexuality with black radical politics" (471); missing, however, in my view, that this intersecting of race, sexuality *and nationality* could only take place "from another place," to quote Pakay's momentous film title once more. I would like to claim this other place to be a *queer* one.

Stranger in the City

Queer uses of time and space develop, at least in part, in opposition to the institutions of family, heterosexuality, and reproduction. They also develop according to other logics of location, movement, and identification. If we try to think about queerness as an outcome of strange temporalities, imaginative life schedules, and eccentric economic practices, we detach queerness from sexual identity and come closer to understanding Foucault's comment in "Friendship as a Way of Life" that "homosexuality threatens people as a 'way of life' rather than as a way of having sex." In Foucault's radical formulation, queer friendships, queer networks, and the existence of these relations in space and in relation to the use of time mark out the particularity and indeed the perceived menace of homosexual life. (Halberstam 1)

Jack Halberstam speaks of the possibilities of "queer time" and "queer space," suggesting the need to view queer lives from angles different from those commonly preordained by the heteronormative society. Baldwin's struggle with expected roles and actual performed *personas*, his being too late to be politically radical and too early to be a queer activist, this being out of "proper" time and place, mark, I believe, his Turkish years. Those years also constitute the precarious period of his middle-agedness that led biographer James Campbell to speak of Baldwin's biographical "enigma," where nothing really "fits" (208). What has puzzled critics—and perhaps why they still shy away from linking Baldwin's Turkish years to his emerging work of the time with its increasing explicitness in sexual matters—is the question of whether to conceive Baldwin's voluntary exile as an "intellectual exile" in the sense that Edward Said articulates it (as a "double perspective" through which "you see things that are usually lost on minds that have never traveled beyond the conventional and comfortable" [380]),[8] or rather to speak of a "sexual exile" in which Baldwin behaved like a sex tourist (in a country reputed in the West for its pervasive sexual potential). A case in point for negotiating such competing claims is what Charles E. Adelson wrote in his 1970 article "A Love Affair: James Baldwin and Istanbul," featured in *Ebony* magazine.

Adelson had attended Baldwin's Turkish staging of John Herbert's play *Fortune and Man's Eyes* about, as Adelson writes, the "deplorable conditions and homosexuality in some Canadian houses of correction" (40). While this play may be of specific concern to the prison affairs of Canada, in other words, may be considered "a regional complaint," as Adelson asserts, it is through the hands of Baldwin that this play has turned into a "poem of universal meaning [...] a '20th century morality play'" (40).

Nevertheless, Adelson seems puzzled, if not irritated by Baldwin's choice of place, i.e. Istanbul, by Baldwin's fascination—Adelson calls it "bewitchery" (42)—with "a 2,000-year-old city squatting in its beauty and its old age on the shores and hills of two continents" (40). Baldwin directed Herbert's play upon Engin Cezzar's (1935-2017) invitation in 1969. Cezzar and his wife Gülriz Sururi were operating the theater company Ümit Tiyatro (Hope Theater) at the time and Cezzar was well aware of the risk he was taking in producing this controversial play, which, as he recalls in his memoir, "was being censored in every country it was staged in" (qtd. in Zaborowska 155). Cezzar had played Giovanni in a stage production of *Giovanni's Room* (by The Actors Workshop, a one-time affair) in New York in 1957-1958, and I believe that through Cezzar in the role of the main protagonist in *Fortune* Baldwin was making a subtle connection between his novel and Herbert's play. The connecting link is the image of the gay prison, an image that incessantly fascinated Baldwin, and that reoccurs in many of his own works, with *Giovanni's Room* being an early

---

8   The full quote reads: "Exile is a model for the intellectual who is tempted, and even beset and overwhelmed, by the rewards of accommodation, yea-saying, settling in. Even if one is not an actual immigrant or expatriate it is still possible to think as one, to imagine and investigate in spite of barriers, and always to move away from the centralizing authorities toward the margins, where you see things that are usually lost on minds that have never traveled beyond the conventional and comfortable." (Said 380)

prime example.[9] While Adelson describes the relation of Baldwin and Cezzar in intimate, yet non-sexual terms, his perspective remains steadfastly American. It is from there that he looks at "Baldwin, the American, on the other side of the ocean, at the edge of the Orient" (44), clearly Orientalizing Baldwin even though comparing Istanbul's landscape to the "many San Francisco-like hills" (44).

There is a lot of "hope" mentioned in Adelson's article, soul-searching and making friends, but Baldwin's answer to Adelson, to the question "Why Istanbul?" stands out, in that he herewith makes a claim for a queer space and time: "A place where I can find out again—where I am—and what I must do. *A place where I can stop and do nothing in order to start again.* [...] To begin again demands a certain silence, a certain privacy that is not, at least for me, to be found elsewhere" (44, original emphasis). Adelson paints a picture of Baldwin that is a double: a happy-go-lucky *flaneur* on the one hand, and then "the other Baldwin as a man-very-far-from-home [...] awash in a special sort of aloneness" (46). This seems a rather melodramatic picture of Baldwin in a place full of strangers looking "toward a friendship tried and trusted where he can anchor his soul for a while, keep himself from drifting further into the stream of loneliness" (46).

What Adelson also fails to mention is the tremendous success Baldwin had with his production of Herbert's play, as well as his amorous entanglements in that "strange, so strangely beautiful, city" (46). In many ways, as Pakay's film has abundantly made obvious, Baldwin here was more of a "stranger" than in Paris, where he mingled with diasporic Algerians, and even stranger than in the far-off "tiny Swiss village," where "no black man had ever set foot" (117), as Baldwin famously wrote in his essay "Stranger in the Village" (1953), but where there were hardly any people who could actually see him. Not so in the metropolis that is Istanbul with millions of inhabitants but hardly any "people of my complexion" ("Stranger" 117).[10] As in many of his texts written

---

9   See also Baldwin's 1961 essay "The Male Prison," where he takes issue with André Gide's "dilemma" of finding "no way to escape the prison of [powerful] masculinity" (235). As Plastas and Raimon point out, "Baldwin insists that this gender prison confines men through the masculinity imperative of men displaying their 'muscles, their fists and their tommy guns.'" To Baldwin, they suggest that "such mandatory and unthinking displays of violence render impossible meaningful love within *or* between the sexes" (690).

10 Baldwin first left the United States in 1948, when he was twenty-four years old, to live in Paris. In 1970 he moved to Saint-Paul de Vence, in the south of France, where he

abroad, in this essay Baldwin links his experience of being looked at in this remote Swiss village as something very strange and unfamiliar, to his "dramatic" experience—and to that of every black man for that matter—in the United States, and he marks a sharp contrast:

> The time has come to realize that the interracial drama acted out on the American continent has not only created a new black man, it has created a new white man, too. No road whatever will lead Americans back to the simplicity of this European village where white men still have the luxury of looking on me as a stranger. I am not, really, a stranger any longer for any American alive. [...] The world is white no longer, and it will never be white again. ("Stranger" 129)

Freaks at the Welcome Table

Baldwin brought this exceptional American experience to Europe and to Istanbul, and amongst other means chose the medium of the theater to negotiate this racial momentum. As in most of his novels, here also the racial is intricately interwoven with the sexual. As Jill Dolan has succinctly remarked:

> Sexual desire has long been a motivating narrative factor in plays and performances, [...] regardless of [the characters'] sexual orientations. Theatre is also a place of fantasy and longing, of fleeting exchange between spectators and performers. With its liminal status as both real and not, as ephemeral

---

remained until he died in 1987. In 1951 he traveled for the first time to Leukerbad, in Switzerland, where his lover Lucien Happersberger's family possessed a chalet, and he returned twice more, relating his experiences in this small village, where people had never seen a black person before, in his essay "A Stranger in the Village." Baldwin traveled to Turkey for the first time in 1961. The following years until 1971 make up a period that "stands chronologically at the center of his multiple journeys—from the Harlem ghetto and [the] Greenwich Village studio, [...] through the churches and lecture halls and freedom marches in the South, to the salons of jet-setting international literati and the vistas of southern France of his later years" (Zaborowska 5). Many dates in Baldwin's life overlap due to his synchronous abodes in different countries and his extensive travels. It is therefore difficult, if not impossible, to track down the exact dates of his times spent in Istanbul, since during his "Turkish decade," as Zaborowska outlines, "he established a pattern of remaining there for extended periods of time, returning home for visits with family and publishers, and traveling elsewhere that would last throughout the 1960s" (8).

and transformational, theatre has long been a site where misfits and the marginalized have congregated. (3)

In his staging of Herbert's play *Fortune* as well as much later of his own play *The Welcome Table*, Baldwin uses this desire that, according to queer theorists such as Dolan, "flows back and forth between the stage and the house in ways that compel the exchange of 'looks' between actor and actor and between actors and spectators" (18). Herbert's play is a prison drama, featuring four inmates and a guard. But it has from its inception been understood not only to present the cruel realities behind bars but also to serve as an allegory of life outside those bars. Towards the ending of the play, Mona, the most vulnerable and sexually ambiguous character, recites Shakespeare's Sonnet 29 that starts with "When, in disgrace with fortune and men's eyes / I, all alone, beweep my outcast state" (qtd. in Herbert 90).

Mona, even though not the main character, was the most crucial one for Baldwin, and, my suggestion is, precisely for her androgynous quality. The stage directions describe Mona as

> a youth of eighteen or nineteen years, of a physical appearance that arouses resentment at once in many people, men and women. He seems to hang suspended between the sexes, neither boy nor woman. [...] His nature seems almost more feminine than effeminate because it is not mannerism that calls attention to an absence of masculinity so much as the sum of his appearance, lightness of movement, and gentleness of action. His effeminacy is not aggressive... just exits. (Herbert 8)

Mona's experience of being sexually assaulted by a group of men, which in turn led to being—falsely—sentenced, is based on Herbert's own experience, and it mirrors Baldwin's constant threat of such a situation during his juvenile years, as he writes in his aforementioned "Freaks and the American Ideal of Manhood" essay:

> On every corner, I was called a faggot. This meant that I was despised, and, however horrible this is, it is clear. What was *not* clear at that time of my life was what motivated the men and boys who mocked and chased me [...]. For when they were alone, they spoke very gently and wanted me to take them home and make love. [...] I was far too terrified to be able to accept their propositions, which could only result, it seemed to me, in making myself a candidate for gang rape. (821-822, original emphasis)

In this essay, Baldwin, contrary to his earlier essays, is quite outspoken about his sexuality and the anxieties this caused for him throughout his life. Writing before the programmatic resurfacing of the term "queer" in the 1990s, Baldwin contends that "[t]he condition that is now called gay was then called queer. The operative word was *faggot* and, later, pussy, but those epithets really had nothing to do with the question of sexual preference: you were being told simply that you had no balls" ("Freaks" 819). Years earlier, Mona as ultimate queer foreshadowed Baldwin's increasingly embracing the androgynous, in a way that anticipates later claims to performativity of queer theorists, such as Judith Butler's, that there is "no simple definition of gender [...] and that [it] is the ability to track the travels of the term through public culture" that matters (184). But Mona also served as reflection for the large transgender community in Istanbul which openly and loudly applauded Baldwin's staging, as Cezzar astoundingly grasped: "I realized that they were all transvestites. They were the ones who claimed the play and supported it: the friends of the 'Friend of the Fallen'" (qtd. in Zaborowska 184).[11]

In *The Welcome Table*, the main character Edith, although cast as a female, is yet another such androgynous figure who, according to Zaborowska, can be understood as embodiment of Baldwin himself:

> The action of *The Welcome Table* takes place during one day, from early morning till 'round around midnight,' in a large Provençal house in the south of France. The play's Turkish and transnational roots can be seen in its cast of main characters, all of them female and [...] all deliberate self-portraits of the author [...]. The protagonist, Edith Hemings, is an intriguing transgender figuration of Baldwin, a veritable hybrid of the charismatic artists he knew and admired in Turkey, the United States, and France: Gülriz Sururi, Eartha Kitt, Beatrice Redding, Josephine Baker, and Nina Simone. (251)[12]

This last play of his thus harks back to his encounters with the gender-bending scene in Turkey (Zaborowska 252), and it stages notions of performing gender of Baldwin's later life, such as articulated in the aforementioned essay

---

11   *Fortune and Men's Eyes* was staged under the title *Düşenin Dostu* (*Friend of the Fallen*) (Zaborowska 145).
12   The manuscript of the play, with annotations by Baldwin, is at the Schomburg Center for Research in Black Culture in New York. As with all papers, the Baldwin Estate does not allow direct quotations (Zaborowska 327, n. 4).

on "Freaks," where he calls for an understanding of gender beyond clear-cut sexual, racial and national borders:

> Freaks are called freaks and are treated as they are treated—in the main, abominably—because they are human beings who cause to echo, deep within us, our most profound terrors and desires.
>
> Most of us, however, do not appear to be freaks—though we are rarely what we appear to be. We are, for the most part, visibly male or female, our social roles defined by our sexual equipment.
>
> But we are all androgynous, not only because we are all born of a woman impregnated by the seed of a man but because each of us, helplessly and forever, contains the other— male in female, female in male, white in black and black in white. We are a part of each other. Many of my countrymen appear to find this fact exceedingly inconvenient and even unfair, and so, very often, do I. But none of us can do anything about it. (828-829)

Baldwin claims in the same essay that the androgynous is an "intimidating exaggeration [of] the truth concerning every human being" (814), insinuating thus a flexibility of sex and gender that we have now come to accept as less disturbing than at the time of his writing the essay, and helping us understand why he was drawn to Herbert's play and especially to the character of Mona: "Directing Herbert's play affords Baldwin the opportunity to present a momentary vision of men's prison that was invisible to much of the world around him," argue Melinda Plastas and Eve Allegra Raimon who point to the abundance of prison images in many of Baldwin's works that provide us with complex depictions of sexual intimacies transcending prison walls: "his sojourn abroad as a beloved literary luminary among avant-garde Turkish artists when he directed *Fortune* and wrote *Another Country* must have encouraged him to imagine and articulate alterities to dominant global scripts of sexualized and racialized imprisonment even as he himself felt the sting of black nationalist homophobia back home" (696-697).

In "Freaks," Baldwin posits the *androgynous* as antidote to the "American idea of masculinity" (815), which he considers a violent and dominant, but above all heterosexist hypermasculinity. In a forceful reassessment of Baldwin as a black queer man, and of his "critique of the racist heteronorm," Marlon Ross maintains that Baldwin's voice is "staged for the public eye through the exhibition of his out-of-gender person" (647), by specifically referring to this late essay, with this quote: "we all exist, after all, and crucially, in the eye of the beholder. We all react to and, to whatever extent, become what that eye sees. [...] and so we move, in the vast and claustrophobic gallery of Others, on up or down the line, to the eye of one's enemy or one's friend or one's lover" ("Freaks" 817). Baldwin understood about the "policing eye" (Ross 647), but he chose to face this eye most successfully through his transnationally removed perspective, up until his last venture into staging queerness in *The Welcome Table*.[13]

In his essay "The Welcome Table: James Baldwin in Exile," Henry Louis Gates writes about meeting Baldwin in Paris in 1973 for a story he was to write for *Time* magazine, entitled "The Black Expatriate." After Baldwin's death, Gates recounts, he met David Baldwin, James' brother, who handed over the manuscript *The Welcome Table*, remarking that it was for Gates. Gates finds himself depicted in the character of Peter Davis, "who has come to interview a famous star, and whose prodding questions lead to the play's revelations" (19), and he links the play's revelatory gesture as well as the title to both Baldwin's novel *Tell Me How Long the Train's Been Gone*, which toward the end includes the line from the old gospel song: "I'm going to feast at the welcome table" (477), and to Baldwin's essay on "Freaks," from which Gates quotes the above-mentioned passage: "Each of us, helplessly and forever, contains the other—male in female, female in male, white in black, and black in white. We are a part of each other" (qtd. in Gates 20).

From Gates' recollection we can conjure Baldwin's vision of the "welcome table" as a truly transnational metaphor. It conjoins friends, brothers and lovers from different cultures, but it is also a working table, mingling Baldwin's love for people with his love for writing. It is a table where black meets white, Turk meets American, gay meets straight, it is a queer table, a meeting site in a certain space at a certain time for people willing to transcend racial and sexual boundaries of identities.

Baldwin's years in Istanbul have left tangible traces in both his works written during that period and his interactions with local culture and people. Especially his engagement with theater while in Turkey led to the creation of Leo Proudhammer, the actor-protagonist of his novel *Tell Me How Long the Train's Been Gone*, the conception of his last play *The Welcome Table*, and the staging

---

13 See Tunc and Gursel, who highlight "The Case of James Baldwin" (13) as pertinent in looking at the transnational turn in American Studies from a Turkish-American perspective.

of Herbert's *Fortune and Man's Eyes* in Istanbul. All three instances are imbued with Baldwin's notion of sexuality being intricately linked to race and nation. Contrary to many criticisms concerning his assumed political ineptness resulting from his geographical distance from American affairs, it is precisely through his self-chosen removed perspective that Baldwin could stay in touch with his Americanness. Only by "seeing from a distance" could he emerge as key player in commenting on the American racial condition, and during much of the 1960s it was Istanbul that served for him as a transatlantic queer space where he could successfully juggle the intricacies of identity politics.

Works Cited

Adelson, Charles E. "A Love Affair: James Baldwin and Istanbul." *Ebony* (March 1970): 40-46.

Avedon, Richard, and James Baldwin. *Nothing Personal*. Photos by Avedon, text by Baldwin. New York: Atheneum, 1964.

Baldwin, James. "Stranger in the Village." 1953. *Collected Essays*. Ed. Toni Morrison. New York: Library of America, 1998. 117-129.

———. *Giovanni's Room*. New York: Dial, 1956.

———. "The Male Prison." 1961. *Collected Essays*. Ed. Toni Morrison. New York: Library of America, 1998. 231-235.

———. *Another Country*. New York: Dial, 1962.

———. *The Fire Next Time*. New York: Dial, 1963.

———. *Blues for Mr. Charlie*. New York: Dial, 1964.

———. *Going to Meet the Man*. New York: Dial, 1965.

———. *Tell Me How Long the Train's Been Gone*. 1968. New York: Vintage, 1998.

———. *No Name in the Street*. 1972. New York: Vintage, 2000.

———. "Here Be Dragons." *The Price of the Ticket: Collected Nonfiction, 1948-1985*. New York: St. Martin's Press, 1985. 677-690.

———. "Freaks and the American Ideal of Manhood." *Collected Essays*. Ed. Toni Morrison. New York: Library of America, 1998. 814-829.

———. *The Welcome Table*. n.d. MS. The Schomburg Center for Research in Black Culture, New York.

Brim, Matt. *James Baldwin and the Queer Imagination*. Ann Arbor: U of Michigan P, 2014.

Butler, Judith. *Undoing Gender*. New York and London: Routledge, 2004.

Campbell, James. *Talking at the Gates: A Life of James Baldwin*. New York: Penguin, 1992.

Corber, Robert J. "A Negative Relation to One's Culture: James Baldwin and the Homophobic Politics of Form." *Homosexuality in Cold War America: Resistance and the Crisis of Masculinity*. Durham and London: Duke UP, 1997. 160-190.

Dickstein, Morris. *Gates of Eden: American Culture in the Sixties*. New York: Basic Books, 1977.

Dolan, Jill. *Theatre & Sexuality*. Houndmills: Palgrave Macmillan, 2010.

Field, Douglas. "Looking for Jimmy Baldwin: Sex, Privacy, and Black Nationalist Fervor." *Callaloo* 27.2 (2004): 457-480.

Fortuny, Kim. "James Baldwin on the Nation of Islam: A Letter from Istanbul." *American Writers in Istanbul: Melville, Twain, Hemingway, Dos Passos, Bowles, Algren, Baldwin, and Settle*. Syracuse: Syracuse UP, 2009. 193-210.

Foster, Guy Mark. "African American Literature and Queer Studies: The Conundrum of James Baldwin." *A Companion of African American Literature*. Ed. Gene Andrew Jarrett. New York: Wiley-Blackwell, 2010. 393-409.

Gates, Henry Louis, Jr. "The Welcome Table: James Baldwin in Exile." *Thirteen Ways of Looking at a Black Man*. New York: Vintage, 1997. 3-20.

Goldstein, Richard. "'Go the Way Your Blood Beats:' An Interview with James Baldwin." *James Baldwin: The Legacy*. Ed. Quincy Troupe. New York: Simon & Schuster, 1989. 173-185.

Halberstam, Jack J. *In a Queer Time and Place: Transgender Bodies, Subcultural Lives*. New York and London: New York UP, 2005.

Herbert, John. *Fortune and Men's Eyes*. New York: Grove, 1967. *Düşenin Dostu*. Trans. Ali Poyrazoğlu and Oktay Balamir. Istanbul: Sander, 1970.

James Baldwin: From Another Place. Documentary. Dir. Sedat Pakay. Hudson Film Works, 1973.

Kaplan, Cora, and Bill Schwarz, eds. *James Baldwin: America and Beyond*. Ann Arbor: U of Michigan P, 2012.

Kenan, Randall. *James Baldwin (Gay and Lesbian Writers)*. Philadelphia: Chelsea House, 2005.

Leeming, David. *James Baldwin: A Biography*. London: Michael Joseph, 1994.

McBride, Dwight, ed. *James Baldwin Now*. New York: New York UP, 1999.

Mead, Margaret, and James Baldwin. *A Rap on Race*. Philadelphia: Lippincott, 1971.

Plastas, Melinda, and Eve Allegra Raimon. "Brutality and Brotherhood: James Baldwin and Prison Sexuality." *African American Review* 46.4 (2013): 687-699.

Reid-Pharr, Robert F. "Tearing the Goat's Flesh: Homosexuality, Abjection and the Production of a Late Twentieth-Century Black Masculinity." *Studies in the Novel* 28.3 (1996): 372-394.

Ross, Marlon B. "Baldwin's Sissy Heroics." *African American Review* 46.4 (2013): 633-651.

Said, Edward. "Intellectual Exile: Expatriates and Marginals." *The Edward Said Reader*. Eds. Moustafa Bayoumi, Andrew Rubin. New York: Vintage, 2000. 368-381.

Taylor, Douglas. "Three Lean Cats in a Hall of Mirrors: James Baldwin, Norman Mailer, and Eldridge Cleaver on Race and Masculinity." *Texas Studies in Literature and Language* 52.1 (2010): 70-101.

Tunc, Tanfer Emin, and Bahar Gursel. "Introduction—The Transnational Turn in American Studies: Turkey and the United States." *The Transnational Turn in American Studies: Turkey and the United States*. Eds. Tanfer Emin Tunc and Bahar Gursel. Bern: Peter Lang, 2012. 11-26.

Zaborowska, Magdalena J. *James Baldwin's Turkish Decade: Erotics of Exile*. Durham and London: Duke UP, 2009.

4. "Built for Europeans who came on the Orient Express:" Queer Desires of Extravagant Strangers in Sinan Ünel's *Pera Palas*

"a fucking palace:" Grand Hotel

When Agatha Christie visited the Pera Palace Hotel in Istanbul in the mid-1930s and allegedly began to write one of her most famous crime novels, *Murder on the Orient Express* (1934), the prime time of grand hotels was already over (Karr 118). The political and economic turmoil of the First World War not only led to a financial crisis and rising nationalism but also to a crisis in the hotel industry. Grand hotels, cherished for their worldliness and opulence, succumbed to the austere living conditions of post-war Europe. In the 1920s, the American Conrad Hilton bought derelict grand hotels and turned their lavish splendor into functional effectiveness. He started to lease the hotels and gradually built up his chain empire. Accordingly, for Europe being in ruins, the Hilton Hotels stood for a future that signaled the "American way of life."[1] Until very recently, however, the Pera Palace withstood this tendency towards corporate hotel business. It was only after extensive renovation measures between 2008 and 2010 that the hotel joined the Dubai-based Jumeirah hotel chain. The hotel's website nevertheless boasts that the building has remained true to its historical legacy:

---

1 See Paul Rösch's claim that "[Hiltons] Erfolgsrezept bestand darin, die verschwenderischen Räume effektiver zu nutzen und den Service zu rationalisieren. Ihm ging es um Funktionalität und Effektivität—dies bedeutete den Tod für die altehrwürdigen Grand Hotels und ihre luxuriöse Herrlichkeit" (39).

> Today Pera Palace Hotel Jumeirah the hotel maintains the elegant classical style that made it famous, with authentic 19th century features serving as a timeless focal point. Additionally, Pera Palace Hotel Jumeirah was designated with "museum-hotel" status in 1981 when, as a tribute to the founder of modern Turkey, Room 101 was converted into the Atatürk Museum. ("Pera Palace Hotel Jumeirah")

Still, this purported history is somewhat misleading, since, although being unique in many ways, the Pera Palace indeed was conceived as part of a chain, which, according to Charles King, was precisely its charm. While the first Orient Express travelers stayed in various hotels scattered throughout the Pera district, which was a highly sought-after area of European tourists, the opening of the Pera Palace not only was located right at the center of this commercial district, but it also differed markedly from the other hotels:

> The hotel had a considerable advantage over the other first-class facilities nearby, such as the Hôtel de Londres, the Bristol, the Continental, the Angleterre, and—its perennial rival—the Tokatlian, situated right on the Grande Rue. It was the only hotel that was part of a pan-European network owned and operated by a single company. Its sister establishments in Nice, Monte Carlo, and other cities offered unprecedented luxury to a new generation of trans-European travelers, and staying at each of the Wagons-Lits facilities became a collect-them-all game, at least for those wealthy enough to afford it. Like the Four Seasons and Ritz-Carlton hotels of later eras, the Pera Palace provided an exclusive experience not because it was wholly unique but precisely because it was part of a chain—a grand community of properties such as the Avenida Palace in Lisbon or the Odyssée Palace in Paris that promised luxury, safety, and a certain degree of predictability in major destinations, all built to a similar style and standard. As the *Guide Bleu* later noted, the Pera Palace was equipped with "all the modern comforts: elevator, bathrooms, showers, radiator heat, and electric lighting, with a magnificent view over the Golden Horn." (King 26)

For Agatha Christie, the grand hotel was above all a site where people met. In this semi-public, semi-private atmosphere, love affairs began and ended, and people could pretend to be somebody else. And yet, in contrast to Vicky Baum's *Menschen im Hotel* (1929), the classic example of the hotel novel of her times, Christie's guests were never anonymously assembled individuals, but instead connected and interrelated in some social or personal way (Karr 116-

117). Grand hotels and the stories set therein had an appeal far beyond their geographical locals, precisely because of their transnational backdrops and densely communal structures.

It is this very hotel, Christie supposedly wrote one of her most celebrated novels that Turkish-American dramatist Sinan Ünel chose as backdrop for his play *Pera Palas* (1998). Set in the 1920s, 1950s, and the 1990s respectively, the play offers a complex spatial and temporal negotiation linking the hotel's history to that of the nation. From the very start, the hotel's grandeur plays a pivotal role in the way the characters position themselves within the spatiotemporal atmosphere they encounter. Evelyn, a young and emancipated English writer visiting Istanbul for the second time in 1918, is the first person we see on stage, and she immediately takes on the role of narrator, which she keeps throughout the play:

> **EVELYN:** Yesterday, I arrived once again at the Queen of cities and I held my breath. As our ship anchored at the Golden Horn, I could see the seven hills, the cypress trees, and the looming minarets stretching to God like devoted believers, all bathed in those wonderful, uncertain and poetical tints which do not belong to our Western world. Nothing had changed. There was the Haghia Sophia and the majestic Süleymaniye just as I had left them. I looked upon this glorious city, my enchanting dream, with the same fascination of that school girl seven years ago. […] I soon discovered, however, that things had indeed changed. The war rages throughout Europe and here there is great suffering. The people are demoralized. Hunger and illness prevail and the city is overcrowded with refugees. (1)[2]

Evelyn serves as an intermediary, a role she intermittently performs throughout the play, reflecting and commenting on her impressions of Turkey towards the end of the First World War and therefore the end of the Ottoman Empire. While she speaks to the audience, Murat and Brian simultaneously enter the scene. Murat is a thirty-three-year-old Turkish man, and Brian is a forty-year-old American; the two are a couple. Their appearance is set in the most current time frame, i.e. 1994, and their profane language strikingly contrasts Evelyn's lyricism. Hence, the action takes place concurrently, and as the stage directions announce, "[a]ll three time frames have one common setting: a room at the Pera Palas Hotel in Istanbul. The rest of the action takes place in various

---

2   Since this is a typescript manuscript, the parenthetical information refers to the pages only.

settings such as the harem, the living room in 1952 or the living room in 1994" (ii). This opening scene already discloses the fact that the characters "speak to each other" in this hotel-room setting although they belong to different eras:

> **BRIAN:** Man, I can't believe this place! I couldn't even grasp that lobby. All that marble and that fantastic ancient elevator!
> **MURAT:** First elevator in the city!
> **BRIAN:** We're staying at a fucking palace! Would you look at this fucking room?
> **EVELYN:** It is only here, in the district of Pera, that the ravages of war are not felt.
> **MURAT:** Built for Europeans who came on the Orient Express.
> **BRIAN:** *(He goes to MURAT, to hug him.)* You didn't tell me! You bastard! (1)

Brian clearly is in awe of the hotel's splendor and location ("Wow! The view!" [2]), and it is he who first makes the link to Agatha Christie and the way the hotel has been part of Western popular culture: "I fucking feel like fucking Hercule Poirot. I'm in a fucking movie with Ava Gardner" (2). Murat, somewhat more somber and less stereotypical in his use of American slang, explains, "Poirot was here, of course. There's an Agatha Christie room somewhere. Some of the rooms are named after celebrities who stayed in them" (2). Murat refers to a fictional character, Inspector Poirot, and its inventor, the British novelist Christie, rather than to Mustafa Kemal Atatürk, which we may well read as an ironic eclipse, silently commenting on hidden or suppressed moments of history that nevertheless haunt the present. It turns out in fact that the gay couple is in one of the celebrities' rooms "called the Evelyn Crawley" (8), which is a reference to Evelyn the fictional character, whom we have already encountered and who has a distinctly different attitude to the hotel and the district it represents. For her, Pera "is the district that Europeans have adopted as their own. […] So here I am, stifled in a room of this distasteful European hotel, finding it rather impossible to write. How I hunger to enter the world of the natives and submerge myself in the luscious experience of the east" (1, 3). Atatürk's stay at the hotel is obscured in the play. Evelyn's residence there takes place shortly before, Brian and Murat's long after, and yet, "[o]n the same day the Allies began their occupation, an Ottoman field commander named Mustafa Kemal checked into a room in the Pera Palace," Charles King writes in his book-length homage to the hotel and its era (52).³

The Pera Palace's strategic location made it the epicenter of this turbulent era of historical transition at the time of Atatürk's arrival there, and it may account for why two years earlier Evelyn railed against "this distasteful European hotel" (3). Established in 1892 specifically to service clients arriving on the Orient Express, the hotel's special features included the "wood-and-iron elevator [which] had only been the second one installed in Europe (after the Eiffel Tower's)" (King 3). Located in one of Istanbul's most fashionable neighborhoods and with its very close vicinity to the major embassies, the YMCA, and legal brothels, the Pera Palace attracted a broad mixture of clients and visitors. For King, as well as for our writer-character Evelyn, "[t]he Pera Palace was meant to be the last whisper of the Occident on the way to the Orient, the grandest Western-style hotel in the seat of the world's greatest Islamic empire" (King 4).

This rather melodramatic way of staging the hotel as harbinger of an empire in decline actually reflects the history of the grand hotel at large, which by the end of the First World War had surpassed its prime. At the turn of century, however, grand hotels were meant to resemble representative aristocratic castles providing a chance for the bourgeois tourist to feel royal. The emergence of the grand hotel thus is closely linked to the dissolution of a strict class society in Europe. As "machines for wish-fulfillment," grand hotels stood for representation and distinction, a space of assembly within larger sites of tourist attractions such as fashionable spas and rising metropolises, which in turn were also highly attractive as cosmopolitan concourses for locals as well as for writers (Rösch 32). It is therefore no surprise that the grand hotel has

---

3   The military occupation of Istanbul on March 16, 1920, brought Atatürk from southern Anatolia as commander against British forces back to Istanbul: "If he needed convincing of how much Istanbul had changed since his last visit, the Pera Palace provided ample evidence. Always filled with foreign guests, the lobby and restaurant were now overrun with British and other Allied officers in uniform" (King 53). Atatürk later recalled that the "ridiculous styles and dress of the women with their made-up faces, half-exposed breasts, and immodest manners occupied my special attention ... [T]he Turkish capital had become a Babylon" (qtd. in King 54). It was especially the Pera district, "the first 'Europeanized' quarter of the city" that, as an experimental area for urban reform, represented the Ottomans' efforts to transform Istanbul into a 'Western' city (Bartu 33). The reforms were to serve as a model for the rest of the city, a plan that failed and eventually led to Istanbul losing its status as capital.

been compared to a stage play with visible and invisible 'actors,' 'directors,' technicians, props, etc. (Rösch 37).

The grand hotel as dramatic stage figures in Ünel's play in various ways. First, it *is* a drama, thus taking up the challenge to double the performativity of the hotel business with the performativity of the stage. But, secondly, Ünel does not choose to transfer the hotel onto the stage as a mimetic act. On the contrary, by using simultaneous action across time and space, he disrupts any semblance of mimesis. Whereas single scenes may come across as 'realist,' they are constantly interrupted by temporal and spatial jump cuts. This technique reinforces the impression of artifice, which in turn could also be said to reflect the artificiality of the hotel scenery. A third element of the inherent theatricality of the hotel that is reinforced in Ünel's hotel play is the tension between presence and absence, between showing and hiding. Much of that tension is localizable in the dichotomy between the public arena of the lobby and the private sphere of the room, the former calls for role-playing, the latter for dropping the masks. "The door, marking the threshold between outside and inside, is the most significant physical barrier in the hotel," explains Bettina Matthias; "Whatever you do in your room cannot easily be detected, but if you choose to, you can open the door and let the outer world in" (60-61).

The literary tradition of hotel crime fiction picks up this very tension of hidden secrets, notably in conjunction with violent acts of sexuality behind closed doors. One could think of Christie's *At Bertram's Hotel* (1965), Stefan Zweig's *Rausch der Verwandlung* (posth. 1982), or John Irving's *The Hotel New Hampshire* (1981), but also Fatih Akin's film *Gegen die Wand* (2004), which partly takes place in Istanbul's Büyük Londra, another late Ottoman grand hotel, located close to the Pera Palace. In these and in many more examples, "hotels are perfect experimental settings […] to study the dynamics between the individual and society or a chosen sub-group thereof and the subject's struggle to find the right balance between feelings of estrangement and liberation" (Matthias 5). In this sense, according to Matthias, hotels represent "social laboratories for writers to test the stability of traditional value systems, and they use the spatial limits of their setting to zoom in on a potential struggle that would be harder to detect or isolate in a less focused setting" (5). Ünel capitalizes on this play between individual and society, of secrecy and disclosure, of presence and absence—also on a visibly performative level, by having characters from one time frame exit through doors and others from a different time frame enter through the very same doors within the same scene. Above all, it is the figure of Evelyn who personalizes the anti-mimetic structure and whose comments enrich the play with an intensified self-reflective bent. Being travelers like her, Murat and Brian follow the promise of the grand hotel being Other, a small-scale model of a utopian metropolis (Seger 8). But people might also gather in such hotels for very different reasons. In his travel account to the Near and Middle East, aptly named *Orient Express*, John Dos Passos recounts a lobby drama taking place at the Pera Palace in 1921. This episode echoes quite the opposite of any utopian comingling of different peoples:

> Downstairs in the red plush lobby of the Pera Palace there is scuttling and confusion. They are carrying out a man in a flock-coat who wears on his head a black astrakhan cap. There's blood in the red plush arm-chair; there's blood on the mosaic floor. The manager walks back and forth with sweat standing out on his brow; they can mop up the floor, but the chair is ruined. French, Greek and Italian gendarmes swagger about talking all together each in his own language. The poor bloke's dead, sir, says the British military policeman to the colonel who doesn't know whether to finish his cocktail or not.
>
> Azerbaijan. Azerbaijan. He was the envoy from Azerbaijan. An Armenian, a man with a beard, stood in the doorway and shot him. A man with glasses and a smooth chin, a Bolshevik spy, walked right up to him and shot him. (qtd. in Fortuny 105)

Dos Passos's memory of the Pera Palace is not one that speaks of promising adventures, nor of thrilling excitement. The murder he witnesses is a token of a collision of political and ethnic forces, publicly played out on the "stage" of the hotel lobby, but speaking of the long-lasting trauma of "the 'Armenian' issue, a determinedly imprecise euphemism," as Kim Fortuny asserts, which is still used today "to avoid placing blame for the unresolved problem of the Armenian diaspora that began during World War I" (106). Rather than analyzing the politic turmoil behind the assassination, Dos Passos depicts the effects of the murder on the hotel's clientele and furniture. In this transnational gathering, the hotel is not a safe haven anymore. Dos Passos's famous camera eye technique captures a moment that speaks of the

> modern condition of Istanbul in 1921 [that] is not the same as that of Paris, London, or New York. Rather than an interim between world wars, in which nations took the opportunity to rebuild themselves, in the case of Europe, or recreate themselves, in the case of the United States, Turkey is simulta-

neously under foreign occupation, under Greek invasion, and mired in civil war. (Fortuny 125)

Dos Passos does not explain this, but here and in the course of his account he does show the confusion of allegiances that happen to fatally collude in this particular time and place: the shift in power from Ottoman to Allied, the Kemalist Nationalists led by Atatürk fighting both, and minority populations such as the Armenians struggling to assess their loyalties. As such Dos Passos's *Orient Express* "creates space for conflicting points of view," and it is the Pera Palace that symbolically marks "both the real and imagined boundaries" of this precarious political ambiance (Fortuny 107, 116). In a similar manner, Ünel does not directly relate to historical events, but rather uses the individual fates of persons as well as innuendo through gossip and rumor as techniques to allude to the social backdrop. One striking moment is Evelyn's sojourn in the harem, which, at the same time, evokes notions of Oriental fantasies and the transnational clash of differing views on gender relations.

"Where memory is, theatre is:" Harem as Memorial

Besides the central locus of the hotel room, *Pera Palas* features another locale by way of contrast: the harem. While the hotel represents the influx of European modernism, the harem emblematizes the legacy of the Ottoman Empire. And yet, the ostensibly striking dichotomies are both reinstated and called into question in Ünel's play. Whereas in the semi-privacy of the hotel room new and modern constellations of gender, ethnicity, religion, and sexuality are being initiated, the harem's ambience seems to belong to a cultural climate that is on the verge of being historically undone. Again, Evelyn is the character that serves most as mediator here: several times she moves between the Pera Palace and the harem. Her initial discontentment with the intrusion of Europeanness into the Pera district in general and into the Pera Palace in particular lures her into accepting the invitation of one of the pasha's daughters, Melek, to stay at the harem of her father, Ali Riza Efendi. The fifteen-year-old Melek is about to enter an arranged marriage, and she persuades Evelyn to leave the "one meager little room" of the hotel to stay with her at the harem: "Oh, please say yes! I would be so happy! We could watch the sunset every evening over the Bosphorus. And we will talk about Turkey and you will tell me all about England and we will take walks in the garden" (6). This vision of cultural exchange and sororal leisurely activities intrigues Evelyn, and her first reaction to the harem is one of tourist curiosity promising exotic thrills:

> This was beyond belief! No European that I knew had been asked to go stay in an actual harem. I was to have the opportunity to live as a real Turkish woman, to see what transpires behind those carefully guarded doors, the great mystery of the eastern world. I was so happy and terrified that I was unable to sleep that night. (7)

Once there, however, instead of the Orientalist fantasy of living "as a real Turkish woman," she quickly adapts her vision of mystery to the realities she encounters, and that is above all a highly gendered and strictly segregated arrangement:

> The large dwelling is divided into two sections. […] The harem for the women and the selâmlık for the men. A man, unless he is a husband or small boy, is forbidden to enter the harem at all times. And the women have access to the selâmlık only through the unfortunate invention called the lattice, more commonly referred to as the cage. In other words, they are allowed to look, but not be seen or heard. (13)

Evelyn is under constant surveillance by the other women and being taken care of by Bedia, a young slave who in the play's middle time frame has married and is mother of Orhan, who in turn is Murat's father. While Evelyn continues to relate her observations in prose intersections, the women of the harem give voice to their own, mostly ironic, observations of Evelyn. Her claim to value independence over marriage, for example, does not make sense for Adalet, an older woman: "*Istiklâlmi? Salak gâvura bak.* [Independence? What a silly infidel; (translation provided by Ünel)] (Laughs. To the other women.) She says she likes her independence. It's because their men are no good in the bedroom. Why else would a pretty thing like that still be a virgin at her age?" (16). Only Melek's half-brother Cavid, who is eighteen and therefore actually too old to still be in the harem, takes Evelyn's side: "I like her. I think she's right to want her freedom" (17). According to Melek, Cavid, to whom I return later, "goes to those meetings where they discuss the issues of women in Turkey and how things should change and that sort of thing" (26).

Evelyn launches a campaign to 'educate' Melek in a modern, feminist thinking that is both at odds with the harem's overall politics and with Melek's personal wishes. Evelyn does not understand why one would want to marry, "a man you have never met," and she thinks that "[i]t must be terrible to have to share your husband with another woman," to which Melek retorts that "that's not done anymore. Things are changing" (25, 26). She has faith in her father's authoritative goodwill: "Papa would never make me marry a bad man or a man who is ugly or old. I trust Papa" (26). In the course of Evelyn's stay at the harem, however, she at first tries to keep a benevolent and distant engagement, and in contrast to her initial wish to "live as a real Turkish woman," she now jokingly fears that "I'm becoming a Turkish woman" (25). This dilemma becomes apparent when she meets other expatriated fellow countrymen such as Sir Robert Cave from the English Embassy, who warns Evelyn about her safety and lectures her about the Turk's boorishness:

> After all, Miss Crawley, we know that these are rather primitive people who do not understand our way of living. And I don't suppose you understand theirs. How do you feel about living in the house of a man with more than one wife? A house where concubines, not servants are employed, and where people use their fingers to feed themselves. (34)

Evelyn is outraged by this blatant xenophobic judgment upon a people that she so dearly embraces and tries to get to know and understand. Hence, although she has strong inhibitions about women's social restrictions, she cannot tolerate Cave's roundabout repudiation of Turkish customs and character:

> Your callowness and condescension are an embarrassment to my country. What do you know about the harem? Next to nothing, I assure you. Do not think I'm unaware of the Englishman's fascination with the harem. When the subject arises at our polite embassy parties, all the eyes of the men light up with curiosity. Wouldn't you like to have a house full of beautiful women ready to satisfy your every whim? [...] Let me tell you something, Sir Robert. If I took you in there it would be an utter disappointment to you because it is entirely different from your childish, misinformed fantasy of it. A harem is a home just like any home. (35)

Whereas she articulates her disregard of Cave's warnings to his face, she takes up some of his arguments when later encountering Ali Riza. Interestingly, she links her discussion of Melek's lack of emancipatory interest to the realm of politics, now accusing Ali Riza of blindly succumbing to the European hegemony by joining in signing the armistice:

> You are an educated, worldly man and you still treat your women exactly the same despicable way Europe, and particularly England, treats your coun-

try. As a commodity. Something to be bought and used for your own selfish purposes. [...] You are naïve, Ali Rıza Efendi. The armistice was signed by a single English official in the name of the allies. They have divided Turkey amongst themselves. And you have put your signature on that obscene document! (60)

The harem episode can be taken to speak of Ünel's awareness of the pitfalls of Orientalist fantasies. One such hazard is to take the slow progress of feminism as a sign of Turkey's stubborn social backwardness. But one has to take into account that older Ottoman models of feminism have been discarded and forgotten by the radical inauguration of the Turkish Republic as a nation modeled on European standards. In fact, already in the nineteenth century, a gradual emancipation of upper-class women was taking place in Ottoman society.[4] As Şerif Mardin states, altogether "there is a remarkable unity in Ottoman upper class concern for the emancipation of women as seen in the Ottoman-Turkish literature of the time" (137).[5] With the transition to a Westernized political hegemony and the adaptation of the Latin alphabet

---

4   Halide Edib Adıvar (1884-1964), for instance, was the first important Ottoman novelist and, as Mardin asserts, "her openness to the world of Western ideas was the consequence of an upbringing that took place at the time of Sultan Abdülhamid II (1876-1909) and was not the result of Young Turk innovations" (137). She took her education at the Robert College, a U.S.-American founded private school that prominently figures in Ünel's play as well: Kathy, Murat's mother, teaches there, and Orhan, Murat's father, went to school there. Edib had particularly strong links to the United States, since she was the leader of the *Wilson Prensipleri Cemiyeti*, the Wilson Principles League, which sealed the surrender of the Ottoman Empire in World War I. The League, a group of Istanbul intellectuals with Edib as only woman, was launched to urge President Woodrow Wilson to protect Ottoman Turkey. As Perin Gurel reflects, the letter "was an appeal for tutelage in the new methods of empire the United States had perfected (e.g. industrialization, professionalization, and liberal developmentalism), sent by an intelligentsia that still imagined an ethnically and religiously diverse Ottoman state" (353). Wilson, however, due to his outspoken hatred of the Turks, never replied to Edib. Owing to Atatürk's famous speech in 1927, called *Nutuk* (i.e. "speech" in Turkish), in which he openly demonized Edib "as a woman in bed with the United States" (Gurel 364), her 'fame' rests on her plea for an American mandate, largely disregarding her important role as spokesperson for women's rights.

5   Amongst other examples of Ottoman feminism is "[t]the first defense of the rights of women (which) appeared as early as 1891 in Fatma Aliye's Nisvan-I Islam [i.e. Women of Islam, R. P.] [...] The rapidity of the emancipation in upper-class families may be gauged by the date at which the first Ottoman emancipated femme fatale, who would have done honor to F. Scott Fitzgerald, is made to appear in Turkish society. This heroine, the

in 1928, former cultural practices including early feminist writings in Arabic were quickly forgotten. In addition, Turkey's modernization, although based on a European model, is not entirely in synchronicity with the Western historical periodization. While the demise of German and Austrian empires at the end of the First World War, for example, can be taken as synchronous to the break-down of the Ottoman Empire, the interwar years and the founding of the Turkish Republic is not analogous with seemingly parallel European developments in nation building. In many ways, the origins of Turkey as a nation state are based on a belated colonial endeavor of European powers, especially the British.

Whereas Evelyn strongly argues against such a colonizing take-over, she seems to be unaware of other historical developments; and what is even more surprising, she is ignorant or does not acknowledge the tradition of—also female—Western tourists fascinated by Turkish customs, especially the harem, she is partaking in. Meyda Yeğenoğlu writes about this "desire to penetrate the mysteries of the Orient and thereby to uncover hidden secrets (usually expressed in the desire to lift the veil and enter into the forbidden space of the harem) [as being] one of the constitutive tropes of Orientalist discourse" (73). And while many male travelers have denounced "the hateful mystery of the harem and the veil" due to this trope of concealment, there have been accounts of female travelers—most notably Lady Mary Wortley Montagu—who have entered this hidden "inner" space (73). Much like these writers of former times, Evelyn could be said to serve as facilitator who voices the 'forbidden,' since according to Yeğenoğlu,

> the only available means for the Western man is to rely on the Western woman's accounts of the harem's forbidden space, her description of the unveiled women, the details of their everyday life, etc. It is thus only through the assistance of the Western woman (for she is the only "foreigner" allowed to enter into the "forbidden zone") that the mysteries of this inaccessible "inner space" and the "essence" of the Orient secluded in it could be unconcealed [...]. (74)

How trustworthy such accounts as Montagu's *Turkish Embassy Letters*, written 1716-1718, are is beside the point here; what is striking, however, is the way

---

central character of Yakub Kadri [Karaosmanoğlu]'s Kiralık Konak [i.e. The Rented Mansion, R. P.] (1922), lives in the years immediately preceding World War I" (Mardin 137).

in which Evelyn fails in her self-ascribed role as a cultural emissary.[6] She remains stuck in the gap between a sympathetic, but historically belated interest in the old Ottoman ways and her reluctance to acknowledge the Turkish modernization in any other way except as European and especially English colonial intrusion. Her final return to the Pera Palace, which she links to this—in her view—fatal Western imposition, marks the end of her self-proclaimed mission there. In turn, her excursion to the harem and the estranging experiences she relates to the audience renders this place a memorial—discarded as outdated cultural practice and yet lingering as crystallized spatiotemporal memorial site. *Pera Palas* therefore both recalls the harem as belonging to the nation's historical past and as casting a shadow on the other characters' respective lives.

Ünel's dramatic technique of simultaneous action at first seems to stress the presentness of all performance in the same way that Peggy Phelan asserts: "Performance's life is only in the present. Performance cannot be saved, recorded, documented, or otherwise participate in the circulation of representations of representations: once it does so it becomes something other than performance" (146). The suggestion that all actions across space and time are interwoven creates an atmosphere of the absolute present. And yet, contrary to such a notion, Evelyn's narrative role and her harem episode also suggest that here performance indeed "becomes something other." In Joseph Roach's words, this kind of performance "stands in for an elusive entity that it is not but that must vainly aspire both to embody and to replace. Hence flourish the abiding yet vexed affinities between performance and memory, out of which blossom the most florid nostalgias for authenticity and origin. 'Where memory is,' notes theorist-director Herbert Blau, 'theatre is'" (3-4).

Ünel's technique of compressing time and space through simultaneous action plays on such "vexed affinities between performance and memory," not only in the present absentness of the harem—as being absent in its utter historicity and yet present in its lasting effect on the inhabitants, visitors and descendants as well as literary documents—but also in his multiple casting method: the actors play different roles in different time frames. This creates an archival effect in the sense that the actors seem to carry traces of multiple characters within their corporeal enactment. This second moment of

---

6   For a longer discussion of Montagu's trustworthiness, see Poole "Das Kopftuch" as well as chapter 2.

present absentness—an actor embodying character traces of other spatiotemporal moments than the present—can be considered queer in that it disturbs ontological conceptions of time and space.

"a place without a place:" Queer Space

Ünel's play abounds with sexual relations that have been considered misalliances in their respective times and places. There is Ali Riza Efendi with his several wives, Orhan (son of former slave Bedia) and his American wife Kathy, their son Murat and his gay American partner Brian, Sema (Murat's sister) and her married lover, and there are two striking single characters, Evelyn and Cavid. These relationships remain a thinly veiled secret (Sema's), are highly disputed (Ali Riza's, Orhan and Kathy's), not discussed at all (Evelyn's and Cavid's), or cause for long-standing rifts (Murat's). *Pera Palas* therefore gives plenty credit to Jill Dolan's claim that theater and sexuality are highly productive spheres of overlapping influence:

> Sexual desire has long been a motivating narrative factor in plays and performances, the force that establishes or destroys relationships, that stirs jealousy and encourages infidelity, or that binds characters or tears them apart, regardless of their sexual orientations. Theatre is also a place of fantasy and longing, of fleeting exchange between spectators and performers. With its liminal status as both real and not, as ephemeral and transformational, theatre has long been a site where misfits and the marginalized have congregated. (3)

Dolan links the plot of a drama to communicative processes between actors and audience concluding that the space thus created—the theater as encompassing stage and auditorium—has the power to serve as safe haven for nonnormative people. Ünel's play *Pera Palas* was first produced at the Lark Theatre in New York, which was founded in 1994 "as a counterpoint to the prevailing commercial, commodity-based culture of theater" and soon "established itself as a platform for free expression and rigorous experimentation" ("The Lark"). *Pera Palas* was one of three initial productions, announced as a "tapestry of East, West, power, and sex." The Lark's mission, in line with Dolan's claim, rests on the belief in the power of theater, in the empathy that results from hearing a new story and the better world that emerges after a shared experience. [...] We recognize that differences in identity including age, background, class, gender, nationality, physical ability, race, sexual orientation and thinking style bring vibrancy to our organization and that such differences help us better connect with the stories that reflect our world. ("The Lark")

The Lark's production of *Pera Palas* in 1997-1998 certainly succeeded in presenting historically and geopolitically underrepresented perspectives on the American stage. Besides New York, *Pera Palas* was presented at the National Theatre in London (1999), the Gate Theatre in London (2000) and the Landestheater Tübingen (2000-2001), the Theater Kozmos in Bregenz (2001), the Long Wharf Theater in New Haven (2002), the Open Stage Theater Co in Pittsburgh (2003), the Antaeus Theatre Company in Los Angeles (2005), the Theatre at Boston Court in Pasadena (2005), and the Arcola Theatre in London (2007). Notably, there has been no production in Turkey so far. Ünel himself calls this irony, since it is a "love story for the city of Istanbul [and] it's my most frequently produced play" ("Sinan Ünel").[7]

Margaret Russett highlights the strategic role of the Pera Palace within the play, but also for the audience providing a possible reason for Turkey's disinterest in the topic: "[I]t is a fantasy of Eastern exoticism, designed explicitly for the West" (631). Is this an American play then, after all? Reluctant to enter the heated debate on the nationality of literature, I certainly concede with what Wai Chee Dimock writes about "American" literature being a shorthand for a complex tangle of relations: "Rather than being a discrete entity, it is better seen as a crisscrossing set of pathways open-ended and ever multiplying, weaving in and out of other geographies, other languages and cultures" (3). If indeed we want to read *Pera Palas* as American literature, then, according to Dimock's *Through Other Continents*, we should also read the play as containing "input channels, kinship networks, routes of transit, and forms of attachment—connective tissues binding America to the rest of the world" (3).

It is in this sense of connectedness that we can perceive Ünel's play as participating in a transnationalization of perceptions about the United States,

---

7   In her essay on the emergence of queer theater in Istanbul, Elif Baş asserts that although there have been a few queer theater productions, LGBT concerns still have rarely been spoken of on Turkish stages: "Taboos about gender identity have not shifted significantly through theatre, but at least small steps have been taken" (133).

which in turn connects Ünel to other writers articulating such views, especially within a Turkish-American context, one prominent example being James Baldwin. After spending much of the 1960s in Istanbul, Baldwin began comparing his experiences as a—black—American to the experiences of Turks, who in turn "helped him to redefine his vocation as a transnational writer," as Magdalena Zaborowska asserts (203). Baldwin like many of his famous fellow American writers chose a life spent mostly abroad as an expatriate. But there is, as MaryAnn Snyder-Körber explains, a "narrower, expected, and [...] seemingly unproductive equation of international American modernism with a roster of writers running on a particular transatlantic route: generally, New York to London or Paris, but more rarely, to Marrakesh and never from Bratislava to Yonkers" (81). Baldwin is one of the writers who ventured beyond the predictable locales of the American modernist roster by taking up lodgings in Istanbul.[8] Tanfer Emin Tunc and Bahar Gursel refer to Baldwin's "'rock star' status" in Turkey as well as to other writers engaging in Turkish-American cultural negotiations such as Twain, Melville, or Hemingway to reassert an ongoing "transnational dialogue" between the two nations. This dialogue, they argue in their introduction to a collection of essays which examine American Studies from the Turkish perspective, takes part in the transnational turn in American Studies "by highlighting the current work that is being conducted by noted Turkish academics, American researchers, as well as foreign scholars working in Turkey, many of whom are living examples of transnationality" (22).

Accordingly, Russett's claim quoted above that Ünel's play has—only—a Western audience in mind, turns out to be highly arguable. But she implicitly points towards another crucial issue: the tension between concreteness and fantasy. And indeed, especially the hotel setting could be called realist in the sense that it actually exists as a "concrete" site; however, the dramaturgical layout of the play undermines any such notions of realism. In this, Ünel follows what theater critics have upheld, above all when speaking about theater experiences relating to marginalized subjects, such as LGBT people, namely

---

8   In *James Baldwin: From Another Place* (1973) by Turkish director Sedat Pakay, Baldwin affirms his transnational status: "I suppose that many people do blame me for being out of the States as often as I am. [...] perhaps only someone who is outside of the States realizes that it's impossible to get out. The American power follows one everywhere. [...] One sees it better from a distance [...] from another place, from another country." See my discussion of the film in chapter 3.

that "theatre doesn't just reflect reality [...]. On the contrary, [these critics] proposed that theatre creates what we consider reality by enforcing conventional notions of 'normal'" (Dolan 14-15). Realist theater, understood in such a manner, represents a closed-off world that not only separates actors/characters from spectators but also encourages audiences "to identify [with] and support worlds framed by conservative ideology that tends to marginalize, demean, or, worse still, exile or murder gay and lesbian characters" (15). A theater that goes against such realist conservatism, according to Dolan, favors postmodernist styles instead, which refuse "the conventions of fourth-wall domesticity" (15).

Ünel's multiple time and space arrangements may not altogether discard the fourth wall separating the stage from the audience, but they certainly disrupt standard notions of linearity, chronology, and spatial coherence. His hotel room scenes are highly versatile in this respect, due to the aforementioned enter-exit dynamic of the characters, which constantly forces spectators to reorient themselves in time and space. Furthermore, such passages seem to speak to each other: for example, Kathy and her sister Anne's conversation about how Kathy's future in-laws are treating her seems to correspond to Brian and Murat's concerns about visiting Murat's parents for the first time. The connection, of course, is a generational one with Kathy being Murat's mother, and intriguing parallelisms across time occur:

> **ANNE:** But living with your in laws ...
> **KATHY:** I don't mind. My mother-in-law is wonderful. She teaches me everything.
> **ANNE:** You have a family here. It's your family.
> **KATHY:** Yes. It's a good family.
> **ANNE:** Come on. Dry your tears before Orhan comes and sees you upset.
> *(MURAT's getting ready. BRIAN enters wearing a tie.)*
> **MURAT:** You packed a tie? You look like you're going to church.
> **BRIAN:** Same difference. Meeting my in-laws. (68-69)

Such scenes of intimate conversation have a special relevance because they relate to sexual and family matters in a transnational context. This is the case with Kathy and Orhan, who are about to get married, although Orhan shows signs of abusive behavior, and above all with Brian and Murat, who are used to being 'out' in the United States, while Murat's parents know nothing of their son's relationship with Brian. After Murat's traumatic coming-out to his parents ended in physical abuse by Murat's father Orhan, Murat had refused to see his parents until he introduces Brian to them. In this sense, the hotel room is a safe haven for them, but it is also a proverbial closet. As such, the hotel room functions as a precarious liminal space, a contested middle ground between the public and the private, between being 'out' and remaining 'in.' Eve Kosofsky Sedgwick has called the knowledge of this curious space between inside and outside an open secret, and she argues that the act of coming out is an endless repetition in view of ever-renewed social mechanisms of homophobia:

> Living in and hence coming out of the closet are never matters of the purely hermetic; the personal and political geographies to be surveyed here are instead the more imponderable and convulsive ones of the open secret. [...] gay identity is a convoluted and off-centering possession if it is a possession at all; even to come out does not end anyone's relation to the closet, including turbulently the closet of the other. (80-81)

The reiterated moment of coming out as performative act, which has "a potential for serious injury that is likely to go in both directions" (Sedgwick 80), is illustrated in Murat's second coming out to his father. Although the main purpose for visiting his home again after many years of exile is to reunite with his parents, once in Istanbul, he is reluctant to do so. The effect of the "pathogenic [open] secret" (Sedgwick 80) of the closet is too strong. Even though he came out to his parents years before, the violent reaction of his father has caused years of silence between them, and neither father nor son are willing to settle the stalemate. When Brian secretly takes action and contacts Murat's sister Sema, a meeting with the parents is set up, which after some initial exchange of niceties quickly escalates into violent verbal battling:

> **MURAT:** Do you remember what I looked like nine years ago? Did you really look at me then? Did you hear my voice? When you walked up those stairs, your eyes popping out of their sockets, stinking stale of alcohol. Came to find me here, your nostrils flaring, your fists, your knuckles, the way you grabbed me, spat at me, <u>spat at me!</u> [...] Don't you remember what you told me before you chased me out of this house? You told me I was an embarrassment to you. That you were ashamed to look at the faces of your friends.
> **ORHAN OLDER:** (*explodes*) Yes you were! You were an embarrassment. Then, and now and the whole time you were growing up! I wanted to pretend I didn't know you. I wish I wasn't even related to you. (92-94; original emphasis)

Instead of reconciliation, both father and son renew their deeply ingrained grudges against one another, and yet, it is Murat who reaches out to his father once again after the latter has fled home seeking refuge on the Bosphorus Ferry. There, on neutral territory, the father finally is able to make contact with his son by way of insisting on their similarities:

> I'm trying to find something I've lost, Murat. Is it a scent? A sound? Something I once touched? You and I are alike that way, searching for the same thing. Do you think you'll find it? [...] I wish I could help you, Murat. But once you assimilate the ideas of another country, once you understand the essence, you have no alternative but to be alienated from your own. I stepped through that threshold when I was young and I've never found my way back. [...] You'll never forgive me, Murat. You know that don't you? (104)

Orhan, most likely referring to his marriage to Kathy and in consequence to 'assimilating' into an Americanness, assumes that Murat has experienced a similar self-estrangement after leaving his family and homeland to live in the United States. Orhan's initial meeting with Kathy is significantly set in the early 1950s, a period in Turkish politics in which, after the landslide victory of the Democratic Party in 1950, Turkey's foreign relations increasingly turned towards the United States: "Turkey in these years became a solid—albeit peripheral—part of the political and military structures the United States and its allies built up to safeguard the continued existence of democracy and free enterprise in their countries. This was a major break with the Kemalist foreign policy of cautious neutralism" (Zürcher 234). Against this transnational background of what Zürcher calls "Atlantic Turkey," it is not incidental that Orhan and Kathy are meeting in 1952, the year Turkey became a full member of the NATO, and it is no less accidental that this last conversation between father and son takes place on the ferry that connects the European and Asian parts of Istanbul (234).

In an essay relating her own experience crossing the Bosphorus on such a ferry, Turkish writer Elif Shafak has described this ferry as a queer space where all kinds of people come together for a moment, "crammed chock-a-block" in "a palette of shades of gray" (Shafak "Transgender Bolero" 26).[9] Watching a transvestite listening to Ravel's "Bolero" on a walkman, Shafak experiences a queer spatiotemporal moment of transcendence which not only

---

9   For a discussion of Shafak's essay and yet another occurrence of the Bosphorus Ferry in her novel *The Saint of Insipient Insanities* see chapter 6.

conjoins silence and sound, melody and sexuality, self and other, individual and collective, but also the past and present of Turkish history. "Bolero" brings Shafak back the year 1928, the year Ravel composed the piece, which in turn reminds her of Turkey's "turbulent days," the dissolution of the Ottoman Empire and the fabrication of the Turkish Republic. As much as Orhan has felt the impact of foreignness through his transnational marriage, Shafak imagines the effect of European influences on the Turkish national psyche. At the same time, her queer moment on the ferry alerts her to the lack of queer thinking about Turkey's past and present:

> Among the ventures of the newly established Turkish Republic aiming to westernize and modernize its citizens as swiftly as possible was an attempt to discourage them from listening to traditional music and instead encourage them to enjoy Western classics, starting with, why not, "Bolero." Everybody hated it. Fortunately, the endeavor was halted shortly after it began, but its impact, the spirit behind it, remained. [...] So little has been studied of Turkey's militarist, masculinist, modernist genealogies. The path-breaking developments in gender studies and women's studies, as well as in gay-lesbian-bisexual-transgender studies, have been strikingly slow to inflect studies of the Middle East in general. Likewise, despite the salient contributions of several feminist scholars both in Turkey and abroad, the question of how individuals managed or failed to transcend gender zones in a society traversing civilization zones remains a marginal topic of research. (27)

Shafak's claim that while modernization seems to constitute a radical break with the past, "when it comes to gender and sexuality, perhaps there are more continuities than discontinuities" (27-28) is reflected in Ünel's play. Murat's innate self-hatred, which may be suppressed while abroad but which surfaces when faced with his father, is a token of the lasting "masculinist" genealogies reaching back across the generations aligning him with the social situation Evelyn encounters. Murat's repetition of a painful coming out mirrors "the story of state, sexuality and modernization in Turkey [as] a song in a repeat track mode, or else, a melody full of repetitions" (Shafak 28). And yet, as much as these processes of modernization required zoning strategies to demarcate the boundaries of gender and sexuality, of the public and the private, Ünel's hotel play points to the volatile state of such boundaries. The moment Murat and Orhan share on the ferry is a singular one—queerly out of time and space, or, put differently, a space, "which draws us out of ourselves, in which the erosion of our lives, our time and our history occurs, the space that claws and gnaws at us" (Foucault 23).

Michel Foucault has famously defined such heterogeneous spaces as heterotopias, oscillating between the real and the virtual, the here and there, the now and then, the present and absent, and between the deviant and the norm. Shafak's repeat melody and Ünel's transgenerational negotiation on the ferry link the heterotopia with the heterochrony in both accumulating and dissolving fixed frames of time and space. It is no surprise, then, that Foucault takes the boat to be such an "other" space "par excellence," "a floating piece of space, a place without a place, that exists by itself" (27). Given the geopolitical as well as cultural-aesthetic importance of the Bosphorus Ferry, Foucault's final comment on heterotopias rings a very special note: "In civilizations without boats, dreams dry up, espionage takes the place of adventure, and the police take the place of pirates" (27). Ünel uses the ferry as other space where—in contrast to the inhibitions of the domestic—a scenario of familial drama may be reimagined that otherwise has repeatedly proven to fail.

The ferry episode is only an interlude, but it leads to the play's finale in the hotel room of the Pera Palace with Murat and Brian deciding to stay on in Istanbul for an indefinite time. Murat's coming to terms with the demons of his past answers Evelyn's last worries, which are the last spoken words of the play: "Once again, I look out of my room in this European hotel, that I have, somehow, grown to like over the years. [...] Will this hopeful nation survive as a western country? [...] Only the future, the frightening, unfamiliar future will show us" (113). Even though Evelyn has made peace with the hotel's 'dubious Europeanness,' she remains unsure as to Turkey's future. Murat *is* that future, and as ambiguous as his character may be, he and what he represents is a marker of what José Esteban Muñoz has called a "queer futurity" that thrives on potentiality beyond the "prison house" (1) of the present:

> We have never been queer, yet queerness exists for us as an ideality that can be distilled from the past and used to imagine a future. The future is queerness's domain. [...] Some will say that all we have are the pleasures of this moment, but we must never settle for that minimal transport; we must dream and enact new and better pleasures, other ways of being in the world, and ultimately new worlds. (Muñoz 1)

Ünel's playful configuration of blending time and space, realized in the synchronicity of the hotel room, takes part in such a queer aesthetics of futurity. This transnational site is open for an intermingling of people with varying cultural, sexual, ethnic, and religious identities, and it is noteworthy that Ünel particularly chooses people with an artistic and educational background—Evelyn as writer, Kathy as teacher, Murat as photographer, Brian as artisan—who are willing to look beyond the present state of affairs. "Queer uses of time and space develop [...] in opposition to the institutions of family, heterosexuality, and reproduction," Jack Halberstam argues (1), and indeed Evelyn, Kathy, and Murat in their respective temporal conditions are representatives of such notions of transgressing normative notions of social conduct and "conventional forms of association, belonging, and identification" (Halberstam 2). As such, they might also be called "extravagant strangers."

"A kiss is just a kiss?" Extravagant Strangers

In his novels, Lawrence Scott, a Caribbean writer of German-French descent, who migrated between his exile in London and his birthplace Trinidad and Tobago, speaks of his exiled protagonists as "extravagant strangers." Based on Latin etymology, "extra/vagary" relates to somebody, who moves outside of traditional boundaries. Scott believes that there are multiple intersections which make one an outsider in this sense, such as race, gender, religion, class, sexuality or age. Scott's concern with "travelling outside the usual frontiers, the usual boundaries" touches upon "the characters in texts doing this travelling and [...] the text itself, [or rather] what becomes of the text" (13). Ünel's play *Pera Palas* is such an extravagantly strange text, with several characters crossing national, cultural, and sexual borders. Ünel himself is an extravagant stranger, moving between various identities and refraining from being labeled this or that. "People generally tend to categorize me as Turkish-American playwright," he says, "I find national identity to be increasingly irrelevant. [...] In terms of identity labels, I'd say I consider myself more 'gay' than belonging to any nation."[10] *Pera Palas* is the only play of his that openly touches on the Turkish-American connection.[11]

---

10   Quoted from personal email correspondence with the author, other information taken from Ünel's homepage <www.sinanunel.com>.
11   Except for *Cry of the Reed*, which is about a journalist abducted in Iraq and her mother in Konya, and *Chatal*, which deals with Western archaeologists excavating a Neolithic site in Turkey, Ünel's playwriting interests lie more in American topics and settings, especially Provincetown (*Tolstoy's Den, Off the Cliff, Lost Gospels of Blankenburg, Thalassa*

With Evelyn, Kathy, and Murat, *Pera Palas* features three characters who are obviously extravagant strangers in Scott's transnational understanding. There is, however, one more character that causes puzzlement: Cavid. He is the only character to appear in all three time frames and he is the most elusive of all. As a young man, he is the only male besides the Pasha to be tolerated in the harem. He therefore is a liminal character from the start, moving clandestinely between strictly gendered spaces. Furthermore, he articulates pronouncedly progressive opinions when he takes Evelyn's side against the other women in the harem: "I like her. I think she's right to want her freedom" (17). Act II starts with a long monologue by Cavid, who is the only one besides Evelyn to engage in this dramatic form. Here, he pronouncedly distances himself from the way he was brought up, especially his father's practice of polygamy:

> Hello. My name's Cavid. Mademoiselle Crawley asked me to address you today. […] I was a happy child until the age of five when my father married for the second time. The rest of my life passed in the bitter and hopeless state of watching my poor mother suffer and age over the years. […] [A]ll I could think about was to leave that house forever and to never marry. […] I pitied [my mother] but increasingly I became angry with her.
>
> No woman of any dignity should be asked to permit a second wife to enter her home. This practice must change! But this change will not come about if you, the women of this country, won't do something to change it. (With disgust) I stand here looking at you in your veils and I think you're despicable. Can't you see how Europe laughs at you? Why do you put up with this iniquitous situation? Why do you still wear those veils, the symbols of servitude? Why can't you come out and free yourselves? (36)

Here, Cavid takes a most outspoken political stance that is clearly aligned with the Turkish process of modernization as propagandized by Atatürk. In the course of the play, however, this stark pro-European view mellows and alters. Although he seeks Evelyn to help his half-sister Melek out of her unhappy marriage, he also accosts her for representing the British nation after the armistice: "How can you still stand here, have you no shame? Your evil government is calling us traitors. We're sent to exile as though we're an embarrassment, as though six hundred years of rule never happened! […] I don't

---

My Heart, Portals), the lives of Russian artists (*Pathétique, A Mad Person's Chronicle of a Miserable Marriage*), or general gay issues (*New Life, Single Lives, The Three of Cups*).

want to go to Europe!" (107). Increasingly, he considers himself an outsider, not only concerning his home country but also in a more general and encompassing way. When Kathy first meets Orhan's parents in 1952, Cavid is also present, purposely acting as mediator between the generations and cultures. By now a man past his prime and having returned after years of enforced exile, Orhan introduces him to Kathy as "our most unfortunate Cavid." Cavid counters: "I am not unfortunate, merely displaced. In place as well as in time. [...] But I'm a stubborn progressive. Many years I lived in Europe" (38). Cavid's reflective model of existence oscillating between self-chosen empowerment and reactive submission resonates with Edward Said's concept of the intellectual expatriate who finds it possible "to imagine and investigate in spite of barriers, and always to move away from the centralizing authorities toward the margins, where you see things that are usually lost on minds that have never traveled beyond the conventional and comfortable" (380). In yet another direct address to the audience, Cavid comments on his experience as refugee in a foreign country:

> This was the saddest day of our lives. To leave our beautiful Istanbul, the magnificent tulips, the sad melodies, our sunsets over the Bosphorus. All in one day gone. It was more than any of us could bear. [...] We were lost in France, like orphans without food or shelter. [...] But I went on [...] and nearly twenty years after our departure, I was permitted to return to my beloved city again. [...] But I was old now. I was poor, homeless ... . (108)

Cavid's experience as refugee is similar to Hannah Arendt's account of Jewish refugees fleeing from country to country, being treated as pariahs, and facing the challenge to balance between being assimilated—turning into "social parvenus [...] ready to pay any price in order to be accepted by society"—and consciously remaining outlaws "in a topsy-turvy world" (119). Arendt's radical stance calls for keeping one's identity even in the face of humiliation.

In terms of historical transitions and transnational existence, Cavid is extraordinarily self-conscious and outspoken. While embracing progress, he abhors his nomadic life as a result of such 'progress.' He is, however, strangely silent, when it comes to his personal life. Assuming that he has never married, there are also no clues as to intimate relationships of whatever sort. In a most striking scene at the very end of the play, he appears in his younger version to Murat in a dream. In answer to Murat's question "Who are you?" he announces himself as "I'm your loss, I'm your sadness" (110-111), stressing a link between the two men that is not blood-related but that relies on being soul mates. In a dialogue, constantly interrupted by Kathy and Orhan's dispute about the deadlock situation of their marriage, Murat and Cavid speculate about what the future might bring for each:

> **MURAT:** You don't know what the future holds.
> **KATHY:** And I can't forgive myself. For not leaving you. Now.
> **MURAT:** Your sadness is a gift. Soon you'll be free. You'll overcome destiny. You'll make your own future.
> **KATHY:** Why won't I leave you? Now?
> **CAVID:** But who will I be? Will I ever know again who I am?
> **ORHAN OLDER:** If you met me today, Kathy, would you still marry me?
> **MURAT:** Yes, you will.
> **KATHY:** Yes.
> **MURAT:** Have courage, Cavid. You belong everywhere. *(MURAT kisses CAVID)*
> **ORHAN:** I'm your destiny.
> **KATHY:** Oh, yes.
> **ORHAN OLDER:** You are everything to me.
> **MURAT:** I release you now. So go. Now. Go. (111-112)

Not only do these conversations crisscross each other, subliminally commenting on one another, they also transcend time and place, and the linear logic of a historical course of events. Kathy in her younger age talks to her husband in his older age, and simultaneously Cavid and Murat communicate in a dream across the span of several decades. Furthermore, contrary to the surface logic according to which Murat in present time 'calls' for late Cavid as a distant soul-mate, it actually is Cavid who in his dream before being sent into exile invocates a future to-be Murat. Accordingly, the dream exists for both of them: they share an intimate moment beyond any spatiotemporal logic. The older Cavid dimly recalls this dream he had as a young man: "The next morning I woke with an unfamiliar feeling. I couldn't remember the dream. But I had hope. What was the dream I'd had? What was setting me free?" (112). Young Cavid, on the brink of becoming the extravagant stranger that he will be, summons a soulmate from the future, a gay, bicultural man, who sends him on his wanderings and seals the promise of becoming with a kiss. The intermingling confirmation of love and destiny, reconfirmed by Kathy and Orhan, reflect on this kiss, which I take to be queer in the sense of transgressing the normative logics of the here and now.

What needs to be taken into account, furthermore, is that this kiss actually happens on stage; although the kiss between Cavid and Murat is the climax of a dream Cavid recalls having and thus cannot be taken as a kiss of this 'real' world, we do witness two real men kissing. The corporeality of actors performing such a kiss reinforces the overall notion of Ünel's play that events from different historical settings are intermingled and relate to each other. This is even further enhanced by Ünel's casting wishes. For example, he suggests a cross-gender casting for some characters such as Bedia: "The actor who plays ORHAN OLDER also plays BEDIA OLDER, his mother" (iii). Again, this encounter interweaves different time frames as well as, in this case, gender performances not only because Bedia is played by a male actor, but because the same actor also plays Bedia's son in a different time frame. Such a practice of cross-gender casting helps to destabilize cultural gender scripts, and therefore adds to the political posture of the play on the corporeal level, namely the performance of cross-dressing bodies on stage. Herewith, Ünel disengages the body from the role, which on the one hand highlights the artificiality of gender norms these characters enact, and on the other hand insinuates resemblances between characters across gender and generation.

Besides such cross-gender casting choices, Ünel suggests that "[t]he actor who plays BRIAN also plays CAVID who appears to MURAT in a dream sequence at the end of the play" (iii). Without further elaboration on this choice, Ünel tightens the web of innuendos here with regard to Cavid. Since Brian is the most 'out' character of the play in terms of his gay sexuality, having Cavid and Brian cast by the same male actor brings Cavid's ambiguous sexuality in closer proximity to queerness. Again, the kiss we see on stage becomes an even stronger queer moment through the double-casting of Brian and Cavid: we literally see them as only one and the same man kissing Murat.[12]

---

12 Kissing scenes are not to be taken lightly. Although famously, just before Rick and Ilsa embrace for their big dramatic kiss in *Casablanca* and Dooley Wilson sings the iconic words "A kiss is just a kiss," film and stage kisses between men remain a disputed topic. Referring to Andy Warhol's film *Kiss* of 1963, Linda Williams asserts that a male-to-male kiss privileges "the surplus perversion of a protogay kiss that shows the engagement of the whole body" (Williams 335), and therefore alludes to the way such kisses make us aware of the genital sex that may accompany it. Williams's Freudian terminological use of 'perverse' in opposition to 'normal' sexual acts refers not to an aberration of a heterosexual norm when two men kiss, but to the representational ('perverse') substitute of a kiss for a ('normal') sexual act due to overt censorship or implicit censor practices that continue even today. Lauren Berlant and Michael Warner relate the underlying coercive sexist ideology to a "national heterosexuality" as the mechanism by which "a core national culture can be imagined as a sanitized space of sentimental feeling and immaculate behavior, a space of pure citizenship" (qtd. in Hariman and Lucaites 128).

Ünel's play features two men kissing and yet it is only a dream kiss. For Cavid, this dream kiss may be a sign of what his life will come to be: lived in a perpetual closet, always remaining the extravagant stranger. For Murat, however, this kiss means something different altogether: it seals his link to his abjected Turkish heritage, making the potential for a renewed home in Istanbul feasible. It is here that the Pera Palace and its confined hotel room setting most notably signifies a queer utopian space in stark contrast to what Matthias claims for hotels and the fictions set therein, when she writes that "hotels are not utopian spaces. Even in the most positive cases, they remain artificial sets where dreams can be acted out but not taken outside hotel's walls into 'real life.' [...] Hotels are there to please, not to change" (7). On the contrary, Murat has changed in the course of his temporary stay that might stretch for a yet undefined time span. Murat together with Brian disrupt the heteronormativity of the space via queer performativity, announcing the imminence of a queer future.

Referring to the iconic "Times Square Kiss," the 1946 photograph of Alfred Eisenstaedt depicting a sailor kissing a nurse on V-J Day, which "is a picture of personal intimacy in a public space" (123), Hariman and Lucaites explain that this kiss icon exemplifies in action what Berlant and Warner describe: "A man kissing a woman in the nation's most famous town square to celebrate military victory is a perfect case of heteronormative citizenship" (128). And precisely because the image enacts such a normative ideology, it can serve as template for challenge as best can be seen in the most famous appropriation of the kiss in the cover illustration of the 1996 *New Yorker* by Bill Blitt, which shows two uniformed men kissing on that very square. Obliquely referring to President Bill Clinton's "Don't Ask Don't Tell" policy allowing gays, lesbians and bisexuals to serve in the military as long as they remain in the 'closet,' i.e. silent about their homosexuality, the picture 'outs' what usually remains hidden in public: men kissing men. The cover thus "creates a sense of scandal, but by showing how supposedly deviant behavior fits seamlessly into the public model of heterosexual normality, it challenges conventional beliefs" (Hariman and Lucaites 129). Much like this "man-on-man public kissing constitutes a paramount political performance" (Morris and Sloop 3), queer kisses on stage have remained taboo until very recently (see Stuart; Morris; Clum 11), which agrees well with Ünel's gender politics in general and his gay kiss on stage in particular. Just as Murat's father claims it is okay for his son to announce his gayness and yet is too repulsed to look Murat in the face, the scandal of the staged gay kiss is both asserted (the kiss is visible on stage) and disclaimed (it is a dream kiss). The sight of two men kissing can still be perceived as a transgression of the given gender order since, "[a] kiss, to paraphrase the old song, isn't just a kiss. Hence its theatrical power" (Clum 11).

Notably, 1993 was the year in which the increasingly visible Turkish LGBT community attempted—and failed—to organize a gay and lesbian pride conference in Istanbul. Originally approved by the Interior Ministry, the event was supposed to be linked to the Gay Pride activities across the globe, but it was banned at the last minute by the governor of Istanbul on the grounds that it would be "contrary to Turkey's tradition and moral values," which led to the detention of 28 foreign delegates who then were deported to Germany. As Hakan Gecim writing for ILGA (International Lesbian, Gay, Bisexual, Trans and Intersex Association) explains, the "most striking result of this event was the establishment of Lambda Istanbul which is one of the most important LGBT organizations in Turkey." Lambda's creed is "to reach homosexuals who have not yet made their coming out process and help them, to establish solidarity within the gay community, to fight the prejudice of the media and society, and to help gays in Turkey to develop their identity and work for equality and liberation" (qtd. in Murray 4).[13] Murat in Ünel's play has come a long way, evolving from a traumatized expatriate to somebody who reconnects with his home. His journey is similar to Ünel's own experience while writing the play which was to be his "love story for the city of Istanbul:" "Writing Pera Palas was a truly cathartic experience. As a dual citizen of two vastly disparate worlds, I always felt psychically divided. This play was the first time I felt those two aspects finally joined together. And it was a dance. A wild, and wonderful dance—and writing it was thrilling" ("Sinan Ünel").

Works Cited

"Pera Palace Hotel Jumeirah." *Jumeirah*. Web. 15 May 2015. <http://www.jumeirah.com/en/hotels-resorts/istanbul/pera-palace-hotel-jumeirah/>

"Sinan Ünel." *Sinan Ünel*. Web. 25 Nov 2021. <http://www.sinanunel.com/pera-palas.html>

"The Lark." *Lark Theatre*. Web. 25 Oct 2015. <http://www.larktheatre.org/>

Arendt, Hannah. "We Refugees." *Altogether Elsewhere: Writers on Exile*. Ed. Marc Robinson. Boston and London: Faber and Faber, 1994. 110-119.

Bartu, Ayfer. "Who Owns the Old Quarters? Rewriting Histories in a Global Era." *Istanbul: Between the Global and the Local*. Ed. Çağlar Keyder. Lanham et al.: Rowman & Littlefield, 1999. 31-45.

---

13 For more on the development of the LGBT community see chapter 1.

Baş, Elif. "From Self-Effacement to Confrontation: The Emergence of Queer Theatre in Istanbul." *Asian Culture and History* 8.2 (2016): 126-134.

Berlant, Lauren, and Michael Warner. "Sex in Public." *Critical Inquiry* 24 (1998): 547-66.

Clum, John M. *Acting Gay: Male Homosexuality in Modern Drama*. New York: Columbia UP, 1992.

Dimock, Wai Chee. *Through Other Continents: American Literature Across Deep Time*. Princeton and Oxford: Princeton UP, 2006.

Dolan, Jill. *Theatre & Sexuality*. Houndmills: Palgrave Macmillan, 2010.

Dos Passos, John. *Orient Express*. New York: Jonathan Cape and Harrison Smith, 1927.

Fortuny, Kim. *American Writers in Istanbul*. Syracuse: Syracuse UP, 2009.

Foucault, Michel. "Of Other Spaces." *Diacritics* 16.1 (1986): 22-27.

Gecim, Hakan. "A Brief History of the LGBT Movement in Turkey." *ILGA*. 1 Oct 2009. Web. 8 Feb 2013. <http://ilga.org/ilga/en/article/420>

Gurel, Perin. "Turkey and the United States after World War I: National Memory, Local Categories, and Provincializing the Transnational." *American Quarterly* 67.2 (2015): 353-376.

Halberstam, Jack J. *In a Queer Time and Place: Transgender Bodies, Subcultural Lives*. New York and London: New York UP, 2005.

Hariman, Robert, and John Louis Lucaites. "The Times Square Kiss. Iconic Photography and Civic Renewal in U.S. Public Culture." *The Journal of American History* 94.1 (2007): 122-131.

James Baldwin: From Another Place. Dir. Sedat Pakay. Hudson Film Works, 1973.

Karr, H. P. "Mörder im Hotel: Eine kleine Beherbergungsgeschichte zu Agatha Christie und ihren Kriminalromanen." *Grand Hotel: Bühne der Literatur*. Eds. Cordula Seger and Reinhard G. Wittmann. München: Dölling und Garlitz, 2007. 111-124.

King, Charles. *Midnight at the Pera Palace: The Birth of Modern Istanbul*. New York and London: W. W. Norton, 2014.

Mardin, Şerif. *Religion, Society, and Modernity in Turkey*. Syracuse: Syracuse UP, 2006.

Matthias, Bettina. *The Hotel as Setting in Early Twentieth-Century German and Austrian Literature: Checking in to Tell a Story*. Rochester: Camden House, 2006.

Morris, Charles E., and John M. Sloop. "'What Lips These Lips Have Kissed:' Refiguring the Politics of Queer Public Kissing." *Communication and Critical / Cultural Studies* 3.1 (2006): 1-26.

Morris, Gary. "Queer Kisses: The Cinematic Taboo Before 2000." *Bright Lights Film Journal*. 1 Nov. 1997. Web. 22 Nov. 2015. <http://brightlightsfilm.com/queer-kisses-cinematic-taboo-2000/#.VlGhQV7Eaqo>

Muñoz, José Esteban. *Cruising Utopia: The Then and There of Queer Futurity*. New York and London: New York UP, 2009.

Murray, Stephen O. "Turkey." *glbtq: an encyclopedia of gay, lesbian, bisexual, transgender & queer culture*. Web. 27 Nov. 2015. <http://www.glbtqarchive.com/ssh/turkey_S.pdf>

Phelan, Peggy. *Unmarked: The Politics of Performance*. London: Routledge, 1993.

Poole, Ralph. "Das Kopftuch unter der Perücke oder der Aufstand der islamischen Töchter gegen den türkischen Kemalismus." *Kopf und andere Tücher*. Eds. Gisela Engel and Susanne Scholz. Berlin: trafo, 2006. 9-29.

Roach, Joseph R. *Cities of the Dead: Circum-Atlantic Performance*. New York: Columbia UP, 1996.

Rösch, Paul. "Das Traumschloss des Bürgers: Zur Kulturgeschichte des Grand Hotels." *Grand Hotel: Bühne der Literatur*. Eds. Cordula Seger and Reinhard G. Wittmann. München: Dölling und Garlitz, 2007. 25-42.

Russett, Margaret. "*Pera Palas* by Sinan Ünel." *Theater Journal* 54.4 (2002): 630-632.

Said, Edward. "Intellectual Exile: Expatriates and Marginals (1993)." *The Edward Said Reader*. Eds. Moustafa Bayoumi and Andrew Rubin. New York: Vintage, 2000. 368-381.

Scott, Lawrence. "'Extravagant Strangers:' Contribution to a Round Table Discussion." *Bridges Across Chasms: Towards a Transcultural Future in Caribbean Literature*. Ed. Bénédicte Ledent. Liège: L 3—Liège Language and Literature, 2004. 13-17.

Sedgwick, Eve Kosofsky. *Epistemology of the Closet*. Berkeley: U of California P, 1990.

Seger, Cordula. "Die literarische Bühne Grand Hotel." *Grand Hotel: Bühne der Literatur*. Eds. Cordula Seger and Reinhard G. Wittmann. München: Dölling und Garlitz, 2007. 7-24.

Shafak, Elif. "Transgender Bolero." *Middle East Report* 230 (2004): 26-29, 47.

Snyder-Körber, MaryAnn. *Modernism in American Centuries: Henry James, T. S. Eliot, Djuna Barnes, James Baldwin*. Habilitationsschrift: FU Berlin, 2014.

Stuart, Otis. "No Tongues, Please—We're Queer: The Same-Sex Kiss on the New York Stage." *The Village Voice* (2 Feb. 1993): 90.

Tunc, Tanfer Emin, and Bahar Gursel, eds. *The Transnational Turn in American Studies: Turkey and the United States*. Bern et al.: Peter Lang, 2012.

Ünel, Sinan. *Pera Palas*. 1998. Unpublished Manuscript.
Williams, Linda. "Of Kisses and Ellipses: The Long Adolescence of American Movies." *Critical Inquiry* 32.2 (2006): 288-340.
Yeğenoğlu, Meyda. *Colonial Fantasies: Towards a Feminist Reading of Orientalism*. Cambridge: Cambridge UP, 1998.
Zabarowska, Magdalena J. *James Baldwin's Turkish Decade: Erotics of Exile*. Durham and London: Duke UP, 2009.
Zürcher, Erik J. *Turkey: A Modern History*. London and New York: I. B. Tauris, 2004.

III. Transnational Queer Poetics

5. "The Wonder of Thy Beauty:" Bayard Taylor's *Poems of the Orient* as an Intermediary Between German Romanticism and American Gentility

The Arabian Indifference to Time—Moving From East to West

"Wir Deutschen sind in der Mitte zwischen Orient und Amerika. Bei den Arabern spielt Zeit keine Rolle. Amerika lebt mit der Uhr in der Hand. […] Wir in der Mitte" (Kerr 221).[1] German traveler Alfred Kerr wrote these lines as part of his hymnal first impressions upon arriving in New York in 1914. Kerr articulates two oppositional cultural tropes: the Oriental calmness and tranquility on the one hand, and the American frenzy and turmoil on the other. Recalling his own enchantment and fascination with the American pandemonium years later, Kerr once more argues on the basis of an intercultural experience. It is only in the midst of American flurry that he comes to rest, whereas German boredom never leaves one in peace: "Die Mittel von Berlin wirken dermaßen langweilig, […] daß man zur Ruhe nicht kommt. Ruhe fand ich hier: weil es rasend geht" (221).

What Kerr in his first statement articulates—the Arabian indifference to time—is one of the enduring stereotypes that Edward Said has argued as being responsible in creating a Western conception of the Orient. This 'timelessness' was something European travelers in the Orient felt to be a threat,

---

[1] Many thanks to Huma Ibrahim for her valuable criticism of this essay. The cited passage originally stems from Kerr's *Die Welt im Licht* (1920). The quote, however, is taken from his later "New York und London: Stätten des Geschicks. Zwanzig Kapitel nach dem Weltkrieg," where in the last New York section, "Amerika—Postskriptum," he cites selected passages of his first text on America.

and according to Said they had to protect themselves from such unsettling influences, since they "wore away the European discreteness and rationality of time, space, and personal identity. In the Orient one suddenly confronted unimaginable antiquity, inhuman beauty, boundless distance" (167). Kerr, however, seems not anxious about this dangerous Oriental trait. He does not feel the need of protection against it, because his take on the Orient is for rhetorical purposes only. In the course of his argument, as can be seen in his second statement, Kerr loses his initial point—and interest—of comparison: the claim of Arabian indifference to time.

Kerr could have constructed a triangular cultural relationship, but he drops the third—'Arabian'—party that would then have served as intermediary in favor of the pronounced contrast between Germany and America. Thus, his opposition is not based on the dichotomy of East and West, but on an inherent Western antagonism of old and new with the East as excluded 'Other,' way beyond any participation in this cultural assessment. Kerr's focus clearly points in the Western direction, from Germany towards America, first recalling but then neglecting the distant East which nevertheless may be said to remain in the back of his mind in a double sense: corporeal and historical.

Geographically, one way to get to America from Arabian countries is by passing through Germany. In this sense, Kerr would literally be leaving the East behind by facing the West. Historically, Kerr calls upon the enthusiastic German reception of Oriental culture exactly a century earlier, starting with Joseph von Hammer's translation in 1812-13 of the *Divan* by fourteenth-century Persian poet Hafiz that set off a broad interest of Germans in Oriental culture and triggered Goethe's *West-östlicher Divan* (1819), which in turn inspired other Oriental poetry, such as August von Platen's *Ghaselen* (1821) and Friedrich Rückert's *Östliche Rosen* (1822). Kerr, as a German, takes this history and tradition of German Orientalism with him on his journey to America.

Another way of situating Germany as middle ground between East and West is by switching the direction of perspective, that is, by traveling from Western America to the Orient via Germany. It is this track that nineteenth-century travel writer and poet Bayard Taylor took, again in the mentioned double sense. Not only did he physically pass through Germany on his way east; in his ethically and aesthetically envisioning the Orient he also fundamentally relied on Germany's Oriental reception. His Oriental travel accounts and above all his own Oriental poetry thus reflect Taylor's actual encounter *with* the East as well as his engagement with German literature *on* the East. Addressing his home audience from abroad—and later at home with lecture tours—, Taylor through his writings held a prominent position in mid-nineteenth century as mediator in the triangular constellation America, Germany, and the Orient. At the same time, through employing the cultural standards of Genteel America, Taylor managed to sidestep the condescending colonial and imperialist attitude that characterized much of European Orientalist literature of the nineteenth century.

From West to East to West—Cross-Cultural Counterpoints

Speaking of the Orient "as a terrain for literary exploitation," Edward Said calls to attention the multiple layers of interest "that covered the Orient as a subject matter and as a territory," especially in the latter part of the nineteenth century. He goes on to argue that even "the most innocuous travel books—and there were literally hundreds written after mid-century—contributed to the density of public awareness of the Orient." What Said has in mind, however, is above all the interest English and French travelers had, even though he parenthetically acknowledges "some American voyagers, among them Mark Twain and Herman Melville" (192).

Said's claim of an exception from the rule actually ignores a quite different story, namely one in which there was an increasing interest in the Orient during the early nineteenth century on behalf of those Americans who cared about the formation of an American self-image apart from European models. "When the young republic strove to complement its political independence from its European origins with declarations of cultural independence," according to Catrin Gersdorf, "the Orient became if not America's surrogate self [...] then an imaginative figure employed to delineate those cultural and historical distinctions it sought between America itself and Europe" (99).

It was the time, when Europe and America competed in staking their mutual claims—geographically and culturally speaking—in the Orient. When Europe's Oriental interest turned especially towards Egypt and India, American writers like Irving, Poe, and Hawthorne took part in the geo-aesthetic fascination that at least in Europe led to an Oriental Renaissance, which Luther Luedtke describes as "a time when the language, literature, and imagination of Europe were reborn through Indic rather than Hellenistic inspiration" (xix). Recent studies like Fuad Sha'ban's define American Orientalism at the turn of the nineteenth century as an amalgamation of European stimulus and American public discourse, or in his own words as a "national cultural dialogue which derives from European background, heritage and influence on the one hand, and, on the other, stems from particular American factors and experience" (vii).

Sha'ban, who grounds his argument on the notion that American Orientalism relies on the self-perception of Americans as the chosen people, goes on, however, to claim that American travelers abroad economically and culturally appropriated the Orient by turning the intercultural encounters into a romanticized souvenir and exotic commodity.[2] With this turn of reasoning, Sha'ban actually asserts what Said himself had claimed as the Orientalization undertaken by Europeans. Whether writers on the Orient chose a more professional or a more personal take on their subject matter, their works, according to Said, "rely upon the sheer egoistic powers of the European consciousness at their center" (158). Thus, "the Orientalist ego" is evidenced by his perspective. Even when trying to be impartial, he writes *for* the European observer and as such is interpreting the Orient: "[T]his interpretation is a form of Romantic restructuring of the Orient, a re-vision of it, which restores it redemptively to the present. Every interpretation, every structure created for the Orient, then, is a reinterpretation, a rebuilding of it" (158).

Whereas the European Orientalists Said is thinking of in this generalized manner may be argued to 'acquire' the Orient in order to domesticate it to European codes and classifications, which "formed a simulacrum of the Orient and reproduced it materially in the West" (166), for American Orientalists the case was somewhat different. Since their perception of the Orient invariably was filtered and enriched through its European artistic response, American writers often took on a double vista that oscillated between a highly aestheticized modus operandi and a more basic fascination with Oriental customs compared to American manners and morals. This shift in perspective is also meant to reconsider the concept of Orientalism apart from its late twentieth-century normative tone that by and large can be seen as a result of Said's

---

2   For a critical reading of Sha'ban, see Gersdorf who writes that Sha'ban's persistent attempt to refer back to "the American vision of Zion" (Sha'ban 177) and to Puritan self-representations as a people "entrusted with the task of rebuilding the Kingdom of God, the 'little American Israel'" (Sha'ban 195) "not only runs the risk of reducing cultural criticism to an ideological exercise whose only concern is to display the one and only foundation for the proclivities and prejudices of late 20th-century U.S. politics in the Near East, it also comes dangerously close to reducing politics simply to a matter of religious zeal" (Gersdorf 101).

powerful argument and that lead to the term being one of the most ideologically charged words in recent scholarship. This tone overlays an originally more sympathetic meaning of the word during the nineteenth century where it conveyed the study of the languages, literatures, religions, arts and manners of the East. As John MacKenzie stresses:

> Orientalism came to represent a construct, not a reality, an emblem of domination and a weapon of power. It lost its status as a sympathetic concept, a product of scholarly admiration for diverse and exotic cultures, and became the literary means of creating a stereotypical and mythic East through which European rule could be more readily asserted. (xii)

Without suggesting that the Orient and Oriental people were not often subject to being stereotypically presented, MacKenzie pleads for a more dynamic historical approach to artistic interests in Orientalism. He speaks of various contrapuntal processes leading to cultural cross-fertilization that in turn produced syncretic forms of art. Said himself admits in a short, rather enigmatic passage at the outset of his study that Orientalism has not always and only been a one-way street. "In addition," he writes, "the Orient has helped to define Europe (or the West)" (1), adding on later that especially for the Romantics the Orient became a means of regenerating and revitalizing Europe (115). Said, however, does not follow through with an argument that the Orient could possibly be seen as the source for a counter-Western discourse which challenges Western conventions and as such would serve as a starting ground for cultural, social, literary, spiritual and artistic resistance. Reading Bayard Taylor's works on the Orient in this light leads to an understanding of how a romantic writer could draw from various artistic influences—both from the East and the West—in order to produce a highly syncretic literary output and at the same time adhere to a national, American, agenda.

"Wahlheimatliteratur"—Taylor Reading Rückert Reading Goethe

POEMS OF THE ORIENT
Da der West war durchgekostet,
Hat er nun den Ost entmostet.
(Rückert)

Bayard Taylor's *Poems of the Orient* (1854) opens with this frontispiece, a quotation of German romantic poet Friedrich Rückert (33).[3] This is significant, for it bears witness to Taylor's having read Rückert's poetical works and to his knowledge of the German language in general. Taylor actually had met Rückert in 1852, when he interrupted his travels in the East for a short visit to Germany.[4] Later recalling this encounter, Taylor in 1866 writes:

> When I first visited Coburg, in October, 1852, I was very anxious to make Rückert's acquaintance. My interest in Oriental literature had been refreshed, at that time, by nearly ten months of travel in Eastern lands, and some knowledge of modern colloquial Arabic. I had read his wonderful translation of the Makamât of Hariri, and felt sure that he would share my enthusiasm for the people to whose treasures of song he had given so many years of his life. (*Critical Essays* 95-96)

From Germany, he took along Rückert's *Morgenländische Sagen und Geschichten* (1837) and, as John Krumpelman has shown, there is evidence in the poems composed subsequent to October 1852 of an almost direct use of Rückert's book, a very prominent example being "Bedouin Song," Taylor's most famous single poem.[5] Taylor's frontispiece reference to Rückert, however, does not

---

3   The sequence *Poems of the Orient* is included in the household edition of *The Poetical Works of Bayard Taylor* 35-67.
4   While Taylor's focus on the Orient was based on first-hand contact, he also sought the aesthetic link to Germany. Taylor himself was partly of German ancestry and his first travel trip to Europe in 1844 at the age of 19 was his initial contact with his German roots. His constantly growing interest in German literature and life led him, for example, to his second marriage with German Marie Hansen, his post as non-resident Professor of German at Cornell University, his scholarly effort *Studies in German Literature*, and it culminated in his metrically faithful translation of Goethe's *Faust* as well as his eventual, but due to a close death short-termed appointment as American minister to Berlin in 1878.
5   Krumpelman convincingly compares Rückert's "Die Liebeslieder und der Koranvers" from his second volume of *Morgenländische Sagen und Geschichten* with Taylor's "Bedouin

originate in Rückert's well-known translation and adaptation of Arabic tales, but is a quote taken verbatim from Rückert's own Oriental poem sequence, *Östliche Rosen*, which were directly inspired by Hafiz (written in 1819, published 1822).[6] At the time, Rückert was under great influence by the recent German translations of the Persian *divans* by the thirteenth-century mystic poet Rumi and the fourteenth-century more profanely oriented, at times even highly erotic poet Hafiz. Rückert became one of the leading Orientalists in Germany, a very important figure for academically establishing Oriental Studies. Like most other Orientalists of his age, he did not travel to the East himself, but his vast language skills allowed him to read Arabian and Persian literature in the original versions.[7]

Rückert is in yet another sense a pivotal character in Germany's romantic yearning for anything Oriental. Rückert followed Johann Gottfried von Herder's and Friedrich Schlegel's ideas of stimulating national poetry by searching for the very origins of language as the seat of all humanity.[8] They all believed to have found these origins not in Romanic or Hellenistic but in Oriental sources:

> Wären uns nur die Schätze des Orients so zugänglich wie die des Altertums! [...] Im Orient müssen wir das höchste Romantische suchen, und wenn wir erst aus der Quelle schöpfen können, so wird uns vielleicht der Anschein von südlicher Glut, der uns jetzt in der spanischen Poesie so reizend ist, wieder nur abendländisch und sparsam erscheinen. (Schlegel 502)

Song." Rückert himself called his poem ein "beduinisch Lied," and it includes the following lines taken in a shortened version from the Qur'an: "Ich las die Verse vom Gericht: / Wenn die Sonn' ist erkaltet, / Und die Sterne veraltet / Und die Berge gespaltet. – / [...] Und das Schuldbuch ist entfaltet." Taylor's refrain reads as follows: "Till the sands grow cold, / And the stars are old, / And the leaves of the Judgement / Book unfold!" Krumpelman shows that Taylor most probably did not take the verses directly from the English translation of the Qur'an, where the related passage is much longer and differently worded, but translated Rückert's quote instead (87). For the dates of composition of the *Poems of the Orient*, see Smyth 302-303.

6   In turn, Rückert's *Ghaselen* were modelled after Rumi's *Divan* (cf. El-Demerdasch 235-236).

7   For an overview of the eighteenth- and nineteenth-century German response to Oriental poetry, see Radjaie 21-34; Weber 39-61.

8   See Herder's *Abhandlung über den Ursprung der Sprache* (1772) and *Ideen zur Philosophie der Geschichte der Menschheit* (1784-1791) and Friedrich Schlegel's "Gespräch über die Poesie" (1800) and *Über die Sprache und Weisheit der Inder* (1808).

By quoting Rückert in his own poems, Taylor therefore situates himself within this German tradition of romantic Orientalism. But a closer look at the quote and its original source reveals that Rückert too has linked his own poems to another author's work. Taylor's quote is taken from Rückert's very first verses of *Östliche Rosen*, a panegyric poem honoring Goethe's *West-östlicher Divan* (1819). Taylor's quote in its context reads as follows:

> Zu Goethes west-östlichem Divan
> Wollt ihr kosten
> Reinen Osten,
> Müßt ihr gehen von hier zum selben Manne,
> Der vom Westen
> Auch den besten
> Wein von jeher schenkt' aus voller Kanne.
> Als der West war durchgekostet;
> Hat er nun den Ost entmostet;
> Seht, dort schwelgt er auf der Ottomanne. (Rückert, *Gedichte* 105)

Goethe's great poetry sequence marks a crucial peak in Germany's perception of the Orient, of course. Like Rückert, Goethe never traveled the Orient; in his "notes" on the *Divan* he writes nevertheless:

> Wer das Dichten will verstehen,
> Muß ins Land der Dichtung gehen;
> Wer den Dichter will verstehen,
> Muß in Dichters Lande gehen. (*Noten* 126)

Goethe does not refer to a journey in the literal sense of meaning. His is both an imaginary-poetical journey as well as a formal-aesthetic project (cf. Boubia). Cultivating the "technique of poetic traveling" (Bahr 148), Goethe insists on the spiritual unity of East and West. To achieve this union, he pleads for an aesthetically equilibristic moving back and forth between the two:

> Wer sich selbst und andere kennt
> Wird auch hier erkennen:
> Orient und Okzident
> Sind nicht mehr zu trennen.
>
> Sinnig zwischen beiden Welten
> Sich zu wiegen lass' ich gelten;

Also zwischen Ost und Westen
Sich bewegen sei zum Besten! (*Divan* 121)

Said declares that "the two most renowned German works on the Orient [are] Goethe's *Westöstlicher Diwan* and Friedrich Schlegel's *Über die Sprache und Weisheit der Inder*" (19). Nevertheless, he believes that "the sheer quality, consistently, and mass of British, French, and [post-World War II] American writing on the Orient lifts it above the doubtless crucial work done by Germany, Italy, Russia, and elsewhere," conceding later on that "I particularly regret not taking more account of the great scientific prestige that accrued to German scholarship by the middle of the nineteenth century [...]" (17-18). Indeed, Said was not very much interested in pursuing Germany's role in the Western perception of the Orient, since there "was nothing in Germany to correspond to the Anglo-French presence in India, Levant, North Africa." His dismissal was mainly due to the fact that "the German Orient was almost exclusively a scholarly, or at least a classical, Orient: it was made the subject of lyrics, fantasies, and even novels, but it was never actual [...]." This "fact" notwithstanding, Said claimed that Goethe partook in the overall Western acquisition of "intellectual authority over the Orient" (19).

Ehrhard Bahr as an aside has drawn attention to Said's consistently misspelling Goethe's *West-östlicher Divan* as "Westöstlicher Diwan." With the omission of the hyphen Said obscures, according to Bahr, "the delicate balance of this hyphenated qualifier" (151). Hendrik Birus, on the other hand, has particularly stressed the importance of this hyphen in his claim that the German hyphenated title *west-östlich* speaks of more than merely a peaceful side-by-side, namely of a "spannungsvolles In-Eins" of East and West (114). Moreover, Goethe actually chose a dual, bilingual—Arabian and German—title with two separate title pages facing each other, a fact Said entirely misses or prefers not to mention. The Arabian title significantly marks a difference for it reads—translated into German—"Der östliche Divan des westlichen Verfassers." Thus, while it is a fact that the Arabian language does not know hyphenated composites, Goethe in choosing these two varying titles pronounces the move towards union as well as the tension between East and West.

Like Goethe's notion of "world literature," Rückert had sought to bridge the cultural gap between East and West in two major ways: on the formulaic level by turning to the syncretistic and polyfunctional model of the *divan*-cycle and the *ghazal*-stanza, and on the broader level of poetics by envisioning a "world poetry." Each in his own way combined a universal approach towards poetry bridging the gap between East and West as well as Old and New with the idea of rejuvenating one's own national literature:

> Ich sehe immer mehr, [...] daß die Poesie ein Gemeingut der Menschheit ist, und daß sie überall und zu allen Zeiten in Hunderten und aber Hunderten von Menschen hervortritt. [...] Ich sehe mich daher gerne bei fremden Nationen um und rate jedem, es auch seinerseits zu tun. Nationalliteratur will jetzt nicht viel sagen, die Epoche der Welt-Literatur ist an der Zeit, und jeder muß jetzt dazu wirken, diese Epoche zu beschleunigen. (Goethe, qtd. in Eckermann 173-174)

> Mög' euch die schmeichelnde Gewöhnung
> Befreunden auch mit fremder Tönung,
> Daß ihr erkennt: Weltpoesie
> Allein ist Weltversöhnung. (Rückert, qtd. in Schimmel 32)

Goethe's idea of world literature serves as a spiritual space, in which peoples no longer speak with the voices of the poets to and about themselves but to another. It is meant as a dialogue between nations, a spiritual interaction, a mutual giving and taking of all spiritual treasures (cf. Strich 18). The outcome of this intercultural encounter should never lead to a levelling of national literatures but to a reciprocal acknowledgement of a common understanding through national characteristics (Blessin 65). Especially Goethe's *Divan* develops this double vision on behalf of the traveling poet that takes him to foreign homelands. "Niemand kann ich glücklich preisen / Der des Doppelblicks ermangelt," says Goethe (73). The *Divan* therefore is a prime example of "Wahlheimatliteratur," since by opting for the old Orient as his newly found 'Heimat,' this chosen relationship henceforth leaves traces through poetical trajectory in one's own country and, indeed, throughout the world (Boubia 70). Inspired by Goethe's *Divan* in this respect, Rückert in a similar mode takes recourse to a poetical homeland in order to invest its traces into one's own writing:

> Die Poesie in allen ihren Zungen
> Ist dem Geweihten eine Sprache nur,
> Die Sprache, die im Paradies erklungen,
> Eh sie verwildert auf der wilden Flur.

Doch wo sie nun auch sei hervorgedrungen,
Von ihrem Ursprung trägt sie noch die Spur. (*Gedichte* 136)[9]

Bayard Taylor through the initial double citation in his *Poems of the Orient* refers to both German poets in different ways. Much like Goethe, at least as Rückert's quote suggests, had made his trial of the West and turned his attention to the East, Taylor himself is about to try his poetic luck with the Orient. And as much as Rückert—the minor poet—through his dedication thrives to participate in Goethe's—the major poet's—fame, Taylor—the yet unknown poet—relies on both poets' reputation to forcefully guarantee his own.[10] And like Rückert and Goethe, Taylor in one of the first of his *Poems of the Orient*, "The Poet in the East," envisions a poetic homeland in the East. Employing a scenery that includes nature imagery of spring air and festive earth, he makes recourse to seeking out the Orient as true homeland of the Western poet:

> The Poet came to the Land of the East,
>   When spring was in the air:
> The Earth was dressed for a wedding feast,
>   So young she seemed, and fair;
> And the Poet knew the Land of the East, —
>   His soul was native there.
> All things to him were the visible forms
>   Of early and precious dreams, —
> Familiar visions that mocked his quest
>   Beside the Western streams, [...] (*Poetical Works* 38)

The poem recalls a moment of recognition and transition. Similar to Rückert's envisioning the trace of poetic origin ("Von ihrem Ursprung trägt sie [die Poesie] noch die Spur"), Taylor discovers this same trace in his romantic dream vision of a poetic quest fulfilled by transcending the national confines ("All things to him were the visible forms / Of early and precious dreams"). The claim of being a "native," of finding his long-sought poetic home-land

---

9   Rückert wrote these verses in 1828 while working on the translation of one of the most important collections of ancient Arabic poetry, the *Kitab-al-Hamasah*. Published in 1846 as *Hamasa oder die ältesten arabischen Volkslieder*, Rückert opens this translated collection with his own famous poem, quoted above (cf. Solbrig 17; El-Demerdasch 240).

10 Ironically, what really guaranteed Taylor his longstanding fame in academia were neither his travelogues nor his poetry but his translation of Goethe's *Faust*, still available and read today.

after being led astray in a mock quest through Western regions, reflects not so much the biographical voice as it might seem. The poet here is a figure of transcendence, a cipher within an ongoing intercultural process, symbolized both by the virginal image of spring time and the bonding ritual of the wedding. Taylor in this poem marks the existing East-West dichotomy only to claim his own overcoming the cultural distinction. He uses spatial and temporal metaphors to focus on paying homage to the Orient. The Eastern poet symbolizes the Orient as a deliberate choice of a poetic and cultural homeland. In a proleptic vision, the poet claims to have always known that here, in the East, his "soul" would find its proper home.

"Unwinding the Turban:" *Poems of the Orient* as American Pastoral

Travels—be they real or imaginary—like the ones Goethe, Rückert, and Taylor undertook suggest movements in space as well as time. They are not only journeys into different cultures but also passages through cultural time zones, juxtaposing the present to both the past and the future. Speaking of Goethe's 'travel' to the Orient, Mirjam Weber remarks: "In der Orientierung an der Vergangenheit (die im Jetzt der Fremdkultur gegenwärtig ist) entdeckt er Richtlinien für die Zukunft, den Stoff für reale Utopien. [...] Goethes Orient-Bild ist also die Frucht der in die Vergangenheit verlagerten Jetztzeit" (43). As a poetic device, this leads Goethe to the concept of relating what is far away to things close and present. In one sense, Goethe's verses in his *Divan* link up to both the syncretism of Oriental poetry as well as the simple and popular *Lied*-formula reminiscent especially of eighteenth-century German Anacreontic poetry (Bahr 146). Rückert, also relying on this syncretistic aesthetic of mixing elements that are 'natural' for both foreign and one's own cultures, coins the apt term "language garden:"

> **DER SPRACHGARTEN**
> Ich hab' in meinem Garten
> Ein Dutzend Sprachen gebaut,
> Und Blüten mancher Arten
> Hab' ich von ihnen angeschaut; [...]
> Begieß es, und erlangen
> Wird's einen neuen Trieb.
> Aber dann bleib nicht hocken

> Bei diesem wieder, bis trocken
> die andern sind, die nun prangen;
> sie sind dir doch alle lieb! (*Werke* I, 210)

Rückert's vision of planting various languages as seeds, and taking care and watching them grow into many different beautiful flowers speaks for a multifaceted approach to poetry. Likewise, Taylor's *Poems of the Orient* harbors such a mixture of various forms, symbols, stiles and references. In the concluding poem of his collection, Taylor once more takes up the notion of 'world poetry' as an intermingling of East and West and refocuses his perspective of the "Poet in the East" as a poet returning finally. Through his physical and poetic traveling, the lyrical vision now has become more complex. The poetical "I" speaks of the traces he hopes to leave through his "songs:"

L'ENVOI
> Unto the Desert and the desert steed
>   Farewell! The journey is completed now
> Struck are the tents of Ishmael's wandering breed,
>   And I unwind the turban from my brow.
>
> The sun has ceased to shine; the palms that bent
>   Inebriate with light, have disappeared;
> And naught is left me of the Orient
>   But the tanned bosom and the unshorn beard.
>
> [...]
>
> I found, among the Children of the Sun,
>   The cipher of my nature,—the release
> Of baffled powers, which else had never won
>   That free fulfilment, whose reward is peace.
>
> [...]
>
> Go, therefore, Songs!—which in the East were born
>   And drew your nurture—from your sire's control:
> Haply to wander through the West forlorn,
>   Or find a shelter in some Orient soul.

> And if the temper of our colder sky
> > Less warmth of passion and of speech demands,
> > They are the blossoms of my life,—and I
> > > Have ripened in the suns of many lands. (*Poetical Works* 65-66)

This concluding poem is both an elegiac farewell to Taylor's own chosen new 'Heimat' in the East *and* a record of the continuous fear of his failure to be recognized as a poet in his old home country. The speaker here no longer seeks entry into Oriental culture and an outlet there for his suppressed longings. He has done all that already ("The journey is completed") and he is ready to "unwind the turban" and face the West once again. His re-entry to his old homeland he had so gladly left behind triggers an imaginary vision of his wandering texts: "Go, therefore, Songs!—which in the East were born." They, so he projects, will always remain at his literally newly found and symbolically regained home in the East, where they have originated in form and substance. But since these texts are part of the poet's very own nature ("They are the blossoms of my life"), they are also meant to remain and travel with him and as part of him.

Aesthetically, he herewith underscores the German romantics' program of a multinational and multifunctional 'world poetics' based on Oriental foundations. But implied are also ethical concerns relating to the state of affairs in his 'old' homeland of America. At this point, the poem is significantly contradictory. On the one hand, the texts may be said to be the better part of the speaking poet's nature. And this better part is closely linked to the Oriental soul that the poet claims to have now gained himself. On the other hand, the poem consistently evokes images of departure, removal, and loss as well as coldness and darkness. All these negatively connoted suggestions are related to the West he is looking ahead to, but not truly forward to.

This obvious paradox grounds on the suggestion, expressed in many of Taylor's Oriental poems, of the poet searching and finding a prelapsarian idyllic pastoral. As such, the seeming contradiction is but a generic device of the pastoral discourse. Taylor's pastoral ideal—at least as articulated in *The Poems of Orient*—differs from that of many American contemporaries in that his is clearly situated far away from his original homeland. Also, it does not oppose the city and the country in a strict sense. It is nevertheless a 'classic' pastoral, since the pastoral in its basic historical form involves the pendulous movement of retreat and return with the pastoral retreat returning insights relevant to the audience at stake (Gifford 2). The contemporary reader thus must understand this pastoral discourse in order to make sense of the cultural context of return. The movement of retreat and return, if not explicit in the text, is, as Terry Gifford asserts, "implicit in the address to an audience for whom what happens in Arcadia has some interest" (81). The essential paradox in the pastoral thus lies in the fact that the retreat to some place experienced without anxieties delivers insights into the culture from which it originates and that had been perceived to be troublesome in some respect.

Shortly before embarking on his travels to the East, Taylor, who grew up in a rural and repressive Quaker community in Pennsylvania, at first seemed to have found his Edenic place of contentment and freedom in the West of America, as can be concluded from his 1850 travelogue *Eldorado; or, Adventures in the Path of Empire: Comprising a Voyage to California* [...]. While Taylor's California in *Eldorado* stands as a model for American democracy, for peaceful relations among diverse ethnic groups as well as for a new, energetic and nature-bound kind of man, the poem "On Leaving California," written at that time, however expresses a telling ambivalence towards this Western idyll:

> Thy human children shall restore the grace
>   Gone with thy fallen pines:
> The wild, barbaric beauty of thy face
>   Shall round to classic lines.
> And Order, Justice, Social Law shall curb
>   Thy untamed energies;
> And Art and Science, with their dreams superb,
>   Replace thine ancient ease. (*Poetical Works* 92-93)

Although he clearly identifies the pastoral with California, he also evokes the impression of a disconcerting present. It is the Edenic past of the Western "wild, barbaric beauty" that needs to—and will, as the speaker assuredly avows—be restored in future again. Both society's rigid rules and laws as well as an unimaginative artistic sensibility are in need of change, so he claims. An essential part of Taylor's struggle with the American present and thus part of his pastoral dream is the realization of manly love (Martin 13). Especially in his later novel *Joseph and His Friend* (first published 1870), he once again returns to the Californian pastoral setting with the promise of a future where love between men may become possible:

> I know [...] a great valley, bounded by a hundred miles of snowy peaks; lakes in its bed; enormous hillsides, dotted with gloves of ilex and pine;

orchards of orange and olive; a perfect climate, where it is bliss enough just to breathe, and freedom from the distorted laws of men, for none are near enough to enforce them! If there is no legal way of escape for you, here, at least is no force which can drag you back, once you are there: I will go with you, and perhaps—perhaps […]. (216)

California once again is envisioned in a temporal and spacial realm of "freedom from the distorted laws of men." Both Californian texts evoke what Leo Marx has called the "middle ground" of pastoral. It is the American ideal of "semi-primitivism," that according to Marx, "is located in a middle-ground somewhere 'between,' yet in a transcendent relation to, the opposing forces of civilization and nature" (23). While critics like Roger Sales and John Lucas have articulated a very bleak understanding of the English pastorals from the seventeenth up to the early nineteenth century for the English reading public by calling them essentially escapist in seeking refuge in an idealized past and thus serving a deeply conservative agenda (Sales 17; Lucas 118), Marx referring to the American context insists on the notion that "the pastoral design, as always, circumscribes the pastoral ideal" (72). There is invariably a "counterforce" undercutting the idyllic vision leading up to a qualification of the retreat within the pastoral design (26). Lawrence Buell, like Marx focusing especially on the American tradition of the pastoral, considers it a versatile form with multiple frames. Accordingly, he argues for careful readings of a pastoral in its specific cultural framework: "American pastoral cannot be pinned to a single ideological position. Even at its most culpable—the moment of willful retreat from social and political responsibility—it may be more strategized than mystified" (44). Buell believes in the pastoral's capacity to assume oppositional stances within otherwise conventionalized "sleepy safe" visions of America. "So American pastoral," Buell points out, "has simultaneously been counterinstitutional and institutionally sponsored" (50). Gifford takes up this anti-simplistic view of the pastoral asserting its capacity for making critical judgments about its inner tensions, its contextual functions and its multiple levels of contradictions: "They are borderland spaces of activity which can be seen through a number of frames" (12).

While Taylor in his relying on the popular pastoral mode was "institutionally sponsored" by his Genteel peers insofar as his texts were widely circulating, his writings do not always comply with the dominant gentile standards of his times that value not so much a natural, corporeal as an abstract, ascetic ideal of beauty, "one closely tied to an emphasis on purity and innocence and one usually symbolized by children and virgins" (Wermuth 178). Pastorals like Taylor's probing into the exploration of various bodily pleasures, even when seen primarily as a discourse of retreat, can still work in two differing ways, either simply as escape from a demanding and dissatisfying present, or as deeper examination of these circumstances. Exploring the present and possibly imagining an alternative future marks the difference between Marx's "sentimental pastoral" and his "imaginative and complex pastoral." Whereas the simplistic, escapist "sentimental pastoral" serves as an "illusion of peace and harmony in the green pasture" that is produced by "the simple, affirmative attitude we adopt toward pleasing rural scenery" (25), the "complex pastoral" productively works with the notion of the "counterforce" undercutting the idyll that shows the discursive mechanism of the pastoral. Taylor's Californian writings belong to Marx's category of complex pastorals, because they are distinctly American Arcadias that are not so much set in the garden of Eden, but in a half-wild, half-innocent state that is presumed to be beyond the 'frontier' in both space and time. Taylor's claim to a better future, for example by realizing a love between men without social restraints, poses an implicit, yet harsh critique of the present repressive culture by relying on an Arcadian past prior to harmful civilizing measures. The nostalgic backward-looking is an essential trademark of the pastoral in general. Quite different from the English counterparts that Sales and Lucas are referring to, Taylor's American version of an Arcadian innocence that is located in a land before colonization and civilization therefore takes hold as the idealized representation of the past and implies a better future conceived in the language of the present.

But not only Taylor's Californian pastorals are complex in their employment of the undercutting counterforce. His Oriental poems also are not simple escapist pastorals that deal with nothing more than a longing to withdraw from the world's affairs to an oasis of harmonious well-being. Taylor's retreat is a yearning for a simpler style of life that at the same time is a movement toward a symbolic landscape and thus "a movement away from an 'artificial' world" with its "disciplined habits of mind or arts" (Marx 9). As such Taylor's pastorals become the embodiment of this middle-ground of "semi-primitivism." Reading Taylor's *Poems of the Orient* in the context of the pastoral construct indeed opens up possibilities of multiple frames. In the exploitation of the Oriental location, Taylor may be said to participate in or even help to form the notion of Orientalism in Said's sense. But adding the frames of the German romantic's aesthetics of finding and recovering a 'world poetry' as well as of the American pastoral ideal of "semi-primitivism," Taylor's Oriental landscapes both envision and transcend these opposing forces and thus form a middle ground that Taylor himself has labeled "semi-barbaric." On a symbolic level, these poetic landscapes evoke what the German romantics referred to as "Weltpoesie," namely the site of all poetic origins. But on a corporeal level, Taylor's experiences with Eastern living habits are no escapist dreams but "the release of baffled powers," as he puts it in his poem "L'Envoi." And thus, as much as he enjoyed these foreign manners, he is well aware that he will not be able to keep up their "barbaric splendour" after returning home. Through the ciphered nature of his *Poems of the Orient*, however, and the aesthetics they call forth, he constructs a poetic *alter ego*. In his dedicatory poem, Taylor tellingly calls this *persona* "shaggy Pan:"

PROËM DEDICATORY
An Epistle From Mount Tmolus.
To Richard Henry Stoddard.

[...]

But were you here, my Friend, we twain would build
  Two altars, on the mountain's sunward side:
  There Pan should o'er my sacrifice preside,
And there Apollo your oblation gild.
He is your God, but mine is shaggy Pan; [...] (*Poetical Works* 35-36)

With this poetic design of installing "shaggy Pan" as representative of his earth-bound, sensual identity, the speaker once more juxtaposes America to the East. It is America that functions as counterforce, as intrusion, to its idyllic Other, the Orient. With his Oriental poems, Taylor sets up a dialogue functioning as intermediary between opposing cultural forces. For Taylor, a "consolatory prospect" (Marx 32) may be found only in syncretizing literalness and figurativeness, that is, in combining intercultural corporeal experience with multidimensional poetic devices. Accordingly in the "Proëm," Taylor—speaking from mythological Mount Tmolus—addresses his poet-friend Stoddard. He clearly marks his own poetical ethics of the "Sprachgarten" in the effort to retrieve his lived experiences of encountering wonderful beauties from a pastoral setting and send them forth as expansively wandering lyrics:

Take, therefore, Friend! these Voices of the Earth,
 The rhythmic records of my life's career,
Humble, perhaps, yet wanting not the worth
  Of Truth, and to the heart of Nature near. (*Poetical Works* 37)

Emblematic Male Oriental Beauty—Emulating Hafiz

Throughout his life, Taylor suffered from being primarily known as the 'Great American traveler.' Although travel writings—at least in his early years—earned his living, what Taylor really longed for and worked towards was to be remembered as a poet. And indeed, *Poems of the Orient* became his most popular poetry collection and was received as a "wonder book" (Smyth 218-219). "To a Persian Boy" is one of his earliest poems from this collection:

TO A PERSIAN BOY
In the Bazaar at Smyrna
The gorgeous blossoms of that magic tree
Beneath whose shade I sat a thousand nights,
Breathed from their opening petals all delights
Embalmed in spice of Orient Poesy,
When first, young Persian, I beheld thine eyes,
And felt the wonder of thy beauty grow
Within my brain, as some fair planet's glow
Deepens, and fills the summer evening skies.
From under thy dark lashes shone on me
The rich, voluptuous soul of Eastern land,
Impassioned, tender, calm, serenely sad,—
Such as immortal Hafiz felt when he
Sang by the fountain-streams of Rocnabad,
Or in the bowers of blissful Samarcand. (*Poetical Works* 62-63)

This poem was first published in 1851, that is, three years prior to the publication of the complete volume. Taylor here pursues a twofold interest. He sets the stage for his audience, describing the perfumed, intoxicating atmosphere of the "Bazaar at Smyrna" with its "opening petals" of "gorgeous blossoms" on a "magic tree." Like a setting taken from *The Arabian Nights* the speaker voices his enjoying Oriental delights. But then the setting turns out to serve as backdrop for the entrance of the protagonist, the Persian boy. The observing speaker makes an effort to intellectualize his feelings ("I [...] felt the wonder of thy beauty grow / Within my brain"), but clearly not only his mind is enchanted. Although he refrains from going into praising the boy's overall physique, he nevertheless focuses on one detail: the boy's eyes. These eyes with their "dark lashes" are not only metonymically linked to the owner's wonderful beauty in its bodily entirety; they also signify the beauty of the boy's culture and origins. The projected allusions to Oriental sensibilities, however, reflect back onto the image of the boy. In the wishful and longing view of the beholder, the boy is all that: tranquil, gentle, melancholic, passionate. Therefore, on the one hand, the speaker seems to evade any straightforward connection between his erotic yearnings and the corporeal object of his desires, transferring them onto the plain of generalized and pleasing cultural attributes. On the other hand, poetically this evasion leads to a metatextual reference that in the end only reaffirms this very desire.

Through a chain of references, Taylor moves from the description of the setting to the appearance of the boy within to stressing the emblematic quality of his eyes which in turn prompts the allusion to Hafiz. With mentioning Hafiz, Taylor thus calls forth the tradition of Persian love poetry, often addressed to boys and therefore suggesting a homoerotic affection on behalf of the speaker (Bürgel 26; Martin 13; Wild 82). This reference that identifies Hafiz with the desiring "I" marks the speaker's implicit positioning of himself both as male voice and as love poet. What is even more striking, however, is the fact that by identifying with Hafiz, the speaker claims to be part of the Eastern landscape that he metonymically discovers in the eyes of the Persian boy. Therefore, what at first seems to be a hierarchical dichotomy of East and West with a Western man looking with a certain distanced attitude at Eastern beauty turns out to be yet another scene of recognition and transition: the speaker becomes enchanted by the boy's beautiful eyes that literally enter the male poet's being. He then not only discovers his own soul as rich as the Orientals', but links up his identity with immortal Hafiz, as lover, as poet, and above all as Easterner.

Taylor here goes a significant step further than Goethe, whose infatuation with the Orient let him to the belief of identifying Hafiz as his own twin brother across time and space:

Und mag die ganze Welt versinken!
Hafis, mit dir, mit dir allein
Will ich wetteifern! Lust und Pein

Sei uns den Zwillingen gemein!
Wie du zu lieben und zu trinken,
Das soll mein Stolz, mein Leben sein. (*Divan* 23)

Aesthetically, Taylor like Goethe chooses in many of his Oriental poems a simple form in both meter and rhyme, some similar to the German *Lied*-stanza and some to the Persian *ghazal*, a richly symbolic kind of love poem, often addressed to a universalized and stylized friend.[11] But unlike Goethe, Taylor in declaring Hafiz his soul mate takes up the distinct homoerotic suggestions that can be traced in Hafiz' poems like this one:

Möge keiner je erleiden,
    was ich durch die Trennung litt,
Denn mein Leben war nur Scheiden,
    mich traf nur der Trennung Tritt.

Fremd, das Herz in Lieb' verloren,
    arm und im Verstande irr,
Schlepp ich überall die Qualen
    und die Glut der Trennung mit.

[...]

Oh, ich will die Trennung quälen
    mit der Trennung, Freund, von Dir,
Daß ihr Lid wie meines träne,
    blutend von der Trennung Schnitt!

[...]

---

11   *Ghazal* originates in the Arabian word 'ghezâlà,' meaning erotic conversation, flirting, love-making, and has in Persian literature (dating as far back as to the tenth century) come to denote a love song or love poem with panegyric function. The first *ghazal*-poet of great consequence was Sànâi who in the twelfth century wrote *ghazals* with a polyfunctional meaning. With his mixture of mystic and profanely erotic motifs, he prefigured Hafiz (cf. Radjaie 55-69). Structurally, a *ghazal* comprises an elaborate string of stanzas each consisting of a couplet of long-verses with all even verses monorhymed, such as aa ba ca da ea fa ga. This consistently homophonic repetition adds to the poem's intended magic effect of a timeless flow.

> Glühend von der Liebe Brandmal,
>   singe ich bei Tag und Nacht,
> Hafis gleich, mit Nachtigallen
>   immerzu der Trennung Lied! (*Gedichte* 80-81)

Hafiz' elegy expresses the suffering of being parted from one's beloved friend. This friend, however, has various guises and may also represent a sovereign as is the case here. This turns the poem from a pure love song into a panegyric oration praising the monarch's supremacy. Johann Bürgel claims this to be one of the major poetic revolutions undertaken by Hafiz, "daß er [...] Fürstenlob und Minnedichtung so miteinander verschmilzt, daß nicht nur der verherrlichte Geliebte für den Fürsten, sondern auch umgekehrt der gepriesene Herrscher für den Geliebten stehen kann" (11). The inherent multidimensionality of such poems calls for further interpretative possibilities. The "I" of the poet, therefore, may turn into a distinct *persona* of the poet, acting as a male muse; and the addressed friend may serve as a variant of the poet's own voice or as the epitome of humankind and beauty. Similarly, in Taylor's poem the gazing 'I/eye' and the object being self-reflectively admired are linked and poetically united through the poet Hafiz. The projection of his own eye onto the other world's wonder of beauty is reflected back onto the perceptive writer in its corporeal and poetic meaning.

Taylor's calling on Hafiz in his own verses therefore brings up this ancient custom of polyfunctional love poetry. Transferring his own romantic longings onto the level of metatextual reference, Taylor strives for poetic immortality in the tradition of Oriental poets like Hafiz. Like in his "The Poet in the East," Taylor in "To a Persian Boy" stresses the East-West dichotomy. But here it is especially the reliance on the bodily presence of the Persian boy that accounts for the overcoming of the cultural chasm. The Persian boy with his erotic attraction—"the wonder of thy beauty"—serves as emblem of the Orient. But by epitomizing Hafiz as the Eastern poet and at the same time proclaiming to emulate Hafiz, Taylor takes a daring step towards mixing his private longings with cultural concerns. This synthesis on the thematic level corresponds to the strategy of fusion on the poetic level. The poem formally recalls the sonnet in iambic pentameters, however not in its Anglophone Shakespearean, but in its older Romanic Petrarchan form with the concluding sestet. The evoked atmosphere is distinctly Orientalized and marks the backdrop for both an erotic and poetic outlet culminating in the union of lover (the speaker), beloved (the boy) and poet (Hafiz). The overall impression is of a homecoming in more than one sense: for Taylor the East relieves him of his cultural restraints. He succeeds in letting go the restrictions that tied his body and his mind to the usual standards of Genteel America.

Taylor's Travels to the Orient—Expanding Genteel Expectations

Taylor's *Poems of the Orient* is but one literary output of his journey to the East. He also wrote three travel narratives—*A Journey to Central Africa, The Lands of the Saracen*, and *A Visit to India, China, and Japan*—, like *Poems of the Orient* all published in 1854-55. Taylor was probably the most prominent traveler of his generation, attesting to the fact that before Twain and Melville toured the Orient, and contradictory to Said's assessment, quite a number of earlier American Orientalists undertook travels abroad. In 1851, Taylor set out for a two-year trip to the East, visiting countries and regions—like Nubia, Sudan and Japan—hardly any American writer had traveled to before. Like other traveling Americans of his time,[12] Taylor's journeys and his ensuing writings on them were motivated partly by curiosity, but also by pecuniary interests. He herewith profited from the special status of writing in antebellum America that contributed to the success of travel writing in general. According to William Stowe, among the many contradictions of the time in structuring societal classes was that "between the neo-Puritan work ethic and the economy's new ability to support more and more economically unproductive members" (10). Taylor indeed was one of a growing number of men in economically marginal occupations, and he took part in redefining the idea of work to include writing as a people's activity. As Stowe points out, Taylor like his contemporary travel writer Margaret Fuller[13] was not rich, but both of them were "members of what [Thorstein] Veblen would call the leisure class because their occupations

---

12 Examples range from Nathaniel Parker Willis, *Pencillings by the Way* (1836), a book that Taylor had read and adored as a boy; John Lloyd Stephens, *Incidents of Travel in Egypt, Arabia Petraea, and the Holy Land* (1837); George William Curtis, *Nile Notes of a Howadji* (1851); John Ross Browne, *Yusef; or, the Journey of the Frangi: A Crusade in the East* (1853); and John William de Forest, *Oriental Acquaintance; or, Letters from Syria* (1856) to Mark Twain, *The Innocents Abroad; or, the New Pilgrim's Progress* (1869) and Herman Melville, *Clarel: A Poem and Pilgrimage in the Holy Land* (1876), who make literary use of the Muslim Near East. See the chapter on "American Travelers in the Levant" by Obeidat 97-126.
13 In the fall of 1846, for example, the *New York Tribune* simultaneously ran two sets of European letters, Taylor's "Glances at Modern Germany, by a Young American" (pub-

produced not material goods, but rather intellectual products in return for which their relatively prosperous society would afford to support their literary activities" (27). Taylor from the start of his traveling career thus succeeded in making money by relating his experiences to an American public interested in narratives about the exotic and the romantic. Robert Martin claims that Taylor's depiction of adventure and romance offered "the new bourgeoisie dreams of travel and excitement, ways of spending their new affluence, and of countering the boredom of everyday life" (13).

fig. 5.1 Portrait of Bayard Taylor by Thomas Hicks (1855), Oil on canvas, National Portrait Gallery, Smithsonian Institution

But besides the pecuniary aspect, Taylor firmly believed in traveling as a source of knowledge and inspiration—for himself as well as for others. In *Journey to Central Africa*, he claims that "the first end of travel is instruction, and that the traveler is fully justified in pursuing this end, so long as he neither injures himself nor others" (132). Many travelers, however, even when they actually went to the Orient, refrained from an effort in truly observing Eastern

lished as the tremendously popular *Views Afoot, or Europe Seen with Knapsack and Staff*) and Fuller's "Things and Thoughts in Europe" (published as *Dispatches from Europe*).

cultures but held on to preconceived images of the strangeness and exoticism of the Orient, thus enhancing the popularization of a romanticized, adventurous representation of anything believed to be 'Oriental.' Paul Wermuth links this attitude to the Genteel tradition that leaned towards idealistic abstraction in general due to a rising middle-class' imitation of aristocratic qualities. Like other Genteel writers, who believed that to "live like a gentleman was a cardinal principle of Victorian gentility" (Wermuth 22), Taylor also felt that he deserved to be a prosperous member of bourgeois society. But his special way of gaining a position within this society first led him to embrace Oriental culture.[14]

Another Genteel poet, Whittier, captured this important aspect of Taylor's approach to travel. In his poem "The Tent on the Beach," Whittier presented Taylor as "One whose Arab face was tanned [...] And in the tent-shade, as beneath a palm, / Smoked, cross-legged like a Turk, in Oriental calm" (16).[15] Taylor himself declared to be "attracted less by historical and geographical interest of those regions than by the desire to participate in their free, vigorous, semi-barbaric life" (*Journey to Central Africa* 2). The implicit aim, that links Taylor's Oriental travel writing to the pastoral's middle-ground of "semi-primitivism," was to help his reader share in that participation of "barbaric splendor." While traveling along the Nile from Alexandria to Cairo he revealed his desire to adopt a new attitude toward life. Juxtaposing America's fast life and hard work with Egypt's luscious languor, Taylor indulged in this newfound splendor in the manner of a man coming to rest. When visiting Egypt a second time in 1873-74, he once more gladly acknowledged that "oriental repose had not yet been seriously shaken" (*Egypt* 52). In this he implied his doubts about Westernization and his deep sympathy with the people: "Alas, for the Orientals! They get but scanty justice, I fear, even from us: we praise the rulers who keep them abject and ignorant, and then revile the people because they are not manly and intelligent" (90). This concern in itself does not create a 'new' discourse on the Orient. It points, however, to Taylor's ultimate interests that reach beyond his at times stereotypically viewing and experiencing the Orient. As can be shown in parts of his travelogues as well as in his Oriental

---

14 For a discussion of Taylor's societal and artistic position within the Genteel circle during the Gilded Age, see Cary and Tomsich.
15 This pose is manifest in Thomas Hicks's *Portrait of Bayard Taylor* of 1855, showing Taylor clad in an Oriental costume amidst an idealized Arcadian setting (see fig. 5.1).

poems, Taylor by referring to the Orient articulates an implicit—sometimes even outspoken—critical and self-reflexive view on his Genteel background.

In particular Taylor's representation of Oriental masculinity touches upon the delicate issue of the popular attitude of feminizing Oriental culture in general and Oriental men in particular. His evocation of semi-barbarism, which for our contemporary ears that have been trained by critical postcolonial theory has the definite ring of the condescending, racist attitude of the colonizing Westerner, for Taylor meant a less pejorative starting point of cultural comparison. Especially in *The Lands of the Saracen*, he repeatedly argues the beauty of the nude male Arab body by comparing it to the American clothed counterpart. Inverting the standard argument of the feminine Oriental men, Taylor claims that by shedding their dresses, for example in public baths, the Arab men appear heroic, muscular and free, whereas American men ignore the existence of their bodies and even lean towards nervousness, a stereotypical trademark of the hysterical female at the time. Describing the Oriental bathing habits and asserting that dress "hides from us much of the beauty and dignity of Humanity," it becomes clear that Taylor notably liked the bodily aspects of the East. And he goes on to appeal to his Western audience that they should similarly "preserve that healthy physical development" (*Lands of the Saracen* 311). Thus, as James Gray puts it, the physical sensuousness that Taylor experiences in the baths "stands in clear opposition to the usual standards of mid Victorianism" (329).

Critics like Robert Martin go even further than that by pointing out that in his travel writing, Taylor "extended the moral options open to a mid-nineteenth century American man and permitted the expression of ideas that were inconceivable at home" (13). In a fairly straightforward fashion and without having to fear censorship, Taylor could rely on the strategy of 'merely reporting' exotic customs. And as Martin asserts, such "travel books thus served a function not unlike some early forms of pornography. Under the guise of science, they offered erotic titillation" (13).

Taylor in his travel writings might not be altogether absolved from drawing "picturesque, often highly romantic, descriptions of what he observed and felt" (Obeidat 115). The same could be said—and has been said—of his Oriental poems. A closer look, however, reveals Taylor's approach to cross-cultural engagement as being deeply self-reflexive and critical towards his own culture. The multifaceted implications of his Oriental poems are based on balancing Eastern habits with both German aesthetics and American ethics. By way of intercultural comparison as well as intertextual reference Taylor managed both to oppose East and West *and* to transcend this dichotomy at the same time. In his "wonder book" he herewith created syncretistic poetry that combined cultural traditions and national agendas. And whereas in the poems he relied on the poetic emulation of Persian poet Hafiz as well as German romantic poets like Goethe and Rückert, his usage of the genre of the travel narrative gave him the liberty of relating his exploration of the more corporeal aspects of his foreign affairs. In these texts, Taylor indulged in describing 'forbidden pleasures' like visiting Turkish baths, smoking hashish, and wearing Bedouin costumes. And in clear contradiction to standard Genteel morality, he allowed himself to reveling over the wonders of male Oriental beauty.

Works Cited

Bahr, Ehrhard. "'East is West, and West is East:' The Synthesis of Near-Eastern and Western Rhetoric and Imagination in Goethe's *West-östlicher Divan*." *Aufnahme–Weitergabe: Literarische Impulse um Lessing und Goethe*. Eds. John A. McCarthy and Albert A. Kipa. Hamburg: Buske, 1982. 144-152.

Birus, Hendrik. "Begegnungsformen des Westlichen und Östlichen in Goethes *West-östlichem Divan*." *Goethe-Jahrbuch* 114 (1997): 113-131.

Blessin, Stefan. "Goethes 'West-östlicher Divan' und die Entstehung der Weltliteratur." *Westöstlicher und nordsüdlcher Divan: Goethe in interkultureller Perspektive*. Ed. Ortrud Gutjahr. Paderborn: Schöningh, 2000. 59-71.

Boubia, Fawzi. "Goethes Entwurf einer interkulturellen Kommunikation zwischen Orient und Okzident." *Kanon und Text in interkulturellen Perspektiven: "Andere Texte anders lesen."* Eds. Michael Auer and Ulrich Müller. Stuttgart: Heinz, 2001. 67-80.

Buell, Lawrence. *The Environmental Imagination: Thoreau, Nature Writing, and the Formation of American Culture*. Cambridge: Harvard UP, 1995.

Bürgel, Johann Christoph. Einleitung. *Gedichte aus dem Divan*. Hafis. Stuttgart: Reclam, 1998. 3-31.

Cary, Richard. *The Genteel Circle: Bayard Taylor and His New York Friends*. Ithaca: Cornell UP, 1952.

Eckermann, Johann Peter. *Gespräche mit Goethe in den letzten Jahren seines Lebens*. Wiesbaden: Brockhaus, 1959.

El-Demerdasch, Mohsen. "Der Orient im Leben und Werk Friedrich Rückerts." *"Das Schöne soll sein": Aisthesis in der deutschen Literatur*. Eds. Peter Heßelmann, Michael Huesmann, and Hans-Joachim Jakob. Bielefeld: Aisthesis, 2001. 231-241.

Gersdorf, Catrin. *The Poetics and Politics of the Desert: Landscape and the Construction of America*. Amsterdam: Rodopi, 2009.

Gifford, Terry. *Pastoral*. London: Routledge, 1999.

Goethe, Johann Wolfgang. *Noten und Abhandlungen zu besserem Verständnis des West-östlichen Divans*. Werke: Hamburger Ausgabe. Vol. 2. München: dtv, 1982. 126-267.

———. *West-östlicher Divan*. Werke: Hamburger Ausgabe. Vol. 2. München: dtv, 1982. 7-125.

Gray, James L. "Bayard Taylor." *Dictionary of Literary Biography*. Vol. 189. *American Travel Writers, 1850-1915*. Eds. Donald Ross and James J. Schramer. Detroit: Gale Research, 1998. 321-335.

Hafis. *Gedichte aus dem Divan*. Ed. Johann Christoph Bürgel. Stuttgart: Reclam, 1998.

Kerr, Alfred. "New York und London: Stätten des Geschicks. Zwanzig Kapitel nach dem Weltkrieg." *Erlebtes: Reisen in die Welt*. Ed. Hermann Haarmann. Berlin: Argon, 1989. 143-302.

Krumpelman, John T. *Bayard Taylor and German Letters*. Hamburg: Cram, de Gruyter, 1959.

Lucas, John. *England and Englishness*. London: Hogarth Press, 1990.

Luedtke, Luther S. *Nathaniel Hawthorne and the Romance of the Orient*. Bloomington: Indiana UP, 1989.

MacKenzie, John M. *Orientalism: History, Theory and the Arts*. Manchester: Manchester UP, 1995.

Martin, Robert K. "Bayard Taylor's Valley of Bliss: The Pastoral and the Search for Form." *Markham Review* 9 (1979): 13-17.

Marx, Leo. *The Machine in the Garden: Technology and the Pastoral Ideal in America*. London: Oxford UP, 1964.

Obeidat, Marwan M. *American Literature and Orientalism*. Berlin: Schwarz, 1998.

Radjaie, Ali. *Das profan-mystische Ghasel des Hafis in Rückerts Übersetzungen und in Goethes 'Divan.'* Würzburg: Ergon, 1998.

Rückert, Friedrich. *Gedichte*. Ed. Walter Schmitz. Stuttgart: Reclam, 1988.

———. *Ausgewählte Werke*. Ed. Annemarie Schimmel. Frankfurt: Insel, 1988.

Said, Edward W. *Orientalism: Western Conceptions of the Orient*. London: Penguin, 1995.

Sales, Roger. *English Literature in History, 1780-1830: Pastoral and Politics*. London: Hutchinson, 1983.

Schimmel, Annemarie. *Weltpoesie ist Weltversöhnung*. Schweinfurt: Förderkreis der Rückert-Forschung e.V., 1967.

Schlegel, Friedrich. "Gespräch über die Poesie." *Kritische Schriften*. München: Carl Hanser, 1971. 473-529.

Sha'ban, Fuad. *Islam and Arabs in Early American Thought: The Roots of Orientalism in America*. Durham: Acorn, 1991.

Smyth, Albert H. *Bayard Taylor*. Boston, New York: Houghton, Mifflin, 1896.

Solbrig, Ingeborg H. "A Nineteenth-Century Ambassador of Asian Literatures: Friedrich Rückert." *Germanic Notes* 20.2/3 (1989): 17-19.

Stowe, William W. *Going Abroad: European Travel in Nineteenth-Century American Culture*. Princeton: Princeton UP, 1994.

Strich, Fritz. *Goethe und die Weltliteratur*. Bern: Franke, 1957.

Taylor, Bayard. *Critical Essays and Literary Notes*. New York: Putnam, 1880.

———. *Egypt and Iceland in the Year 1874*. New York: Putnam, 1874.

———. *Joseph and His Friend: A Story of Pennsylvania*. New York: Putnam, 1879.

———. *A Journey to Central Africa*. New York: Putnam, 1854.

———. *The Lands of the Saracen; or, Pictures of Palestine, Asia Minor, Sicily and Spain*. New York: Putnam, 1854.

———. *Poetical Works*. Household Edition. Boston: Houghton, 1880.

Tomsich, John. *A Genteel Endeavor: American Culture and Politics of the Gilded Age*. Stanford: Stanford UP, 1971.

Weber, Mirjam. *Der "wahre Poesie-Orient:" eine Untersuchung zur Orientalismus-Theorie Edward Saids am Beispiel von Goethes 'West-östlichem Divan' und der Lyrik Heines*. Wiesbaden: Harrassowitz, 2001.

Wermuth, Paul C. *Bayard Taylor*. New York: Twayne, 1973.

Whittier, John G. *The Tent on the Beach and Other Poems*. Boston: Ticknor and Fields, 1867.

Wild, Inge. "Goethes *West-östlicher Divan* als poetischer Ort psycho-kultureller Grenzüberschreitungen." *Westöstlicher und nordsüdlicher Divan: Goethe in interkultureller Perspektive*. Ed. Ortrud Gutjahr. Paderborn: Schöningh, 2000. 73-88.

6. Bastardized History: Elif Shafak's Transcultural Poetics

Comic Survival or the Endless Repeat Melody

> [Asya] offered one of the headphones to Armanoush. Armanoush accepted the headphone warily and asked: "Which Johnny Cash song are we going to listen to?" "'Dirty Old Egg-Suckin' Dog!'" [...] And the song started, first a listless prelude, then country melodies fusing with seagull shrieks and Turkish vocalizations in the background. [...] There were a few tables scattered outside on the sidewalk. A grim couple settled themselves at one of them, and then another couple, with stressed-out, serious urban faces. Armanoush watched their gestures with curiosity, likening them to characters from a Fitzgerald novel. (Shafak, *The Bastard* 200, 205)

This urban scene taken from Elif Shafak's novel *The Bastard of Istanbul* (2007) not only mixes dissonant sounds and clashing images, it also envisions a transnational encounter on several semantic levels: Asya, the Turkish girl and native Istanbulite, takes Armanoush, her American cousin of Turkish-Armenian descent, on a tourist tour accompanied by local city noises as well as American country songs, while her visitor compares this foreign urban setting of Istanbul to her own, yet fictionalized American background. It is a scene that while with "a touch of enchantment" above all offers a disturbing and dangerous vision "full of contradictions and temper, utterly disharmonious [...] and ready to explode at any time" (200). This hypersensitive urban locale, focalized through the young female visitor's stunned gaze, alludes to interpersonal and transnational intersections crisscrossing familial, cultural, and ethnic histories. Even though employing the standard trope of a tourist's first-encounter perspective, Shafak evokes Istanbul not so much as the mythologized city located on two continents joining Europe and Asia, but as a chaotic, puzzling, and multifarious "hodgepodge of ten million lives. It is an open book of ten million scrambled stories" (243). Istanbul thus figures both as distinctly Turkish cultural focal point and as a global city that shows resemblances to multi-million cities across the world and history, especially including U.S.-American metropolitan sites.

It was Leo Marx, who in his effort to un-puzzle (anti-)urbanism in classic American literature, sharply distinguishes American from European cities. Tying together the unlikely couple of Hawthorne's *The Scarlet Letter* and Fitzgerald's *The Great Gatsby*, Marx shows that while often negative images like the scaffold or the valley of ashes represent facets of the dominant culture of industrial capitalism, there are also abundant moments of alternative "pastoral" visions not so much of resistance, but of simple withdrawal into nature and thus into the realm of the "pre-socialized resources of the self" (78). This notion of reclusive and idyllic life prior to social and political turmoil stands, of course, in stark contrast to the actual development of American cities. "Most American cities, after all, have been built since the onset of industrialization," claims Marx and "unlike London, Paris, or Rome"—and I want to include Istanbul in this list here—

> they embody relatively few features of any social order other than that of industrial capitalism. If the American city is perceived chiefly as the locus of a particular socio-economic order, that view accords with the historical fact that millions of Americans have moved to cities, not because they preferred urban life to rural life, but rather because of the inescapable coercion of a market economy. (Marx 78)

Nevertheless, writers like Shafak expand this intra-American dichotomous perspective to encompass a transcultural scope of lived metropolitan experience both in the New and Old World. Shafak accordingly writes against an "etherialization" of history that Lewis Mumford discusses in his study on *The City in History* as counterpoint to the materiality of the city. Instead of the notion that cities have taken part in "etherializing" history, Mumford argues for an oscillation between the ethereal and material, between the symbolic and the concrete:

> The rhythm of life in cities seems to be an alternation between materialization and etherialization: the concrete structure, detaching itself through a human response, takes on a symbolic meaning, uniting the knower and

the known; while subjective images, ideas, intuitions [...] likewise take on material attributes. (113)

Ihab Hassan takes up this idea of a city design being linked to a social process of materialization and points towards the abstract, theoretical, and hidden 'nature' of cities, for the city, he says, "acts as mediator between the human and natural orders, as a changing network of social relations, as a flux of production and consumption, [...] as an arena of violence, play, desire, as a labyrinth of solitudes, as a system of covert controls, semiotic exchanges" (95). Hassan's effort is to reveal "the city as a fiction composing many fictions" (97) and thus to claim a complicity between fiction and the city that against all experiences of disaster, terror, and destruction remains a visionary space for writers: "We stand as ever between history and hope. And standing there I perceive the postmodern city as a place of ecumenism" (108).

Shafak's metropolitan novels envision such ecumenical spaces in a more literal sense than Hassan may have had in mind. In her earlier novel *The Saint of Insipient Insanities*, she brings together three male roommates from three different countries, all students in Boston between 2002 and 2003. Abed, the devout Moslem from Morocco, engaged to marry a girl back home in an arranged marriage and watching slasher films at night to soothe his multitudinous worries, and Piyu, the devout Catholic from Spain, very much in love with the bulimic Mexican-American girl Allegra, are joined by Ömer, the Turk, who is not so religiously inclined, sexually very agile, but falling in love with Gail, a half-Jewish, half-Protestant lesbian, feminist, and vegan chocolate maker, who is also very much prone to suicidal tendencies.

All three students in different ways pursue romantic longings, none of them succeeding very well. It becomes obvious that their struggle for survival within an often hostile American environment brings them closer together, even though they vastly differ in their respective cultural and personal backgrounds. But all agree, for example, on their love for food, a topic that in *The Bastard of Istanbul* is explored in even greater detail and depth, where the 'surprising' similarities between traditional, yet transculturally available Armenian and Turkish cuisines are starkly contrasted against a globalized McDonald-fast food culture devoid of long-standing local practices.

The three unlikely roommates of *The Saint of Insipient Insanities* judge their lives in exile in terms of balancing the gains and losses, be it through engaging in food, alcohol, education, relationships, or religion. It is, however, above all the intercultural relationships between Ömer and Gail as well as Piyu and

Allegra—and Abed's significant lack thereof—that the novel represents as intersecting and mirroring instances of transcultural negotiations leading up to an uncanny climax in the end: Gail kills herself during their honeymoon in Istanbul by jumping off the bridge crossing the Bosporus. What is at stake here is, in particular, the issue of time, sequence, and development. As much as the novel's narrative structure denies any logically motivated linearity of plot, with the first chapter taking place rather towards the end—but not quite the end—of the plot, the many chapters mostly taking a specific character into focus add up to a scattered mosaic of ironically comic survival situations in an alien location.

The importance and vagaries of time are especially articulated through the voice and actions of Ömer. As primary embodiment of Shafak's displaced migrant, the "stranger in a strangeland" as she herself claims in an interview ("Migrations" 57), his measurement and thus perception of time relies not on the passing of seconds, minutes, hours, and days, but on an individualized pattern of recurrence instead:

> Ömer Özsipahioğlu was, in every single layer down to the lowest echelons of his soul, demoralized and unsettled, poo-scared and exhausted into slow motion by the hyperspeed of that crepuscular hologram called "time." Anyhow, *what was time?* [...] it wasn't the definition, and not even time per se that got on his nerves, but what she was supposed to be doing all the time: flow . . . and flow . . . and flow . . . It was precisely this flowing part, and flowing not as in lyrical meandering but as in galloping at full speed, that made him so tense about it. (*The Saint* 75, original emphasis)

Having the feeling that time always needed to be compartmentalized, analyzed, and measured, "and yet never accumulating into a meaningful whole" (*The Saint* 75), made him come to a conclusion how to handle this puzzling phenomenon 'time.' Instead of giving in to the purposeful linearity of time as measured through clocks and watches, he chooses to rely on the time's circular quality measured through yet a very different media: the endless loop of music.

> Rather than hours, minutes, and seconds, he used albums, songs and beats. The length of a period between two succeeding things was tantamount to the length of a certain song played over and over again. Basically, it was good to be reminded that unlike time, music could always be rewound, paused, and replayed. [...] It did not glue itself to the one-way current of

time heading toward a phony notion of progress. The circular loop of songs eased the burden of the irreversibility of linear time. (*The Saint* 76-77)

As much as Ömer's habit of measuring time seems to be a product of his exile existence, it actually predates his arrival in Boston and is thus a cultural 'baggage' that he brings along from Turkey. Is it, however, a distinctly personal habit, or rather a cultural distinction pointing towards an East/West-dichotomy? Since Ömer's songs, and overall they are Western, are comments on his current situation, the first conclusion seems quite obvious. Here Ömer could be said to be one of those "personal-stereo users," who according to sound researcher Michael Bull manage time as part of everyday life through the use of technological devices such as the walkman or "personal stereo" as he calls it:

> The ritualized journey and the pressing demands of the everyday come with a recognition that the cyclical and linear components of the day constitute either a threat or an unacceptable incursion to their everyday life. Users' experiences are rather understood in terms of their desire to operationalize a 'compensatory metaphysics' in which time is transformed and experience heightened through its technologically mediated management. (161)

Ömer's effort to control and manage his everyday life and thus to keep civilizational fears and threats at bay indeed participates in such "technologically mediated" strategies of urban "lifeworld" partitioning that Bull describes. Taking a side-glance at one of Elif Shafak's essays, however, leads more in the direction of the second conclusion of alluding to a culturally distinct and historically specific context. In "Transgender Bolero," she alludes to yet another "circular loop" that is significant in this context since it attests to Turkey's enforced Western transformation in the early twentieth century.

Shafak first reflects about her debut novel on the hermaphrodite Sufi mystic. Its title *Pinhan* refers to a mystical term meaning "covertness," and she claims to have followed "in the footsteps of a certain tradition of disclosure—the way of telling things without saying them, disclosing without exposing, speaking through silences, just like the Sufis used to do in the past. *When the society is not ready to hear what you have to say*, advised the Sufi, *say it to no one other than your soul and your soulmates*" ("Transgender Bolero" 27; original emphasis). Within the essay, Shafak then frames this poetological statement with the encounter of a transsexual that she watches on a ferryboat crossing the Bosporus. This encounter is strikingly "bizarre" due to its transgender implications with the transsexual making visible in broad daylight what usually remains hidden within Istanbulite nightly dark corners. But it is her specific action of putting on a walkman and listening with increased volume to Ravel's "Bolero" that brings Shafak into her very own cultural loop of time:

> As she leaned back listening to the world's longest crescendo, for a fleeting moment the world's sexiest smile crossed her lips. All of a sudden, past and present, she and I, the silences within my novel and her clamorous existence on earth got connected to one another, as if everything had fallen neatly in this place, each and every one of us transforming into personal scraps of repetitions along the protracted and yet equally abrupt social transformation that the Turkish state and society has undergone. ("Transgender Bolero" 27)

Maurice Ravel's "Bolero" of 1928, a "piece lasting 17 minutes and consisting wholly of one long, unbroken crescendo" (Ravel, qtd. in Shafak 27), nevertheless was structured as a seemingly repetition of a single melody—actually two alternating melodies—, culminating in a tremendous climax that many took to resemble a sexual orgasm. As Shafak asserts, along with the dissolution of the Ottoman Empire and the fabrication of the Turkish Republic as a modern and secular nation-state came the attempt in discouraging the practice of traditional Anatolian folk music and the encouragement to rather listen to Western music. As one of the controlled incentives, Ravel's "Bolero" was played on the public ferryboats travelling along the Bosporus in an endless loop. Not only does this radically disregard the composer's musical intentions, turning the climactic experience in its ironic opposite with the repetitive melodic structure now meaning nothing but boring, annoying repetition instead of the ultimate and ecstatic crescendo. This practice also attests to the official cutting-off of local traditions in favor of Westernized modernization, whereas unofficially these very traditions have continued till today. Shafak here claims that "perhaps it can be plausibly argued that the story of state, sexuality and modernization in Turkey resembles a song in a repeat track mode, or else, a melody full of repetitions" ("Transgender Bolero" 28).

Like the transsexual listening to the "Bolero," in yet another cross-cultural appropriation Asya's habit in *The Bastard of Istanbul* to constantly—endlessly one might say—listen to Johnny Cash's aggressive-mournful tunes paradoxically reflects Asya's own dissociate mental state ("Asya had decided she too was born in the soul of misery" [*The Bastard* 63]) as well as the city's explosive influence on its inhabitants. But I believe that especially Ömer's habit of measuring time in endless repetition rather than progressive linearity demonstrates Shafak's idea of a "deluge of perpetual repetition alongside underlying transformation, a long, drawn-out melody of modernization" ("Transgender Bolero" 47) that characterizes Turkey's difficult stance as intermediary between East and West. The novel's ending with newly-wed American Gail jumping the Turkish bridge and exiled, visiting-home Ömer once again listening—repeat track—to one of his American songs, ironically, but in its prolepsis appropriately titled "Gimme Danger"—by punk rocker Iggy Pop, although not mentioned in the text—turns the endless repetition into a drastic and highly explosive full stop: Gail's death.

Elegiac Metropolis or "A Bridge in Between"

The novel's tangled mosaic plot builds up to an astounding climax. The last pages can truly be called a crescendo as well as accelerando in musical terms. This *stretto* connects and interweaves all the novel's motifs. While the first chapter with Ömer's bemoaning his difficult lot as a forlorn foreigner *and* desperate husband embarked on the topic of cultural misunderstandings due to migratory processes, the overlapping synchronicity of the novel's ending points towards a contrary direction: no matter where you are or whom you are with, a feeling of belonging, sharing, and intimacy is fluctuating and temporary at best. The three roommates all embark on revelatory intimate experiences at the exact same time, two of them in Boston and Ömer in Istanbul. And while Piyu finds out about Allegra's secret bulimia and Abed finally gives in to his sexual needs, Ömer must face Gail's suicide. The novel of immigration that starts out as a cultural critique of America's global imperialism filtered through Ömer's—but not only his—sense of loss of identity ends with a huge step towards the claim of cultural relativism: individual estrangement and suffering supersedes collective or national dilemmas.

Ömer, while listening—repeat track—to "Gimme Danger," once again has the feeling of "lagging behind the speed of time, unable to catch the cadence of life, except that this time it is the cadence of death he is running after" (*The Saint* 349). As much as "the cadence of life" seems like an oxymoron, since in musical terms it comprises a harmonized ending and thus "cadence of life" metaphorically would come to signify life's opposite, namely death, Ömer's feeling of "lagging behind the speed of time" actually equals that musical motion of *ritardando* with which a piece slows down towards its finale. Whereas, therefore, Ömer's habit of listening repeat track can be seen as a defiance of an untimely ending, his wish to be in accord with the "cadence of life" can also be read as the equivalent to a latent death wish or as "incipient insanity" in allusion to the novel's enigmatic title. In any case, this incongruity there and then coalesces to make perfect, if tragic sense. Belatedly running after Gail, he has one last—and fatally false—consolation: "She won't die. No, she'll not. People do not commit suicide on other people's soil, and this is not her homeland" (350). Departing from Ömer's fallacious belief in survival and in a sudden shift of focalization, the omniscient narrator takes over and brings the reader to acknowledge the transcultural tragedy within repeatedly failed comic survival efforts: "But did she ever have one [i.e. homeland]? Who is the real stranger—the one who lives in a foreign land and knows he belongs elsewhere or the one who lives the life of a foreigner in her native land and has no place else to belong?" (350-351). Thus, while Ömer until the end remains stuck in his lack of understanding the complexity of cultural crosscurrents, the reader may capture the tragic sense of such dissonant chords. Ultimately, the novel ends in a bleak juxtaposition of untimely time sequences:

> The bridge is sixty-four meters above sea level. A song plays on Ömer's Walkman. The song lasts three minutes, twenty seconds, but if you keep repeating the track it can last an eternity.
>
> Gail's fall lasts only 2.7 seconds. (351)

Everlasting suspension—the illusion of eternal life—and sudden closure—the reality of imminent death—meet producing an explosively discordant finale instead of an elaborately expanded harmonious cadence. Shafak here recalls Georg Simmel's idea of the separateness *and* connectedness that meet in the bridge, since walking on the bridge, "before we have become inured to it through daily habit, [...] must have provided the wonderful feeling of floating for a moment between heaven and earth" ("Bridge and Door" 173). Shafak refrains from glossing over the eccentric vagaries of the lives of her transculturally migrating characters, highlighting instead the eccentricities of their idiosyncratic choices. This last chapter, appropriately called "A Bridge in Between" draws on a transnational poetics that on the one hand 'bridges' cultures, but on the other hand leaves people homeless for no "apparent reason" as Gail's suicide symbolizes: "Once again in her life, she started watching herself falling down, and the falling down accelerate at a bewildering pace, eroding her desire to live bit by bit, like blood oozing from a wound inside, except that there was no apparent wound, and, therefore, no apparent reason why" (346) *Apparent* being the key word here.

In a diary entry of 1925, Virginia Woolf asks herself whether a novel could be an elegy: "I have an idea that I will invent a new name for my books to supplant 'novel.' A new—by Virginia Woolf. But what? Elegy?" (qtd. in Kennedy 1). In a sense, I believe Shafak's novel to be such an elegy, here on an idealized vision of transculturation within a global sphere. Even though the novel is set directly following the fatal 9/11 incidents and features Muslim characters, it makes no particular references to any specific cultural war being waged against Islamic immigrants in the United States. Her elegiac approach is not so much political here than personal: it is the intimacy between people that has been corrupted and lost in this time and age. This links her to urban theorists who claim that the modern Western city has become a "world of strangers" with a logic of sexuality of its own that depends upon the "large, dense and permanent cluster of heterogeneous human beings in circulation" (Bech, qtd. in Knopp 151). Shafak's notion, however, includes Istanbul and thus a metropolis located between East and West in her depiction of the idiosyncrasies of exiled identities.

Even though her characters are not so much forced into exile, their migrating across the globe as well as their stubbornly remaining at an allotted spot is a sign of their internal state of exile. And consequently, not only are evolving intimate relations prone to be transitory at best, fatal at worst; intimacy as such seems to be bound to the fundamental dread of loss—personally *and* culturally. As Abed, the Moroccan who steadfastly believed in the truth of his love only to be betrayed by his far-away beloved Safiya, ruminates when in the end he negates all that he has believed so far and gives in to a fleeting moment of anonymous intimacy with an older woman at the laundromat. Feeling "as if pulled by an invisible rope," he comes to realize that he has deserted Safiya long before she has:

> He sensed but could never explain to anyone, no less to himself, that his loyalty for Safiya had been abstrusely interwoven with his devotion not only to their common past, but also to their country. The effect of losing bit by bit his connection to Safiya was a subtle loosening of the moorings that tied him to his homeland. Not that he felt less connected to Morocco now. But he somehow felt more connected to his life in the United States. (*The Saint* 348)

Shafak's metropolitan elegy is not one that bemoans nostalgic notions of 'homeland,' but that calls forth a sense of loss and suffering as a world-wide ailment, beyond national borders. The synchronicity at the end of her tale of two cities stages the coincidental acts of Gayle's suicide, Allegra's ferocious eating binge, and Abed's sexual hysteria as temporally, but not logically interconnected. And while Shafak calls upon Istanbul's bridge as literally connecting the two halves of the city, but above all symbolically connecting East and West, the synchronic actions of those various individuals in different parts of the world also create cross-cultural lineages way beyond geopolitical log(ist)ics. Shafak in this joins critics like Leslie Adelson, who in writing on the trope of "betweenness" in relation to Turkey's location on the cultural map of our time forcefully argues "against between" claiming that this "discursive model that repeatedly situates Turks and other migrants 'between two worlds' relies too schematically and too rigidly on territorial concepts of 'home' (*Heimat*)" (23). Accordingly, we need to read Shafak's effort in balancing the gains and losses of transnational migrants not as a nostalgic yearning for the "tired bridge 'between two worlds,'" but as beckoning of transitional spaces, an invitation to cross transnational thresholds as sites "where consciousness of something new flashes into view" (Adelson 24). Here the image of the door supersedes that of the bridge, because "the door represents in a more decisive manner how separating and connecting are only two sides of precisely the same act. [...] Thus the door becomes the image of the boundary point at which human beings actually always stand or can stand" (Simmel, "Bridge and Door" 172).

The Saint of Insipient Insanities is Elif Shafak's first novel written in English. Before making this linguistic move towards the *lingua franca* of world languages, she already has been, as an extensive, thirty-page interview in the American academic journal *Meridians* of 2003 announced, "an accomplished and award-winning novelist in her home country of Turkey" ("Migrations" 55). Although *Meridians* introduces Shafak to the American audience as somewhat of a surprise novelist, she proves to have actually been a successful and versatile writer for some time with novels dealing with hermaphrodite mystics (*Pinhan* [*The Sufi*], 1997), estranged and deterritorialized Sephardic Jews (*Şehrin Aynaları* [*The Mirrors of the City*], 1999), traumatized obese women (*Mahrem* [*The Gaze*], 2000), and degraded apartment buildings (*Bit Palas* [*The Flea Palace*], 2002).

All of these novels in one way or another focus on Turkish nationality, history, and sexuality, mostly highlighting the cultural history of Istanbul, which might account for the lack of interest in her novels outside of Turkey. With her fifth novel of 2004, *The Saint of Insipient Insanities*, however, Elif Shafak has entered a different plane, namely that of transnational literature, since not only this novel originally is written in English, it also is set mainly in east-coast metropolitan North America. She has continued writing in English with her highly disputed sixth novel of 2007, *The Bastard of Istanbul*, which with its predominantly urban setting of Istanbul but also of Tucson, Arizona, and San Francisco could be said to be a counter piece to *The Saint* in its Turkish-American connection. In both of her English-language novels, Shafak deals with the questioning of ethnicity and nationality from postcolonial and global perspectives, and thus on the one hand departing from her narrower focus on Turkish cultural history of her earlier novels, but on the other hand suggesting to read post-Ottoman Turkey's national setting against the backdrop of postcolonial national histories across the world.

To be sure, the Turkish republic of today cannot easily be integrated within a postcolonial discourse, but a set of developments makes this feasible, after all. For once, as Ismael Talib in his study on the language of postcolonial literatures asserts, the association of the introduction of writing with the colonial power may open up the discussion in the case of Turkey "which was not colonized by a Western European power, but which also introduced the romanized script for the writing of Turkish, because of the belief that it was more efficient for writing the language" (72). This already shows the influence of the West on the shaping of the Turkish nation-state, a process that Shafak likens to disenchantment: "The Turkish language has been cleansed, Turkified—the reformists got rid of Persian words, Arabic words, Sufi expressions. The language has been disenchanted. [...] When you try to limit language, you limit your own imagination" ("Crossover Artists" 25-26). Deniz Kandiyoti and Ayşe Saktanber further claim in their introduction to *Fragments of Culture*, even in countries such as Ottoman Turkey "that did not experience direct colonial rule, European hegemony and the perceived 'backwardness' of their [...] societies created a terrain for ideological contest in which notions of 'catching up,' imitation of the West, cultural corruption and authenticity continued to have purchase on political discourse" (3). Instead of relying on the traditional East/West binaries, postcolonial scholarship especially in the aftermath of Edward Said's *Orientalism* has successfully dismantled such cultural clichés pointing toward "the processes of cultural hybridization that characterize alternative modernities" (Kandioyti and Saktanber 3) such as Turkey's. And above all, literature has taken on a pivotal role to reflect these cultural transitions as

Shafak herself claims: "In Turkey, the novel especially served this end because it was a new genre. It was the voice of Westernization when the Turkish reformers were trying to accelerate the process of Westernization" ("Crossover Artists" 24).

Shafak on various levels has taken up the lastingly problematic center-periphery model of power to disclose how Western perceptions of Turkey, but also Turkish self-perceptions at times easily position Turkey within the culturally less privileged peripheral location. Ömer's awareness of how Americans might perceive him is mirrored by Asya's self-deprecatory statements that she turns into her "Personal Manifesto of Nihilism:"

> Back in Turkey, he used to be ÖMER ÖZSİPAHİOĞLU.
> Here in America, he had become an OMAR OZSIPAHIOGLU.
> His dots were excluded for him to be better included. After all, Americans, just like everyone else, relished familiarity—in names they could pronounce, sounds they could resonate, even if they didn't make much sense one way or another. Yet, few nations could perhaps be as self-assured as the Americans in reprocessing the names and surnames of foreigners. (*The Saint* 5)

> Asya Kazancı was still lying in bed under a goose-feather quilt, listening to the myriad sounds only Istanbul is capable of producing while her mind meticulously composed a Personal Manifesto of Nihilism:
> Article One: If you cannot find a reason to love the life you are living, do not pretend to love the life you are living. (*The Bastard* 121)

But besides letting her characters take on opposing cultural standpoints, Shafak herself is keenly aware of her own cultural position as Turkish author aspiring to 'conquer' the American literary market including the linguistic adaptation of her own name from Turkish "Şafak" to Americanized "Shafak." Additionally, she is forced to think of herself as an ethnicized woman, because in the United States she is being perceived as "colored" due to her cultural background. While most Turks would consider themselves as "white" or "Caucasian," she refers to this dubious category of "skin color" within the context of "deterritorialization, non-belonging, and the constant feeling of being an 'outsider,' in addition to outside perceptions of what it means to be from an Islamic country, Muslim or Turkish, even though I am not a practitioner of Islamic religions, that makes me a 'woman of color'" ("Migrations" 61). In this awareness of cultural double-standards, Shafak's transnational poetics and above all ethics become apparent as a field of experimentation that reconsiders established cultural premises and literary canons. She therefore projects and delineates, as Jahan Ramazani suggests, "models of transnational imaginative citizenship that are mobile, ambivalent, and multifaceted" (354). In this sense, Shafak's poetics of transnationalism can help us

> both understand and imagine a world in which cultural boundaries are fluid, transient, and permeable, and thus read ourselves as imaginative citizens not of one or another hermetically sealed national or civilizational block, but of intercultural worlds that ceaselessly overlap, intersect, and converge. (Ramazani 355)

In her English language novels, Shafak participates in that shift towards opening up the fixed boundaries of a nationalist literature to embrace a transnational poetics of overlapping, intersecting, and converging qualities, which here also includes envisioning herself as a "woman of color" for strategic reasons. As Diana Fuss succinctly reminds us there are times and places, where "strategic essentialism" can be employed as powerful tool to dismantle fixed either/or constructions, if one keeps in mind that there is difference between "deploying" or "activating" essentialism and "falling into" or "lapsing into" essentialism:

> "Falling into" or "lapsing into" implies that essentialism is inherently reactionary—inevitably and inescapably a problem or a mistake. "Deploying" or "activating," on the other hand, implies that essentialism may have some strategic or interventionary value. (20)

Shafak in this sense politically invests her marginal position as a female writer from a Muslim country to address issues relevant not only for her own 'homeland,' but for her targeted American audience as well. She uses the "soft-power" of literature to recall Turkey's historical investment of such power as means of cultural homogenizing "to promote the establishment of a nation-state and the Turkification of language," and calls for a strategic use of such power once again, but to different, namely transnationally oriented ends. Remembering the multicultural Ottoman past, she makes strategic use of the relinquished and forgotten merits of a Turkish heritage without falling back to a proto-colonial attitude of dominance and hierarchy: "Now, it is time to use soft power in the opposite direction. This time, through words and stories, newspapers and novels, we Turkish writers can uphold the cultural, ethnic, and religious diversity that was dismantled but never completely lost" ("Accelerating the Flow of Time" 26).

She therefore imagines through her novels the particularities and histories of a nation-state like Turkey as well as the globalized phenomenon of world travelling and urban migration, and she excels, I think, especially when being most ironic. Humor is a trait that Shafak expressly values in the English language, because of its possibility of relinquishing the "either/or framework," whereas Turkish humor for her is direct, "political humor, but not irony. [...] In English, I found more gates for that humor, additional doors" ("Crossover Artists" 26). And so, instead of peacefully affirming or adamantly renouncing the metaphor of the "tired bridge 'between two worlds,'" she lets an angry, young girl like Asya sardonically smirk at such an overwrought allusion when her aunt suggests acting as translator for her American visitor Armanoush:

> Therefore, dear, you will be her translator. You will ferry her words to us and our words to her. [...] Like a bridge extending over cultures, you will connect the East and the West.
>
> Asya crinkled her nose, as if she had just detected an awful stink in the house that was apparent only to her, and screwed up her lips, as if to say, "You wish!" (*The Bastard* 134)

Edible City, or the Etho-Poetics of Food and Sex

Much like the tragic-comically overlapping synchronicity that characterized the climax of *The Saint of Insipient Insanities* and was acted out on the Bosporus Bridge as well as in Boston's urban center, Shafak's later novel *The Bastard of Istanbul* reinforces the notion of the idiosyncrasies of exiled identities. Here, the sole male heir of an old Istanbulite family hides in Tucson, Arizona, only to return to Istanbul after twenty years to face his past trauma and follow the fate of every single male in the family, i.e. a sudden early death:

> Like an evil spell put on the whole lineage, generations after generations of Kazancı men had died young and unexpectedly. [...] Yet it was one thing to move away from the city where he was born, and another to be so far removed from his own flesh and blood. Mustafa Kazancı did not so much mind taking refuge in America forever as if he had no native soil to return to, or even living life always forward with no memories to recall, but to turn

into a foreigner with no ancestors, a man with no boyhood, troubled him. (*The Bastard* 29, 285)

Returning to Istanbul to recapture his run-away stepdaughter Armanoush, he has to face his "cultivated denial," fully aware that "if he stayed here any longer, he would start to remember" (335). Mustafa has manufactured amnesia for good reasons: his flight to America years ago was brought on as aftermath of raping his sister and in turn fathering Asya unbeknownst to everyone else in the family. His involuntary return home not only brings him back to a household of women of three generations he had escaped from, but to a trip down memory lane: "The moment he had stepped into his childhood home, the spell that had shielded him all these years against his own memory had been shattered" (335).

Through Mustafa's guilt, shame, and denial that in turn caused Asya's mother's—his sister's—hard-edged, cynical behavior as the family's "black sheep" (174), Asya herself lacks a stable sense of identity and home. She is the victim of a family secret that not only socially stigmatizes her as "bastard," but psychologically forces a dark past upon her own young life. And while she wishes to "have no past," to be "a nobody" with "[n]o family, no memories and all that shit" (148), she is painfully aware of her status as "outcast in that house, eternally exiled from dreadful family secrets. In the name of protecting me, they have separated me from them" (175). Calling her own mother "aunt" and having no father that she knows of, her familial identity is suspended in a space of non-being, a last "bastard" in a long chain of fatefully forsaken ancestors, which due to historical and political circumstances has continuously been disrupted leaving its members scattered all over the world.

While metropolis, translated from the Greek, literally means mother-city and thus etymologically links the urban space to motherhood, Shafak makes it very clear that whatever haven these large mega-cities may offer, they have certainly lost their quality of a safe motherly home. In her novel, she delicately interweaves the story of two very different and culturally very distinct Ottoman families: one Armenian and diasporic, living in San Francisco, and the other Turkish and remaining in Istanbul. And yet, as the novel's ending suggests, these families' histories have connecting points both in the distant past and the immediate present as do many others: "Family stories intermingle in such ways that what happened generations ago can have an impact on seemingly irrelevant developments of the present day. The past is anything but bygone" (*The Bastard* 356). Through the lens of mostly female characters of multiple generations, the novel recounts the interconnected fate of these women and links them to a common history that was cut off through the demise of the Ottoman Empire in general and the injustices committed against Ottoman Armenians in 1915 in particular. Several passages clearly stake out this volatile political terrain, for example when Armanoush refers to herself as part of "a diaspora people" (178) being "the grandchild of genocide survivors who lost all their relatives at the hands of Turkish butchers in 1915, but I myself have been brainwashed to deny the genocide because I was raised by some Turk named Mustafa!" (53-54). While ironically, Armanoush and her step-father have common ancestors and therefore, Mustafa actually is part of several relatives of Armanoush's that she believes to lack, Asya's mother has a lover who is also Armenian, but who does not want to be assigned to a diasporic fate claiming instead a multicultural and -ethnic urban heritage as his own:

> This city is my city. I was born and raised in Istanbul. My family's history in this city goes back at least five hundred years. Armenian Istanbulites belong to Istanbul, just like the Turkish, Kurdish, Greek, and Jewish Istanbulites do. We have first managed and then badly failed to live together. We cannot fail again. (*The Bastard* 254)

This Armenian's account refers to the radical urban changes that affected Istanbul's ethnic, non-Muslim inhabitants during the transition from the Ottoman Empire to the Turkish Republic, drastically decimating the Christian population who made up a large part of the Istanbul's intelligentsia, a fact Shafak mentions several times in her novel: "Writers, poets, artists, intellectuals were the first ones within the Armenian *millet* to be eliminated by the late Ottoman government" (*The Bastard* 96). Sociologist Çağlar Keyder also asserts: "Between 1915 and 1925, a total of more than two million Armenians and Greeks were killed, expelled, exchanged, or departed of their own will. This Christian population had constituted a disproportionate portion of the wealthier urban dwellers of the late empire" (145). Shafak, who in the historical Armenian Conference on the events of 1915, which after being postponed due to nationalist political pressure but was finally held in September 2005 in Istanbul, presented a paper on the only female Armenian intellectual Zabel Esayan, stresses the importance that against a "nationalist smear campaign" a growing "network of intellectual solidarity between Turkish and Armenian intellectuals" has joined forces in collective efforts to improve Turkey's human-rights record. She herself quotes from Marc Nichanian's *Writers of Disaster*:

Armenian Literature in the Twentieth Century (2002), a quote that might as well stand for her own effort in *The Bastard of Istanbul*:

> The years will pass, the political enmities and hatred will fall into oblivion, the new humanity, beguiled with new hopes and new desires, will forget today's mourning and misery, but one thing will remain, which cannot be healed or forgotten, that is the protracted agony of a whole people under torture, of which you will find but a pale image in the following pages. (Nichanian, qtd. in Shafak, "Accelerating the Flow of Time" 25)

For this effort, Shafak was put on trial for "denigrating Turkishness" under the Turkish Penal Code, because some of the Armenian characters spoke of the "Armenian genocide" in the novel. Even though the charges were dropped—after PEN International organized a campaign of appeals on her behalf—ruling that she could not be prosecuted for something said by a fictional character, the novel does hit a sore spot. As much as the novel's title refers to the youngest daughter of the Istanbulite family literally being a 'bastard,' the overall concern of the novel hints at a larger meaning of the term 'bastard.' The mysterious death premise of all male family members leaves this particular family not only without a proper patriarch, it also makes perfectly clear that it is the weakness and failure of the fathers as leading figures that has led to this state of cultural, ethnic and historical bastardization, the anomaly of rupturing a wholesome multiethnic society, breaking its structure and dispelling its units.

Shafak brutally dismisses the last male descendant through murder. And it is food that plays the crucial role in both executing the murder and reuniting all others. The novel abounds in food and food metaphors. All chapters are titled with food names from "Cinnamon" to "White Rice," and some include elaborate recipes. In one particularly striking scene, Armanoush experiences her step-father's Turkish family as they wish to excel in their famous Turkish hospitality only to be taken aback and then rejoicing in the fact that this girl knows all those meals and their names, because they remained the same in Turkish and Armenian cuisines. It is here that Shafak makes a strong argument in favor of cultural understanding across historical divides, namely that food as cultural phenomenon mirrors and transcends cultural processes at large. Especially when looking at diasporic situations, the editors of *Eating Culture: The Poetics and Politics of Food* argue that "cooking performs memory: food and recipes are links to cultural 'roots' and are, at the same time, testifying on the contact zones and 'routes' which their producers and consumers have gone through" (Döring, Heide, and Mühleisen 7). This certainly attests to the effort of Armanoush's diasporic Armenian family in San Francisco to uphold the culinary tradition of Armenian cooking at every family gathering. As Armanoush's uncle remarks on one such occasion:

> Dikran Stamboulian gazed longingly at the food set out on the table, and reached for a jar of yogurt drink, Americanized with too many ice cubes. In multihued clay bowls of different sizes were many of his favorite dishes: *fassoulye pilaki, kadın budu köfte, karnıyarık*, newly made *churek*, and to Uncle Dikran's delight *bastırma*. [...] his heart warmed at the sight of *bastırma* and entirely melted when he saw his favorite dish next to it: *burma*. (*The Bastard* 51)

This heart-warming and communal culinary experience—even when 'watered down' as partially Americanized—links its exiled participants to their lost home. It also captures the diasporic community's struggle to maintain what Roger Bromley has termed "a critically imagined collective community" (9), critically here in the sense, as Peter Brooker explains, that although the diasporic experience "can invite nostalgia for an 'authentic' homeland," as a critical concept it is reflexive and politicized, "always in a dialogic relation with the dominant and with the past, drawing upon both for its critical resources in the present" (20-21). Armanoush's Armenian family takes part in this retelling and reworking of a collective historical sense, and especially Armanoush herself is not only a cultural hybrid, but also takes on the role of transcultural mediator literally migrating across the globe and thus opening up spatio-temporal possibilities of reimagining a "hetero-cultural present" (Brooker 23) where much may seem unassimilable at first.

However, stretching the argument beyond the diasporic, Elspeth Probyn in her study on *Carnal Appetites: Foodsexidentities* goes on to claim that "eating reconfigures us in local, global and sexual ways" (145). It is through food and eating that love and shame, virtue and vice, passion and poison may all be mixed up together. This claim of an "etho-poetics" of food and sex (75) is not as far-fetched as it might seem, even within the diaspora. It is certainly not meant in a way that one may supersede the other: food instead of sex or vice versa. Rather, this is a claim to combine cultures and histories of our lives, "the pasts and present within which we live" (146). And it is food and eating that "can foreground the sense and sensuality of the timing and touch of precise combinations." As Probyn remarks: "The imperative to bring together different elements, and at the same time to not lose sight of their individual flavors, textures, and inherent possibilities, extends across a wide range of sites" (146). It was Georg Simmel who made two famous, seemingly contradictory statements: eating and drinking "is the most egotistical thing, indeed the one most absolutely and immediately confined to the individual" ("Sociology of the Meal" 130). But this strict individuality of the eating act may be overcome in the temporal and special experience of community: "The shared nature of the meal, however, brings about temporal regularity, for only at a predetermined time can a circle of people assemble together—the first triumph over the naturalism of eating" (131).

This captures the turning of the natural into the social, the elemental into the alimentary. Shafak's novel indeed revels in the celebration of the culinary community. It is at the table where the daughters—one Turkish, one Armenian-American—unite in a feast of making up bastardized histories. But food is also the site, and maybe Simmel here was right after all, where one eats utterly alone, when passion and poison clash fatally. The last chapter is entitled "Potassium Cyanide" and it refers to the poisonous ingredient, tasting like almonds, which is mixed up in the dessert of Mustafa, the family's last male heir. He eats it, fully knowing, and also fully aware of his shame, namely of raping his sister and fathering a bastard. This most private incident, however, is encompassed by a collectivized and naturalized metropolis that is aligned with the etho-poetics of food. Through the eyes and the nose of the Armenian-American girl Armanoush we sense the olfactory quality of the sexiness of an edible city:

> The breeze shifted direction just then, and Armanoush caught a pungent whiff of the sea. This city was a jumble of aromas, some of them strong and rancid, others sweet and stimulating. Almost every smell made Armanoush recall some sort of food, so much so that she had started to perceive Istanbul as something edible. (*The Bastard* 246)

The city has metamorphosed into a communal feast to be relished beyond a cursed history. Like Ömer who craves for Turkish raki in Boston only to find Greek ouzo, Armanoush will remain a stranger in a strangeland, whether in Istanbul, Tucson, or some other city. And yet, even strangers may mysteriously fall for such strangelands. "Life is coincidence," Shafak's narrator claims in the end, "though sometimes it takes a *djinni* [i.e. a ghost or demon] to fathom that" (*The Bastard* 356). Whether this is meant to be taken as witty irony or at face value is for the reader to decide.

Works Cited

Adelson, Leslie A. "Against Between: A Manifesto." *New Perspectives on Turkey* 28-29 (2003): 19-36.

Bech, Henning. "Citysex: Representing Lust in Public." Paper presented at Geographies of Desire Conference, Netherlands' Universities Institute for Co-ordination of Research in Social Sciences, Amsterdam, 1993.

Bromley, Roger. *Narratives for a New Belonging: Diasporic Cultural Fictions*. Edinburgh: Edinburgh UP, 2000.

Brooker, Peter. *Modernity and Metropolis: Writing, Film and Urban Formations*. New York: Palgrave 2002.

Bull, Michael. *Sounding Out the City: Personal Stereos and the Management of Everyday Life*. Oxford and New York: Berg, 2000.

Döring, Tobias, Markus Heide, and Susanne Mühleisen, eds. *Eating Culture: The Poetics and Politics of Food*. Heidelberg: Winter, 2003.

Fuss, Diana. *Essentially Speaking: Feminism, Nature & Difference*. New York and London: Routledge, 1989.

Hassan, Ihab. "Cities of Mind, Urban Words: The Dematerialization of Metropolis in Contemporary American Fiction." *Literature and the Urban Experience: Essays on the City and Literature*. Eds. Michael C. Jaye and Ann Chalmers Watts. New Brunswick: Rutgers UP, 1981. 93-112.

Kandiyoti, Deniz, and Ayşe Saktanber, eds. *Fragments of Culture: The Everyday of Modern Turkey*. London and New York: I. B. Tauris, 2002.

Kennedy, David. *Elegy*. London and New York: Routledge, 2007.

Keyder, Çağlar. "The Housing Market from Informal to Global." *Istanbul: Between the Global and the Local*. Ed. Çağlar Keyder. Lanham et al.: Rowman & Littlefield, 1999. 143-159.

Knopp, Lawrence. "Sexuality and Urban Space: A Framework for Analysis." *Mapping Desire: Geographies of Sexualities*. Eds. David Bell and Gill Valentine. London and New York: Routledge, 1995. 149-161.

Marx, Leo. "The Puzzle of Anti-Urbanism in Classic American Literature." *Literature and the Urban Experience: Essays on the City and Literature*. Eds. Michael C. Jaye and Ann Chalmers Watts. New Brunswick: Rutgers UP, 1981. 63-80.

Mumford, Lewis. *The City in History*. New York: Harcourt, Brace, and World, 1961.

Nichanian, Marc. *Writers of Disaster: Armenian Literature in the Twentieth Century*. Princeton: Gomidas Inst., 2002.

Probyn, Elspeth. *Carnal Appetites: Foodsexidentities*. London and New York: Routledge, 2000.

Ramazani, Jahan. "A Transnational Poetics." *American Literary History* 18.2 (2006): 332-359.

Shafak, Elif, Minae Mizumura, and Shan Sa. "Crossover Artists: Writing in Another Language." *PEN America: A Journal for Writers and Readers* 7 (2006): 24-31.

———. "Accelerating the Flow of Time: Soft Power and the Role of Intellectuals in Turkey." *World Literature Today: A Literary Quarterly of the University of Oklahoma* 80.1 (2006): 24-26.

———. "Migrations: A Meridians Interview with Elif Shafak." *Meridians: Feminism, Race, Transnationalism* 4.1 (2003): 55-85.

———. "Transgender Bolero." *Middle East Report* 230 (2004): 26-29, 47.

———. *The Bastard of Istanbul*. New York et al.: Viking, 2007.

———. *The Saint of Insipient Insanities*. New York: Farrar, Straus and Giroux, 2004.

Simmel, Georg. "Bridge and Door." *Simmel on Culture: Selected Writings*. Eds. David Frisby and Mike Featherstone. London et al.: Sage, 1997. 170-174.

———. "Sociology of the Meal." *Simmel on Culture: Selected Writings*. Eds. David Frisby and Mike Featherstone. London et al.: Sage, 1997. 130-135.

Talib, Ismail S. *The Language of Postcolonial Literatures: An Introduction*. London: Routledge, 2002.

IV. Performing Queer Turkish Cultures

7. Precarious Masculinities in the New Turkish Cinema

"New Turkish Cinema" is a disputed label. It is grounded on "one of the biggest crises" in the history of cinema in Turkey, since after 1990 spectators "no longer (a) went to the cinema in general, and (b) when they did, they especially avoided Turkish films" (Atam 202). The label therefore, as Zahit Atam asserts, "is used as part of a simple and pragmatic discourse, rather than as an appropriate term to characterise the new cinema in Turkey" (202). Asuman Suner (12) sees two separate forms emerging from this crisis: 1) a new popular cinema with considerable box-office success that is trying to emulate the style of Hollywood productions (e.g. *Kurtlar Vadisi—Irak*, see discussion below) and 2) an art cinema based on European auteurism and receiving critical acclaim and prestigious awards in national and international festivals, but attracting no Turkish audience, or only a very limited and elitist one (e.g. *Güneşe Yolculuk*).

Popular Turkish cinema up to the 1980s is called "Yeşilçam cinema," literally meaning "pine-tree cinema." The name stems from a street in Istanbul that housed the film production companies. During its golden years in the 1960s and early 1970s, an annual average of 200 films was produced (Suner 3). Before director Yılmaz Güney entered the scene, Yeşilçam cinema was a highly commercialized cinema of stars with little power granted to directors. Relying mostly on melodrama and comedy, but also historical action adventure and gangster films, this changed in the 1970s with the advent of social and political turmoil and the ensuing politicization of cinema.

Güney first starred in this cinema as an actor playing a rough lower-class anti-hero type at odds with the former polished image of middle-class heroes, which made him the most popular star in Turkey and earned him the nickname "Ugly King" (Suner 5). He then turned to directing and became known for his politicized social-realist films such as *Umut* (*Hope*, 1970) and especially

Yol (*The Way*, 1982), which won the Golden Palm at the 1982 Cannes Film Festival. Arguably the most internationally acclaimed Turkish film to date, *Yol* had an astounding production history with Güney being imprisoned for his political views and actions—charged initially for sheltering anarchist refugees, but also for smuggling forbidden films like his *Umut* out of the country, he later was accused of murder—and writing film scripts that were executed by assistants (Şerif Gören in the case of *Yol*). With the film industry still being highly controlled by state censorship that lasted until 1986 and beyond, it is a miracle that this film was realized at all. *Yol* was not shown in Turkey until 1999, and yet the film marked a decisive shift in politics as well as aesthetics in the development of Turkish cinema. It deals with Kurdish protagonists—who had to speak Turkish, because the use of the Kurdish language was still prohibited in Turkey at the time—in conflict with law; it is about women's rights, family honor and ethnic differences filmed in a multifocal, poetic visual style. The main plot revolves around a group of prisoners on furlough, who are travelling as far as Kurdish East Anatolia. The film eventually turns into an allegory with the disillusioned prisoners having to realize that they are physically and mentally freer in their prison microcosm than in a seemingly modern democratic republic that does not allow any kind of nonconformist dissidence and is controlled by military force. For the first time, Turkey appeared on the international film scene with formally challenging aesthetics combined with social criticism paving the way for a New Turkish Cinema.

Yol is famous not least for some of the most gruesome depictions of female suffering in cinema history, but noteworthy is also the depiction of masculinity. On the one hand, traditional Turkish gender relations seem to be affirmed; most conspicuously female sexual digression causes a rift in the family honor system and is consequently punished by male family members. On the other hand, the film also portrays a hitherto unacknowledged male vulnerability. Eylem Kaftan explains this vulnerability as an outcome of a traumatized society subjected to both a feudal patriarchy and military rule. While there is no space for women to act at all, men are shown to have a limited agency, yet fail to overcome the power systems at work. At first repressed by older male relatives, they then take on the role of oppressor in handling their own female relatives. Kaftan speaks of a precarious subjectivity with the failure of men in their families and homes as allegory of a national power system in crisis that, at least in southeastern Turkey, still seems to be valid (cf. 160-161).

From Yeşilçam to New Turkish Cinema: Black Turks and Nationalist Masculinity

Güneşe Yolculuk (Journey to the Sun), a milestone of the New Turkish Cinema, has a lot in common with Güney's *Yol*, and yet it sets a new standard in the depiction of ethnic conflicts, of the urban/rural divide, and especially in its focus on masculinity. But it also marks a new development in Turkish cinema which increasingly becomes European in terms of production and reception as well as narrative. *Güneşe Yolculuk* is a Turkish-German-Dutch coproduction from 1999 and it earned Turkish female director Yeşim Ustaoğlu the "Blue Angel" at the Berlin Film Festival as best European film. The film's socio-geographical location is the working-class milieu of Istanbul and it depicts the friendship between Mehmet, a migrant from Turkey's west coast, and Berzan who stems from the Eastern Kurdish village Zorduç. Without ever using the word "Kurdish" in the film, Mehmet due to his dark skin and friendship with Berzan is repeatedly taken as Kurdish himself. After Berzan is killed in street riots, Mehmet starts his journey east with Berzan's coffin. This journey entails bidding a final good-bye to his German-Turkish girlfriend Arzu, who, despite having grown up in a liberal German milieu, cannot free herself from the restraints of her traditional Turkish family. Again, like in *Yol*, the journey east points towards repressed political and ethnic conflicts in modern Turkey, but here, in contrast, the voyage serves as initiation for the male protagonist who evolves from a naive malleable young man to a hardened defiant hero. His corporeal experience of being treated as "black" (a pejorative term for Kurdish) Turk and thus as second-class citizen leads him to acknowledging a pluralistic society that is at odds with Turkish founding father Atatürk's enforced secular Kemalist ideal of a homogenized nation modeled after European pattern.[1] Metropolitan centers, and especially Istanbul, prove to be a far cry from this

---

[1] On the lasting impact of foreign films and especially American films on urban Turkish youth—above all those living in Istanbul—in the early years of the Turkish Republic see Boisseau, who claims: "By the end of the 1920s American films outpaced all other foreign imports, cementing not only the cultural connection between cinema and Western expressions of 'modernity' but also Hollywood (and by extension the United States itself) as the apotheosis of what it meant to be 'modern.' Hollywood provided a model of modern relationships between men and women and a sounding board for the emerging youth of Turkey to negotiate their new-found national identity and generationally specific self image" (170). For years to come, foreign cinema was the most powerful and widely available form of media from abroad in Turkey, and it would

ideal and turn out to be hybrid, Arabesk spaces of migration, transformation and negotiation, and accordingly the narrative center of much of New Turkish Cinema.[2]

fig. 7.1 *Güneşe Yolculuk. Mehmet carries Berzan's coffin*

fig. 7.2 *Güneşe Yolculuk. Mehmet's tortured body*
fig. 7.3 *Güneşe Yolculuk. Mehmet's tortured body*

---

    remain associated with 'the West' in general and 'America' more specifically until the heyday of Yeşilçam cinema during the 1960s and 1970s.

2   On the concept of "Arabesk" see Stokes. I will expand on "Arabesk" in the following chapter.

From the very first image, we see a world that is topsy-turvy. As prolepsis, it shows Mehmet carrying the coffin on his long odyssey to Zorduç. His image, however, is reflected in water and thus upside-down (see fig. 7.1). The film was released during a period of escalating conflict between the Turkish military and the Kurdistan Workers' Party (PKK), and its narrative reflects this conflict through Mehmet's body. The director inserts Mehmet's involuntary involvement in street riots, hunger strikes, and police harassment into documentary footage. Mehmet's body progressively becomes the site of the ethnic-nationalist confrontation: being taken as a "black Turk," i.e. as a Kurd, he is tortured by the police and shunned by his colleagues. Setting, camera, and lighting drastically emphasize the visible traces of abuse on Mehmet's body (see fig. 7.2 and 7.3). At the same time, he physically gets closer to Berzan, with whom he starts to share his life in an increasingly intimate haven of privacy secluded from the outside turmoil until Berzan is killed. At this point Mehmet claims to be Berzan's closest relative, thus tightening the homosocial bond with seeming blood ties. The physical and emotional intimacy between the two men is striking, also in its visual presentation, giving credence to queer theorist Eve Kosofsky Sedgwick's claim of a "potential unbrokenness of a continuum between homosocial and homosexual—a continuum whose visibility, for men, in our society, is radically disrupted" (1-2). Thus, when speaking of homosocial male bonding as is the case with Berzan and Mehmet, this marks non-sexual social interactions between two men that in general often feature a strong homophobic undercurrent, which, however, is totally absent here. Even given habitualized male-male interaction, which in Mediterranean cultures does not necessarily prohibit the display of physical affection between men, I would argue that the intensity of such displays between Berzan and Mehmet exceeds the culturally sanctioned degree of homosociality. Instead, the two men's bonding must be seen as deliberately embracing the notion of being 'othered' by society, and they accordingly cross the divide of heteronormative prescriptions that society forces onto men's interactions with one another. When Mehmet decides to act as a close relative and to take Berzan's coffin home to Eastern Turkey, Mehmet further intensifies their 'Othering' bond even beyond death by symbolically choosing a new identity and homeland for himself. His 'journey to the sun' therefore reverses the migrant Western direction towards the metropolis Istanbul. Mehmet's final refusal to be part of a falsely homogenized nation comes with a strengthened sense of self. The assertion of manhood has eventually taken a somewhat utopian turn in being based on an abject ethnic minority (cf. Atam 218).³

Quite the contrary can be said of *Kurtlar Vadisi—Irak* (*Valley of the Wolves: Iraq*), one of the most remarkable and controversial films emerging from Turkey in recent years. This 2006 film by Serdar Akar "is an action movie set in contemporary northern Iraq that has become a box office hit in Turkey and ended up as the highest-grossing Turkish film [...] since reliable box office returns began to be compiled in this country" (Özkaracalar 165). The film is a mix of many things: evidently, it is a spin-off from the popular television series *Kurtlar Vadisi* featuring a super-violent undercover officer, Polat Alemdar, who has been idolized by far-right wing young Turkish nationalists especially prone to terrorizing the Kurds. But more importantly, the film starts off with several factual events, most significant amongst which is the incarceration of a group of Turkish undercover military personnel in northern Iraq by the American forces in 2003. This event caused a public outcry in Turkey because the Turkish detainees were marched off hooded, their heads in sacks, by the American captors, which was perceived as an open demonstration of shaming (see fig. 7.4). The film then tells the fictional story of Alemdar going after the American officers who humiliated his compatriots. "At a basic level," as Özkaracalar claims, "it is a crude revenge fantasy to heal hurt national pride" (166).

Fig. 7.4 Kurtlar Vadisi—Irak. Hooded Turkish prisoners
Fig. 7.5 Kurtlar Vadisi—Irak. Human pyramid

 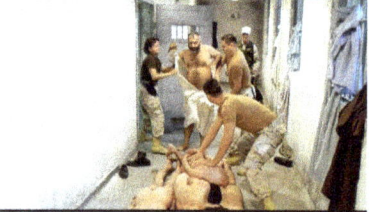

The film includes "almost every single atrocity known to have been committed by the occupation forces in Iraq, including the notorious 'human pyramid' torture at Abu Gharib [sic] prison" (Özkaracalar 166, see fig. 7.5). It is

---

3 For an extended discussion see Poole, "Unsichtbarer Kurde."

therefore "saturated with anti-American imagery," and yet, as Özkaracalar rightly points out, it "fails to qualify as a progressive anti-imperialist text" (166), mainly because the protagonists are driven by extremely nationalist and chauvinistic motivations glorifying their own imperial past of the Ottoman Empire and because of its anti-Kurdish and anti-Semitic representations. In contrast to the films by Güney and Ustaoğlu, this economically most successful film of the New Turkish Cinema remains within the patriarchal order of the republican regime if not blatantly propagating Prime Minister (now President) Recep Tayyip Erdoğan's increasing Islamist political shift in recent years. Thus, this masculine action-adventure melodrama depicts, as Savaş Aslan concedes, "male bonding among the tough heroes and their sidekicks, codes of patriarchal honor, and the domestic role of women" as parts of the dominant nationalist discourse. The "power play among secret agents, military, and terrorists" leaves no room "for the utterances of alternative male subjectivities" (261).

On yet another level, i.e. that of the film's international and especially American reception, it can be said that "Turkey is still the land of *Midnight Express* for many. For human rights groups, journalists, intellectuals and others still come to Turkey with preconceived images branded in their minds by this film. And perhaps so do the officials of the European Union who refuse to admit Turkey" (Şahin). *Kurtlar Vadisi—Irak* has therefore been understood as revenge against the humiliation of Alan Parker's *Midnight Express* (1978).[4] Gardels and Medavoy even assert that the

> Turkish backlash has manifested itself precisely in cultural reassertion, using America as a foil. [...] Capturing the sentiments of ordinary Muslims throughout the region, it [i.e. *Kurtlar Vadisi—Irak*] portrayed a Muslim Rambo who sets out on a mission of revenge against Americans in Iraq, who are shown as looting and raping sadists. (67)

Asuman Suner includes this film in the corpus of New Turkish Cinema because it reflects the rising internationality of Turkish Cinema while also proclaiming a trend to restorative nostalgia based on a conspiratorial worldview. While blatantly anti-American, the film also employs American cinematic models, above all the American-style action hero, who is inserted into this contemporary culture-clash setting as "all-powerful, undefeatable and

---

4   For a further discussion of the link between Serdar Akar's and Alan Parker's films see Poole, "Foltern."

devotedly patriotic," and who yet functions "as reincarnation of the Ottoman/Turkish legacy" (47-48) at the same time.

Precarious Masculinities in the New Turkish-German Cinema: The Melodramatic Penis and Trans-Masculinity

Like Serdar Akar, Fatih Akın and Kutluğ Ataman both arguably belong to the cadre of New Turkish Cinema directors, but unlike Akar both present male subjectivity in a much more volatile and vulnerable manner. Aslan has called their films "alternative fictions"—in contrast to Yeşilçam's "dominant fictions"—relating them to art house or auteur cinema, especially in depicting the loss of belief in "Oedipal normalization" and offering "overt instances of the portrayal of gendered and sexual identities which runs counter to the dominant fiction and its masculinist logic" (261). More and more, contemporary urban life becomes entrenched with transnational and diasporic experiences, and the cinema accordingly turns to international co-operations and multinational narratives.

Whereas Suner contradictorily claims that the films of Fatih Akın are not part of the New Turkish Cinema and yet includes him in her discussion of this cinema due to Akın's representation of Istanbul, other critics such as Deniz Bayrakdar list Akın in their corpus of New Turkish Cinema. Akın's films are variously said to be part of New European Cinema (Bayrakdar), Cinema of New Arrivals (Süalp), Kino der Normalität (Nicodemus), Accented Cinema (Naficy), Cinema du métissage (Seeßlen), Transnational Cinema (Göktürk), Post-Migrant Cinema in Transit (Lornsen), New German Transnational Cinema (Esen), Deutsch-Türkisches Kino der Gegenwart (El Hissy), 'New' New German Cinema (Fachinger), etc. With regard to German-Turkish film productions, it is safe to say that Fatih Akın has been the most important and most prominent director to date. Akın calls himself a "child of European Cinema" (qtd. in Bayrakdar, "Introduction" xviii) and indeed his fourth film, *Gegen die Wand* (*Head-On*) from 2004 was a major European success receiving amongst other prizes the Golden Bear award at the Berlin Film Festival and the "Best Film" and the "Audience Award" at the 2004 European Film Awards.[5] Part of why Akın is considered to be the essential force in shaping a *new*

---

5   In 2007, Akın's second part of his trilogy "Liebe, Tod und Teufel," *Auf der anderen Seite* (*The Edge of Heaven*), won the prize for best screenplay at the 60th Cannes Film Fes-

German-Turkish cinema is what Levent Soysal calls his "visual theory of migration" (109). By shifting the focus from a stereotypical victim-focused, Orientalized representation of the male migrant 'Gastarbeiter' and the veiled, submissive woman of former times, a cinema that therefore has been labeled "Suleikarism" (Lornsen 14), Akın's films are corrective to such conventions of visualizing immigrants (cf. Soysal 117) and instead promote an Otherness that has turned from showing German 'multikulti'-society to a transnational, globalized outlook (cf. Bayrakdar, "Turkish Cinema" 121). Besides featuring very resilient and self-assertive women, far from any "Suleika"-stereotype, Akın's male protagonists are equally very different from the standard Turkish male macho. They are often at a loss, struggling with their diasporic existence, showing a rather fluid subjectivity at odds with traditional gender norms, are unsure of their male prowess (such as the 'hero,' Nejat, of *Auf der anderen Seite*), and are often depressive if not outright suicidal, as is the case with the protagonist Cahit in *Gegen die Wand*.

Already the title signifies the protagonist's crisis of masculinity. The film's opening scene shows Cahit in his menial job, a drunkard being repeatedly and unrightfully cursed as "bum and fag," epithets that he later also uses, adding Kanake, to ironically belittle himself. Only a few minutes into the film, Cahit drives full-force into a wall, thus providing the literal meaning of the film's title, *Gegen die Wand*. However, he survives and while in psychiatric treatment, Cahit meets equally suicidal Sibel who asks him to marry her as a means of escaping her traditional Turkish family. He agrees, and although their marriage is a contract allowing the pursuit of one's own pleasures, which includes sleeping with whomever one wants, Cahit starts his metamorphosis from an un-stable existence that lacks a center into a caring partner. This growing into the role of husband, and thus into a heteronormative masculinization, however, entails an increasing violent streak and possessive jealousy, which leads to an attack on one of Sibel's one-night stands who then dies. Cahit's ensuing imprisonment ends the first part, located in Hamburg. The film then focuses on Sibel's move to Istanbul. This is an interesting element in terms of sex and gender performance, since I see Sibel's immediate reaction to Cahit's imprisonment as a transitory moment of female masculinity. She discards all elements of overt femininity such as long hair and short skirts, and dresses similarly to Cahit's street style. She starts to roam the city and bars like Cahit

---

tival and was awarded the first edition of the LUX prize for European cinema by the European Parliament. The trilogy's final part, *The Cut*, was released in 2014.

did, drinks, takes drugs, picks fights, and dances until she falls unconscious (see fig. 7.6 and 7.7). These scenes have been heavily criticized for their misogyny and depiction of Turkish machismo, but I think that her male masquerade rather serves to act out mourning and anger. Cahit, on the other hand, towards the end of the film after his release, tracks her down and asks her to go with him to Mersin, his birthplace on the Mediterranean coast of southern Turkey. Sibel, who by now has a new partner and a daughter, at first agrees to join him, but then does not show up at the appointed time of departure. So Cahit, much like Mehmet in *Güneşe Yolculuk*, travels alone towards his new/old home, which is the film's final image.

fig. 7.6 Gegen die Wand. Sibel drinking
fig. 7.7 Gegen die Wand. Sibel fighting

Gegen die Wand has been called a melodrama (cf. Lornsen 15, Eren 181, Göktürk 216), and even though it has comic moments, I would agree. The humorous scenes probably stem from Akın's original plan to write a romantic comedy in the style of Peter Weir's *Green Card*. However, the first draft of the script coincided with the terrorist suicide attacks of 9/11, and Akın had too many "angry thoughts," as he claims, that entered the plot to sustain the plan of a comedy (cf. Lornsen 26). The surviving scenes of comedy are mostly rooted in transcultural moments of linguistic and heteronormative failure, due to Cahit's rusty Turkish, but also his deadpan sense of humor, for example when he counters Sibel's effort in cutting off his long, unruly hair and thus 'beautifying' but also taming him with the rhetorical question: "Willste aus'm Bauer 'n Modell machen?" ("D'you wanna turn a farmer into a model?").

The film features two interesting mirror moments concerning precarious masculinities. The first was mentioned already: Sibel's male masquerade that almost gets her killed. The second relates to Cahit's performing maleness as an ethnicized variant of what Peter Lehman has called the spectacle of the melodramatic penis. Mainly focusing on American films, Lehman considers "one of the most significant developments in the representation of the penis" in recent years the melodramatic penis as a third category besides "the phallic spectacle" and "its pitiable and/or comic collapse" (235). One of the problems that Lehman mentions is that the "privileged signifier of the phallus" (236) retains its awe and mystique best when the penis remains hidden: "The melodrama surrounding the representation of the penis paradoxically cries out to reaffirm the spectacular importance of the penis even as the very assault on the taboo seeks to dislodge that importance" (252). This melodramatic paradox basically continues "to assert that showing the penis must be of some special, if bizarre, significance. The one thing a penis cannot be is simply a penis" (255). Cahit's physical representation shares many traits of such a paradoxical melodramatic penis. On the one hand, his marriage to and ensuing love for Sibel triggers a process of masculinization leading to jealousy and manslaughter, his formerly deviant masculinity as loser turns into a dominant hegemonic masculinity, and a very stereotypical Turkish masculinity above all. And yet, the continued depiction of his vulnerable body, repeated shots of his bare behind and, indeed, his penis, mark him as a feminized object to be gazed at and pitied (see fig. 7.8). His hopeless love, of course, adds to this structurally feminized position, marking the precariousness of his masculinity.

fig. 7.8 *Gegen die Wand*. Cahit naked

While the film in general paints a stereotypically negative portrait of Turkish masculinity—especially through Sibel's father and brothers—, Cahit's volatile masculinity stands out in stark contrast. Leal and Rossade, however, take this to be a limited existence that Cahit in the end leaves behind with his return to Turkey, which releases him "from the negatively charged conception of masculinity" (72). Viewed this way, Cahit's troubled hyphenated Turkish-German masculinity gives way to a notion "that Turkey might in fact offer an alternative and potentially less fraught context in which to define new masculine identities" (72). I agree that *Gegen die Wand* is "resolutely heterosexual," at times even manifestly homophobic, thus relegating alternative sexualities to the margins and revealing "how threatening these can be to those constructions of heterosexual masculinity potentially destabilized by the experience of social exclusion" (81). But I also believe Cahit's portrayal as described above undercuts this heteronormative logic in a way that differs from Leal and Rossade's reading. Moreover, the casting of Cahit with actor Birol Ünel adds to a subversion of Turkish(-German) masculinist cliches. Ünel's star *persona* has been described as eccentric and has also been compared to that of Klaus Kinski, which in turn highlights Ünel's own ethnic masculinity: "The comparison to the sexualized, eccentric, ill-tempered star [Kinski] certainly gave Ünel an edge, connecting him to an actor who represents New German Cinema and German Culture with an ethnically ambivalent body, since Kinski had a Polish father" (Gueneli 145). As Gueneli points out, Ünel's repeated filmic appearances that link him to "high alcohol consumption, a lower-class milieu [and] a complex sexuality tied to ethnic masculinity" (146) is further complicated in *Gegen die Wand* through explicit nudity, which at first lacks eroticism but becomes increasingly sexualized, albeit in an ethnically romanticized way. This romanticization in turn highlights Akın's move from a narrower Turkish-German to a broader transnational filmic agenda. As Deniz Göktürk asserts, the multilocal affiliations and frequent travels across borders as well as the interchangeable use of German, Turkish and English puts *Gegen die Wand* within "a new trend in European cinema, namely a shift of some transnational directors out of the niche of 'exilic' or 'diasporic' cinema, aptly described by Hamid Naficy as an 'accented cinema,' into mainstream popular cinema or the international festival circuit" (216).[6] Several critics especially stress Akın's mix of Turkish,

---

6   For an application of Naficy's "accented cinema" in *Gegen die Wand* see Esen, who claims that "the film utilizes both closed and open forms, the epistolary form, multilinguality, and the notion of 'journey' that transforms lost and drifting characters who are looking to kill themselves in the beginning of the film to open and responsible characters in the end: [...] on a journey of being and becoming" (153).

German, and American cinematic traditions and genres that characterize his transnational move, above all his reliance on American melodrama (Douglas Sirk), the New Turkish Cinema, the New German Cinema (Rainer Werner Fassbinder), the new German comedy of the 1990s, and MTV's video-clip style, as well as his fascination with the Italo-American gangster film (Martin Scorsese, John Cassavetes) and the postmodern film noir, with Cahit as a European version of John Travolta's character in *Pulp Fiction* (cf. Eren 181, Fachinger 254, Göktürk 221, Lornsen 20).

Kutluğ Ataman's *Lola + Bilidikid* (1999) is yet another prominent film that strives towards a transnational perspective, partly by mixing cinematic genres such as the female-identified melodrama and the 'male' action thriller. It is also a film which focuses on the penis in a very literal manner, namely as the "little problem" that needs to be taken care of, i.e. by having a male-to-female sex reassignment surgery, thus "queerly challenging the audience's expectations of genre conformity" (Clark 563). In contrast to Akın's oeuvre, Ataman's film indicates another crucial moment in the development of a New Turkish Cinema relocated in Germany but with numerous international links. Whereas Rob Burns claims that the recent Turkish-German cinema, although aiming to be transnational, is a "new male-oriented cinema" which marginalizes women (142, qtd. in Fincham 60), both Sibel in *Gegen die Wand* as well as Lola and the other transgender characters in Ataman's film transcend this limited perspective. Other critics, like Christopher Treiblmayr, while acknowledging the U.S.-American commercial and generic influence, nevertheless stress the 'Germanness' of *Lola* and include the film in the corpus of the post-Fassbinder "Junger Deutscher Film" alongside Sönke Wortmann or Tom Tykwer (cf. 192). Certainly, when viewed from this angle, Ataman's film gestures toward "the difficulty of articulating what German national cinema has come to mean in the new millennium" (Gemünden 181, qtd. in Frackman).

In contrast to Akın, Turkish-born Ataman is not German-Turkish, in that he has no binational background. His academic training at the University of California, Los Angeles, and his Berlin film, however, transport him into a transnational field of production and reception. Already his film's title suggests its intertextuality, by mixing the allusion to the legendary American Western hero Billy the Kid with references to German female heroines such as Marlene Dietrich as Lola in Josef von Sternberg's *Der blaue Engel* (1930) and Rainer Werner Fassbinder's *Lola* (1981). What is most impressive, however, is the fact that all this is played out against the backdrop of what has been called "transness" as a "moment of in-betweenness," simultaneously representing the emergence of a new category of sexual and cultural liminality, and revealing "the instability of all categories" (Clark 556). This playing out of gender and ethnicity via "transed" sexualities and, thus, national "transness," links *Lola* to yet another American filmic genre: the New Queer Cinema. Ataman, although claiming to be the only gay Turkish director who is out of the closet (cf. Treiblmayr),[7] is actually part of a small but growing number of directors, who tackle Turkish gay sexuality, either from an exiled point of view, such as Ferzan Özpetek, most famously in his Italian-Turkish-Spanish coproduction *Hamam: Turkish Bath* (1997),[8] or from a foreigner's perspective, such as Guy Lee Thys in his Belgian film *Mixed Kebab* (2012). What these "queer diasporic" films (Williams 197, 213) all have in common are depictions of parallel societies, i.e. gay Turkish lives as being marginal within an already marginalized minority of Turkish immigrants.

Ataman's film came out at the same time as the much more famous Tom Tykwer Berlin film *Lola rennt* (1998), as yet another cinematic link in the ever-growing "Lola culture" (Kılıçbay 113). In it, the redhead Lola also 'runs' through Berlin's streets, but here she is a performer on stage, part of a transvestite group called "Die Gastarbeiterinnen" (see fig. 7.9). Off-stage and like her co-performers forced to wear male clothes in Turkish Kreuzberg, she 'runs' from her Turkish-German cultural heritage as much as from her macho lover who wants to turn Lola into a 'good' Turkish wife and *Hausfrau*, which is, of course, where the penis comes into play (see fig. 7.10). In order to have this wish fulfilled, i.e. to live with Bili as 'normal' husband and wife in Turkey, Lola would have to get rid of the "little problem," as her lover calls the allegedly superfluous mark of manhood: "Wir werden verheiratet sein. So wie diese deutschen Schwuchteln können wir nicht zusammenleben. [...] Aber da gibt es noch ein kleines Problem. [...] Wenns sein muss, schneid ich dir den Schwanz ab." ("We will be married. We can't be together like those German fags. [...] But there still is a little problem. [...] I'll cut off your dick if I have to.")

---

7   As Karin Hamm-Ehsani points out, homosexuality is still largely a social taboo in Turkey, and even within the German-Turkish community, openly queer people are mostly rejected. While the film was successful internationally, the reaction in Turkey was so fiercely negative that Ataman faced death threats when the film premiered, which partly led to the director's decision to flee Turkey for London (cf. Hamm-Ehsani 371, 378; Smith 54).

8   For a discussion of Özpetek's *Hamam* see chapter 2.

fig. 7.9 Lola + Bilidikid. "Die Gastarbeiterinnen"
fig. 7.10 Lola + Bilidikid. Bili und Lola

While Cahit in Akın's film metamorphoses into an ambivalent specimen of Turkish heteronormative manhood, Bili in Ataman's film is equally ambivalent in his Turkish machismo, which is based on a structurally internalized homophobia, claiming: "Ein Mann ist ein Mann and ein Loch ist ein Loch. Sei niemals ein Loch." ("A man is a man, and a hole is a hole. Never be a hole.") Bili's masculinity, however, is precarious in various ways. He works as a hustler, and yet his troubled homosexual desire is at odds with his acculturated heterosexism, and his heroic, yet diminutive and juvenile name "Bilidikid" points towards a performed, 'fake' hypermasculine identity, a "Macho-Drag" (El Hissy 249-250). Lola resents and resists relinquishing her penis to become Bili's "w/hole woman" (Kılıçbay 107), a decision that she comments on in a dystopic tale which not only paints a bleak picture of Bili and an imagined penis-less Lola in Turkey, but foreshadows her own violent death shortly after: "Warum glaubst du hat Bili Lola verlassen? Weil die Frau, die er geheiratet hat, nicht mehr der Mann war, in den er sich verliebt hatte." ("Why do you think, Bili left Lola? Because the woman he married was not the man he fell in love with anymore.") Towards the conclusion, in a spectacular showdown, Bili, before getting killed himself, castrates, not Lola (who is dead by then), but Lola's presumed murderer, a Neo-Nazi. As it turns out, Lola was not a victim of hate crime but of family honor instead, since it was Lola's older brother who sexually abused and later killed her. Lola's younger brother, who masquerades as his dead brother, and thus acts as yet another Lola running through Berlin's streets, eventually solves the crime and exposes his abusive older brother as a homophobic killer acting in the name of family honor. The film's title heroes are ultimately both dead, perhaps because they represent failed attempts in dealing with a multifarious "transness." Nevertheless, there are other survivors claiming a queer utopic space of precarious masculinity, above all Kalipso, one of the "Gastarbeiterinnen," who is the only character in the film to decide to make the transition from performing transgender on stage to also being transgender off stage. Kalypso's chosen name refers to a sea nymph in Greek mythology that literally means "I will conceal," which is very appropriate since "she is portrayed as a drag queen who finally breaks free after years of concealing her orientation in her daily life" (Kılıçbay 108). In a humorously campy epilogue, the film's last moments and words are given to Kalypso, who, while triumphantly riding in a taxi towards "the glorious queered Berlin 'Siegessäule'" (Hamm-Ehsani 379), calls out in Turkish: "I am a woman with balls." In the end, she has surpassed the melodrama of the penis, celebrating a precarious trans identity that has moved beyond dichotomous national and sexual borders.

It is with such films that European cinema both stays true to its own diverse national traditions and moves into a transnational sphere of a supranational cinema. While many films of the New Turkish Cinema such as *Güneşe Yolculuk* and *Kurtlar Vadisi—Irak* incorporate multiethnic perspectives, migratory narratives, and transnational, especially American generic modes, they still highlight primarily national issues. In contrast, films like those of Akın and Ataman radically break open such national framings. Especially through depictions of fractured, destabilized, and liminal masculine identities, these films engage in a transnational agenda of negotiating multiple ethnic and gendered cinematic representations across national borders.

Works Cited

Aslan, Savaş. "Venus in Furs, Turks in Purse: Masochism in the New Cinema of Turkey." *Cinema and Politics: Turkish Cinema and the New Europe*. Ed. Deniz Bayrakdar. Newcastle: Cambridge Scholars, 2009. 258-267.

Atam, Zahit. "Critical Thoughts on the New Turkish Cinema." *Cinema and Politics: Turkish Cinema and the New Europe*. Ed. Deniz Bayrakdar. Newcastle: Cambridge Scholars, 2009. 202-220.

Bayrakdar, Deniz. "Introduction. 'Son of Turks' Claim: 'I'm a Child of European Cinema." *Cinema and Politics: Turkish Cinema and the New Europe*. Ed. Deniz Bayrakdar. Newcastle: Cambridge Scholars, 2009. xvii-xxxii.

———. "Turkish Cinema and the New Europe: *At the Edge of Heaven*." *Cinema and Politics: Turkish Cinema and the New Europe*. Ed. Deniz Bayrakdar. Newcastle: Cambridge Scholars, 2009. 118-129.

Boisseau, Tracey Jean. "Kiss-Kiss Bang-Bang Nation: Hollywood and the En-Gendering of Modernity in the Youth of the Early Turkish Republic." *The Transnational Turn in American Studies: Turkey and the United States*. Eds. Tanfer Emin Tunc and Bahar Gursel. Berlin et al.: Peter Lang, 2012. 169-189.

Burns, Rob. "Turkish-German Cinema: From Cultural Resistance to Transnational Cinema?" *German Cinema Since Unification*. Ed. David Clarke. New York: Continuum, 2006. 127-149.

Clark, Christopher. "Transculturation, *Transe* Sexuality, and Turkish Germany: Kutluğ Ataman's *Lola und Bilidikid*." *German Life and Letters* 59.4 (2006): 555-572.

El Hissy, Maha. *Getürkte Türken: Karnevalske Stilmittel im Theater, Kabarett und Film deutsch-türkischer Künstlerinnen und Künstler*. Bielefeld: transcript, 2012.

Eren, Mine. "Cosmopolitan Filmmaking: Fatih Akın's *In July* and *Head-On*." *Turkish German Cinema in the New Millennium: Sites, Sounds, and Screens*. Eds. Sabine Hake and Barbara Mennel. New York: Berghahn, 2012. 175-185.

Esen, Adile. "Exoticism, the 'Orient' and the Fetish in the 'New' German Transnational Cinema: Fatih Akın's Experimentation on Cities and Genders in *Gegen die Wand*." *From Weimar to Christiana: German and Scandinavian Studies in Context*. Eds. Florence Feiereisen and Kyle Frackman. Newcastle: Cambridge Scholars, 2007. 153-168.

Fachinger, Petra. "A New Kind of Creative Energy: Yadé Kara's *Selam Berlin* and Fatih Akın's *Kurz und schmerzlos* and *Gegen die Wand*." *German Life and Letters* 60.2 (2007): 245-260.

Fincham, Victoria. "Violence, Sexuality and the Family: Identity 'Within and Beyond Turkish-German Parameters' in Fatih Akın's *Gegen die Wand*, Kutluğ Ataman's *Lola + Bilidikid* and Anno Saul's *Kebab Connection*." *GFL: German as Foreign Language* 1 (2008): 40-72.

Frackman, Kyle. "The Curious Case of the Turkish Drag Queen: Film and Social Justice Education in Advanced German." *Neues Curriculum: Journal for Best Practices in Higher Education German Studies* (August 2012). Web. 7 Dec. 2014. <http://www.neues-curriculum.org/papers/Frackman2012.pdf>

Gardels, Nathan and Mike Medavoy. *American Idol after Iraq: Competing for Hearts and Minds in the Global Media Age*. New York: Wiley-Blackwell, 2009.

Gegen die Wand. Dir. Fatih Akın. Perf. Birol Ünel and Sibel Kekilli. Arte, Bavaria Film International, Corazon International, NDR, Panfilm, Wüste Filmproduktion, 2004.

Gemünden, Gerd. "Hollywood in Altona: Minority Cinema and the Transnational Imagination." *German Pop Culture*. Ed. Agnes Mueller. Michigan: U of Michigan P, 2004. 180-190.

Göktürk, Deniz. "Sound Bridges: Transnational Mobility as Ironic Melodrama." *European Cinema in Motion: Migrant and Diasporic Film in Contemporary Europe*. Eds. Daniela Berghahn and Claudia Sternberg. Houndmills: Palgrave Macmillan, 2010. 215-234.

Gueneli, Berna. "Mehmet Kurtuluş and Birol Ünel: Sexualized Masculinities, Normalized Ethnicities." *Turkish German Cinema in the New Millenium: Sites, Sounds, and Screens*. Eds. Sabine Hake and Barbara Mennel. New York: Berghahn, 2012. 136-148.

Güneşe Yolculuk. Dir. Yesim Ustaoğlu. Perf. Nazmi Kırık, Newroz Baz, and Mizgin Kapazan. Istisnai Filmier ve Reklamlar, Medias Res Filmproduktion, The Film Company, 1999.

Hamm-Ehsani, Karin. "Intersections. Issues of National, Ethnic, and Sexual Identity in Kutluğ Ataman's Berlin Film *Lola and Bilidikid*." *Seminar: A Journal of Germanic Studies* 44.3 (2008): 366-381.

Kaftan, Eylem. "Allegorical Failure in *Sürü* (The Herd) and *Yol* (The Way)." *Cinema and Politics: Turkish Cinema and the New Europe*. Ed. Deniz Bayrakdar. Newcastle: Cambridge Scholars, 2009. 154-162.

Kılıçbay, Barış. "Impossible Crossings: Gender Melancholy in *Lola + Bilidikid* and *Auslandstournee*." *New Cinemas: Journal of Contemporary Film* 4.2 (2006): 105-115.

Kurtlar Vadisi—Irak. Dir. Serdar Akar. Perf. Necati Şaşmaz, Billy Zane, and Ghassan Massoud. Pana Film, 2006.

Leal, Joanne and Klaus-Dieter Rossade. "Negotiating Gender, Sexuality and Ethnicity in Fatih Akın's and Thomas Arslan's Urban Spaces." *GFL: German as Foreign Language* 3 (2008): 59-87.

Lehman, Peter. *Running Scared: Masculinity and the Representation of the Male Body*. New Ed. Detroit: Wayne State UP, 2007.

Lola + Bilidikid. Dir. Kutluğ Ataman. Perf. Gandi Mukli, Baki Davrak, and Erdal Yıldız. Boje Buck Produktion, WDR, Zero Film GmbH, 1999.

Lornsen, Karin. "Where Have all the Guest Workers Gone? Transcultural Role-Play and Performative Identities in Fatih Akın's *Gegen die Wand* (2004)." *Finding the Foreign*. Eds. Robert Schechtman and Suin Roberts. Newcastle: Cambridge Scholars, 2007. 13-30.

Naficy, Hamid. *An Accented Cinema: Exilic and Diasporic Filmmaking*. Princeton: Princeton UP, 2001.

Nicodemus, Katja. "Ankunft in der Wirklichkeit." *Die Zeit*, 19 Feb. 2004. Web, 13 Nov. 2014. <http://www.zeit.de/2004/09/Berlinale-Abschluss>

Özkaracalar, Kaya. "Representations of Imperialism in Turkish Cinema Within a Pendulum of Nationalism and Anti-Emperialism [sic]." *Cinema and Politics: Turkish Cinema and the New Europe*. Ed. Deniz Bayrakdar. Newcastle: Cambridge Scholars, 2009. 164-171.

Poole, Ralph J. "Unsichtbarer Kurde und schwarzer Türke: *Güneşe Yolculuk (Reise zur Sonne)* und das neue türkisch-europäische Kino." *Werkstatt Geschichte* 14.40 (2005): 103-114.

———. "Foltern, Schänden und Entehren: Das mediale Spektakel des gefangenen Mannes." *Extreme Erfahrungen: Grenzen des Erlebens und der Darstellung*. Eds. Anja Tippner and Christopher F. Laferl. Berlin: Kadmos, 2017. 139-166.

Şahin, Haluk. „Midnight Express 20 Years Later: A Turkish Nightmare." Web. 27 Nov 2021. <https://turcoman.net/turk-world-articles/contents-1/midnight-express/>

Sedgwick, Eve Kosofsky. *Between Men: English Literature and Male Homosocial Desire*. New York: Columbia UP, 1985.

Seeßlen, Georg. "Das Kino der doppelten Kulturen / Le Cinema du metissage / The Cinema of inbetween." *epd Film* 12 (2000): 22-29.

Smith, Paul Julian. "*Lola + Bilidikid*." *Sight & Sound* 10.4 (2000): 53-54.

Soysal, Levent. "Visual Travels to Other Places: Politics of Migration in Reel." *Cinema and Politics: Turkish Cinema and the New Europe*. Ed. Deniz Bayrakdar. Newcastle: Cambridge Scholars, 2009. 108-117.

Stokes, Martin. *The Arabesk Debate: Music and Musicians in Modern Turkey*. Oxford: Clarendon, 1992.

Süalp, Zeynep Tül Akbal. "The Glorified Lumpen 'Nothingness' Versus Night Navigations." *Cinema and Politics: Turkish Cinema and the New Europe*. Ed. Deniz Bayrakdar. Newcastle: Cambridge Scholars, 2009. 221-231.

Suner, Asuman. *New Turkish Cinema: Belonging, Identity and Memory*. London: I. B. Tauris, 2010.

Treiblmayr, Christopher. "'Ein Mann ist ein Mann, und ein Loch ist ein Loch:' Männlichkeit, Homosexualität und Migration in Kutluğ Atamans *Lola und Bilidikid* (Deutschland 1998)." *Identitäten in Bewegung: Migration im Film*. Eds. Bettina Dennerlein and Elke Frietsch. Bielefeld: transcript, 2011. 191-225.

Williams, James S. "Queering the Diaspora." *European Cinema in Motion: Migrant and Diasporic Film in Contemporary Europe*. Eds. Daniela Berghahn and Claudia Sternberg. Houndmills: Palgrave Macmillan, 2010/2014. 196-214.

Yol. Dir. Yılmaz Güney and Şerif Gören. Perf. Tank Akan, Halil Ergün, Şerif Sezer, Meral Orhonsay. Güney Film, Cactus Film, Antenne 2, SRG, 1982.

8. Arabesk: Nomadic Tales, Oriental Beats, and Hybrid Looks

The role of a particular musical style within a specific cultural setting may well attract cultural anthropologists, ethnomusicologists, sociologists or—as in my case—a literary scholar with leanings toward popular culture. Coming from diverse disciplines and employing different analytical tools, what they/we all share is the effort to inquire how musics as forms of performance are intermingled and preoccupied with issues of nationalism, ethnicity, transculturation and hybridity, or as David Coplan puts it "the complex, indeterminate relationships between cultured sound-making and cultural sense-making in specific social contexts" (592). With emerging modern nation states, the status of music was likely to be split between political alignment and cultural tradition, with certain musical styles being favored over others. But through various developments of the media, a dissemination and dispersion of neglected or forgotten musics in many nation states has led to a contemporary scene with a wide range of musical styles and musical languages representing multitudinous ethnic and other identities within and at times in opposition to official nationalist statutes. Turkey is such a nation state that is "quite understandably nervous about musical appropriations and expressions used to foreground or fashion a sub-national 'ethnic'—as opposed to cultural—identity" (Coplan 594). Music has played a crucial role in the self-definition of the Turkish nation state as well as in the self-fashioning of various groups both of which have employed music as tuning the state politics and performing (resisting) traditions.

"Arabesk" in particular is a musical style that is closely connected to Turkey's recent national and cultural history. Besides its immense and at times subversive power, which is mostly at odds with the state-regulated efforts to forge a common national identity, Arabesk also pays tribute to a questioning of how to situate an overwhelmingly popular and socially pervasive music genre within the discourse of globalized pop music. After first taking a look at the roots, emergence and development of Arabesk music, I will then discuss how the ambiguous polysemic body politics of Arabesk reflect *and* subvert the basically inflexible dichotomous gender structure—still—reigning in Turkey. This paradox of compliance and transgression that has led to an ever-increasing dissolution and dissemination of the music genre Arabesk will then be regarded *vis-a-vis* the needs of a global market of pop music for steadily increasing, yet clearly defined target audiences. My argument here will be that as much as Turkish national politics in general tries to uphold its traditional gender structure even through the means of regulating popular music, the Arabesk performers themselves are much more versatile players within the pop-cultural scenario of creating hybrid and multifaceted *personas* like nostalgic macho Tatlıses, flamboyant transsexual Bülent Ersoy, or Orientalized sex icon Tarkan.

Arabesk's Impurity: From Anatolia to Istanbul

The phenomenon of Arabesk is situated at the crossroads of two notable trends in Popular Music Studies described by Martin Cloonan as on the one hand works "which have tried to document the 'local' music scene, and on the other hand, accounts of processes of globalization." Cloonan, however, goes on to claim that both trends tend to downplay "the continually important role of the National-State" (193). Arabesk culture is a truly urban phenomenon paying tribute to substantial social and political transformations of Turkey. Today, the label is used as broadly as to denote not only a musical genre, but a film genre, a novel genre—like the novels of Orhan Pamuk—as well as the cultural habitus and lifestyle of its fans.

This cultural practice emerged on the fringes of Istanbul during the 1950s and '60s, where the traditional habits of immigrants from predominantly impoverished southeast Anatolian—mostly Kurdish—rural areas blended with contemporized urban life-styles. As music ethnologist Martin Stokes puts it, many of the Arabesk singers "are migrants from a remote and barbarized Turkish 'orient,' the Arab speaking and Kurdish regions of south east Anatolia, who occupy the urban spaces between squatter town and metropolitan centers" ("Islam" 213). This mass-migration peaked in the 1970s but is still continuing. Recent attempts in tearing down those ghetto-like districts notwithstanding—making way for new villa-type, guarded residential areas of an emerging 'yuppie' upper class and leaving literary millions of people homeless as a consequence—, the migrant influx has not only drastically changed the face of Istanbul's ever-growing cityscape with the bulk of those migrants accumulating in the *gecekondular* (squatter towns, also aptly called Arabesk districts).

Moreover and from an architectural perspective, the development of those squatter districts in large cities like Ankara and Izmir, but especially Istanbul also attests to the changing attitudes of a rapidly transforming society. Speaking of the "predicament of modern architecture in Turkey," Sibel Bozdoğan claims that today's dilemma of a dissociate urban landscape stems from Turkey's profoundly ambivalent Kemalist aspiration "to be Western in spite of the West:"

> Turkish architectural culture of the 1930s adopted the formal and scientific precepts of Western modernism and yet posited itself as an anti-imperialist, anti-Orientalist, and anticolonialist expression of independence, identity, and subjecthood by a nation hitherto presented only by the Orientalist cultural paradigms of the West. (137)

The concept of Kemalism, therefore, was hybrid from the very start. Inaugurated by Turkey as it became a republic in the 1920s through its founding father Kemal Atatürk, Kemalism has been trying to consolidate remnants of urban Ottoman culture like 'pure' Turkish folk *(balk)* music and modern Westernized, i.e. reformed notions of Turkish culture. Within this already precarious nationalist model, Arabesk's foreignness and alienness—its 'Arabic' style[1]—clearly could not be assimilated and therefore posed a threat to the politics of the Turkish nation state. Alev Çınar remarks that this classing strategy of constituting the "provincial other" as "the alien infesting the city" has created personifying depictions of Istanbul as a beleaguered place on display suffering from corruption, alienation, and degeneration, as being "open to penetration and destruction, a place that is defenseless in the face of the modernizing and Westernizing influences of the secular state" (386).

The musical and urban history of Arabesk gives evidence that what has started as a fiercely contested and 'dissociated' life style of marginalized rural migrants has moved to the center of public—and political—appreciation across class, age, and ethnicity. Even balanced voices such as Bozdoğan's who

---

[1] Etymologically, the adjective "arabesk" or "arabesque" derives from the "French, from Italian *arabesco* Arabian in fashion, from *arabo* Arab, from Latin *Arabus*" ("arabesque.").

try to take on "a less polemical and more fruitful approach" in order to "face the historical complexity and ambiguity of the project of modernity in architecture" seem at odds with more recent developments which embrace cultural diversity and aesthetic diversification:

> [I]n a potentially democratic impulse, educated elites became increasingly more aware of the multiplicity of taste cultures, and especially of popular culture as the manifestation of the struggle of marginalized peoples for cultural expression and self-representation. We all began learning to suppress our contempt for *geekondu* taste, *arabesk* music, *kebab* houses, intercity bus terminals, and cheap little mosques with aluminum domes, if we did not actually begin rather to like them, as we confronted our own ambivalent experiences of modernity. (148)

Gülsüm Baydar Nalbantoğlu more forcefully argues "that the cultural border between the city and the village, which architectural discourse has sharply delineated, is a fluid one" (193). Instead of holding on to the notion of the distinction between the modern Turkish city and its 'Other,' that is, rural Turkey, Nalbantoğlu takes up Michel de Certeau's proposal of "tactics" as calculated actions that de-privileged subjects cleverly use due to the lack of a proper locus. In this instance, rural migrants found ingenious—resisting—ways to utilize a land belonging to others and "thus lend a political dimension to every day practices" (de Certeau, qtd. in Nalbantoğlu 203). Nalbantoğlu claims that what those *gecekondu* squatters achieved was a display of survival tactics: "Rural immigrants assimilated, subverted, and mimicked" (206). Part of those spatial and architectural tactics were the actual practices of improvised houses that could easily be moved as well as an outlay of street networks that resembled a maze and were hard to control by legal forces from the outside, but easy to manage by its inhabitants from within. What city officials, who from the 1950s onwards aimed at installing an "international style" of architecture (Bozdoğan 140; Nalbantoğlu 207), continuously described as "ugly" and "unsightly," as "the city's garbage to be disposed of" and responsible for the "ruralization of cities" (qtd. in Nalbantoğlu 203, 208),[2] the maze-like urbanscape of the *gecekondu* mirrored the aesthetics of Arabesk arising from those very spaces. Like the Arabesk songs that mixed and merged different cultural

---

2   See Latife Tekin's novel *Berji Kristin: Tales from the Garbage Hills* (orig. 1984) for semi-autobiographical descriptions of the process of migration and settlement in Istanbul's *gecekondular*.

sources most of which belong to unofficial and unacknowledged musical languages, *gecekondu* settlers operated both within and through the city language they encountered overriding conventionalized borderlines.

Originally, the epithet Arabesk was coined by Turkish musicologists to describe what they believed to be a regressive musical genre that employs 'impure' Arabicized Turkish language and complex, chromatic melodies and harmonies, very different from the diatonic system of traditional Turkish folk music (Stokes, "Music" 29). Arabesk musical sources were decidedly not rural Anatolian, but Arabic dating back to mostly Egyptian popular music and films of the 1920s and '30s, especially the custom of belly-dancing music, called *raks sharki* (also spelled *raqs sharqi*). It paradoxically reached wide Turkish audiences in translations and imitations after the Turkish ban on such Egyptian musical art after 1948. Not only did the ban actually trigger an unwanted counter-effect by spurring the creation of a booming local industry through translating and imitating the originals. But through the need to alter the Egyptian sources to accommodate the Turkish censorship, this musical culture also took on specific Turkish social concerns in its song lyrics. Moreover, since these Egyptian compositions often also were augmented with a Western-style string section, "Western influences seeped into Turkish art music via Egypt" (Özbek 213) thus further complicating the effort to control musical production. Accordingly, one can say that it is paradoxically due to the state-controlled music industry—especially restrictions on radio and later television broadcasting—that Arabesk came into being.

Increasingly intermixing Egyptian film music with powerful dance rhythms, Arabic vocal and orchestral conventions, and later still Western rock, pop, and dance music, Arabesk continued to be vastly successful within the low-income working-class milieu *and* chastised as thoroughly alienated cultural artefact by Turkish officials as well as by the Kemalist bourgeois urban intelligentsia. At the same time, Arabesk's leaning towards a philosophy of fatalism also clashed with Turkish Islamic orthodoxy, where belief in fate still leaves persons the freedom of choice whereas the fatalism of Arabesk depicts images of subjects being utterly trapped by fate and society alike (Stokes, "Music" 29). Again, the *gecekondular* with their aura of misery due to hard economic conditions and social ostracizing are evidence of Arabesk's image of being 'the music of suffering.' Although poverty and alienation were rarely explicitly addressed as themes in the songs, they were alluded to through a feeling of dissatisfaction or, as Martin Stokes puts it, "'Arabesk without pain' would simply cease to be Arabesk" (Stokes, "Music" 30).

From Tatlıses's Nostalgic Anatolian Machismo to Emrah's Sexed-Up Hard Body

Arabesk singers like Orhan Gencebay, Ferdi Tayfur, or Ibrahim Tatlıses have acquired cult status. In contrast to Gencebay and Tayfur, however, who have refused to have their work labeled as Arabesk because of its 'unclean' and 'Arabic' implications, Tatlıses boldly embraces this very label (Özbek 222). For many, especially Turkish expatriates living abroad, Tatlıses—a chosen name which means "sweet voice"—has become the symbol of Arabesk. With Arabesk's endless variations of the story of a poor peasant boy, who leaves his homestead to seek fortune and success far away, Tatlıses's own story reads exactly like one of his songs, since for 40 years now he is probably the most successful singer in Turkey. Coming from a bitterly poor Anatolian family and after child laboring and roaming the country as menial worker, he succeeded in establishing himself as one of the leading Arabesk singers ever with his first hit song and album "Ayağında Kundura" (1977), a nomadic tale reflecting his own experience of longing and suffering—here depicted as the yearning for a lost "sweetheart" who has literally moved ("shoes are on her feet") beyond his grasp:

Ayağında kundura	Shoes are on her feet
Yar gelir dura dura	And my sweetheart comes stopping from time to time
Yar gelir dura dura	And my sweetheart comes stopping from time to time
Ölürem ben ölürem vay	I die (for her) I die

(Tatlıses, "Ayağında Kundura". For the translation see <www.allthelyrics.com>.)

An important aspect of his success is the fact that he never made a secret of his mixed Arabic-Kurdish origins; on the contrary, in his songs he cultivated a noticeable Eastern Anatolian Turkish accent spoken by many Kurds at a time when Kurdish language was prohibited in schools and media. This added, naturally, to the nostalgic aura surrounding the performer as did his emphasis on a specific brand of masculinity, which as Özbek claims, "resulted in much criticism and in his ultimately being branded a vulgar *maganda*" (223). While on the one hand, Arabesk lyrics leaned towards characteristics like passivity and depression that commonly may be held as rather feminine traits, the unambiguously hyper-masculine *maganda* stereotype on the other hand originally refers to a cartoon figure, but entered "popular vocabulary to describe and denigrate arabesk aficionados as vulgar, sexist, and uneducated" (Özbek 222). Tatlıses, being well aware of that public branding, self-assertively parodied himself as a *maganda* as well as making fun of his critics by doing so. At the same time, the explicit identification with Arabesk culture reconfirmed his social ties to "his own people."

Tatlıses in the course of his career, however, has moved from clearly discernible Arabesk songs to more mainstream pop-oriented arrangements like his version of the traditional song "Ağrı Dağı (Cano Cano)" from the album *Bulamadım* (*I Couldn't Find*) of 2007, which many artists, including Tarkan,[3] have covered:

Ağrı dağın eteğinde	At the foot of Ararat
Uçan güvercin olsam	I wish I was a flying pigeon
Türkü olsam dillerde	Wish I was a folk song on mouths
Diyar diyar dolansam	Wish I wandered from land to land
Başımdaki sevdayı	The love on my head
Karlı dağlara mı yansam	Shall I complain on snowy mountains
Bu bendeki aşk değil cano cano	This I have is not love dear
Söyle bana nere gidem	Tell me where I shall go

(Tatlıses, "Ağrı Dağı [Cano Cano]". For the translation see <www.allthelyrics.com>.)

While in general Arabesk singers like Tatlıses enact a style of masculinity within a changing urban landscape that harks back to older rural mores like "the virtues of loyalty, unselfishness, and moral rectitude, but with a bitter undertone of perpetual betrayal and disappointment" (Kandiyoti, "Gendering the Modern" 124), he gradually changed his clothing fashion discarding the conservative suit-and-tie outfit for a leisure look of sunglasses, silver necklace, unbuttoned shirt, and leather jacket, albeit never relinquishing the

---

3 See Tarkan's video <www.youtube.com/watch?v=HpGh7ypBGto> (accessed 13 December 2021).

trademark Islamic 'Turkish' moustache.[4] What's more, Tatlıses also changed musical arrangements and even added techno-remixes on his albums, which is significant since in pop music remixes mark the victory of electronic sound criteria over melody and harmony as major distinctive criteria (Gebesmair 54-55).

Tatlıses's altered, rejuvenated look gives way to a musical mainstreaming taken on by a younger generation of Arabesk performers like Emrah, who in their musical and visual style have increasingly joined forces with Tarkan to mix Arabesk with pop and rock. They do so, however, with different means, especially with regard to their visual presentation. Emrah, like Tatlıses of Kurdish origins and bringing a specific regionalism—that of southeastern Turkey—to Istanbul, represents a revamped model of Arabesk, which no longer is connected to the 'trash' style of the squatter towns. He is most outspoken in his presenting—unlike Tatlıses—a strongly sexualized body and herewith, I would argue, marks a link with Western images of male rock singers that is also reflected in his music. It is striking that in his albums he even highlights his well-defined, muscular body by including headless body-only shots, a style at odds with the usual face-centered presentation of Arabesk singers.

Emrah's still somewhat softened masculine representation with ethno-necklace and abstract-ornament shirt stitching on his album, *Kusursuzsun (You are Without Blemish)* of 2004 gives way to an ultra-masculine body-image on his later album *Adın Ne Senin (What's Your Name)* of 2006. Unshaved with goatee and longer, wilder hair, and strictly clad in either plain unadorned white tank top or shirt: this is a body even more hardened and built-up, as his self-indulging pics reflect that show him working out and proudly sweating in a fitness studio. His fans, nevertheless, have not accepted this new image of sexed up and Westernized Arabesk performer as his plummeting album sales prove.[5] All in all, Emrah's position within the array of Arabesk stylizations

---

4   Mark the interesting retro-style of the album cover *Metamorfoz* (2007), where Tarkan for the first time dons formal clothing with suit and tie, whereas Tatlıses album *Neden* (2008) shows him in loose shirt and jeans.

5   This trend towards a more Westernized rock and pop style continued with his album *Dön* (2007), and his 2008 album *Yelpaze* even experimented with R&B, resulting in the lowest sale figures of any of his albums. Emrah could reverse this downward trend with the 2011 album *Terzinin Oğlu* by returning to his Arabesk roots with a visually matured look.

illustrates the marked shift of this most popular musical genre in Turkey towards hybridization and crossover. Emrah's sexed-up masculine hard body performance as well as the hard beats of his songs have moved much closer to Western notions of rock and thus away from the melodramatic poetics of standard Arabesk.

Flamboyant Transgression? Bülent Ersoy

The modification in the visual stylizing of Arabesk stars from Tatlıses to Emrah raises the larger question of the link between music and gender, which in the case of Arabesk proves to be a particularly complex one. Whereas female Arabesk singers are still scarce and—like Ebru Gtinde and Sibel Can—tend to reinforce a stereotypical image of woman as seductive Oriental dancer-singer, male singers have relied on a "sedate manliness" like Orhan Gencebay or on a "gloomier," rather tearful version like Ferdi Tayfur respectively. On the whole, the genre has remained in the stronghold of a masculine culture that "is strongly associated with mustaches, masculine friendship, and *rakı*-drinking, cigarette-smoking rituals" (Özbek 223). Nevertheless, the long-standing 'Othering' of Arabesk singers as well as the melodramatic lyrics of their songs have put these male performers in a somewhat ambiguous category of masculinity. Especially when considering most Arabesk singers' background of Anatolian peasantry, their former hierarchically uncontested position as family patriarchs has increasingly disintegrated with the migration from rural to urban environments due to the demands of housing, employment, and child-raising, and with wives and daughters visibly entering public spheres and therefore gaining considerable empowerment. With the manliness of Arabesk singers always already in danger of being culturally feminized—or, as shown, marked as vulgarly hyper-masculinized—, the considerable popularity of transsexual performers in this genre further adds to the complexity of body politics that distinguishes Arabesk in general.

Writing about the male body in the context of house music, Stephen Amico modifies Ellen Koskoff's inquiry into *Women and Music in Cross-Cultural Perspective*, adapting the offered four ways in which music may function *vis-a-vis* gender structures to questioning masculine signification in pop music performances. According to Koskoff, these are the four categories of music performance that emerge in connection with inter-gender relations:

(1) performance that *confirms and maintains* the established social/sexual arrangement; (2) performance that *appears to maintain* established norms in order to protect other, more relevant values; (3) performance that *protests, yet maintains*, the order (often through symbolic behavior); and (4) performance that *challenges and threatens* established order. (10, emphasis added, qtd. also in Amico 359)

Whereas Tatlıses for the most part embodies the traditional Muslim Turkish male look of his generation, Emrah does the same thing for his younger, now more Westernized generation. Both can be said to confirm and maintain established social and sexual norms through their visual representation. Emrah, however, even though a clear descendant of his older idol belongs to a generation that is much more influenced by Western rock music than Tatlıses has been. And, as critics like Diane Railton have shown, the stronghold of "rock hegemony" (323) still calls for strictly exclusionary gender distribution: rock stars have recreated a male and masculine public sphere with their physical performance being clearly targeted at an appreciative and relishing and above all female audience.[6] Even though Arabesk at times was in conflict or even in contradiction to the Kemalist interests or the nation state, performers like Tatlıses and Emrah certainly posed no threat to the prevailing gender politics of Turkey.

On the other hand, "The Gendered Carnival of Pop" as Railton calls it, opens the dance floor for yet very different ways of presenting and receiving gendered codes and messages. Arabesk with its roots in "low culture" belongs to the realm of popular entertainment that not only in the U.S. has traditionally been associated with "mindless" enjoyment and bodily pleasure and as such has been "inextricably linked to the feminine" (325). For the Turkish state, therefore, faced with the fact of a rising popularity of unruly Arabesk, it certainly did not help matters that the singers and performers of Arabesk music have often stemmed from ambiguously sexed and socially marginalized urban tenants like Kurds, gypsies, homosexuals, transvestites, and young children. Following the 1980 military coup, the restrictive politics included a policing of Arabesk music and films that in turn resulted in the exile of Arabesk stars like transsexual Bülent Ersoy, to pick an especially notorious and famous example.

---

6   See also Rosa Reitsamer who speaks of rock culture's gendered dichotomy as accepted realm to articulate normative male sexuality: "Rock offeriert einer Reihe gesellschaftlich akzeptierter, sexualisierter männlicher Posen den Rahmen, sich in Stereotypen auszudrücken" (173).

Ersoy was one of the first widely known Turkish transsexuals, quickly gaining cult status within the Arabesk community. After her sex reassignment surgery in 1981, she not only faced transphobic reactions from the government leading to her ban from public performances, her petition to be legally recognized as a woman was rejected at the time as well. Her operation was performed abroad in London, because local sex reassignment surgery was illegal in Turkey at the time. Her highly visible stardom might even have accelerated the restrictive measures of the military government on Arabesk. Being forced to leave the country due to persecution, she, however, successfully continued to perform in West Germany until her return in 1988, initiating yet another development of Arabesk culture: the rising translocation of Arabesk musical production to Western European countries like Germany and the —at times illegal—re-import and distribution of those very products through the channels of a vast black market in music-cassettes. This explosion of the music market especially during the 1980s brought with it a vast expansion of venues for listening to Arabesk performers, literally to every corner of the urban space:

> Although arabesk music was excluded from state-run radio and television because it did not fit into any of the officially sanctioned musical modes, by the mid-1970s it was everywhere. [...] Arabesk invaded virtually every private and public sphere, from theaters that showed movies of arabesk singers to thoroughfares were street peddlers sold cassettes. (Özbek 218)

After Ersoy returned from forced exile, she filed a court case, fighting for her legal recognition as a woman. Due to the changed Turkish Civil Code in 1988, which added the amendment that male-to-female post-operative transgender people could now obtain the "pink card" to certify their new female gender (Yüksel 279), Ersoy continued her career as a female performer in Turkey, although retaining her rather male first name Bülent. Ersoy not only managed to regain her position as one of the leading Arabesk singers, she also successfully entered various other performance spaces like starring in the musical genres of Turkish folk and classical music as well as with an almost daily presence on television as popular guest star in talk shows, as juror in talent shows, and as moderator and performer in her own shows. Whether her transsexual *persona* protests or challenges the established order remains to be discussed, nevertheless.

At first glance, it seems that her status as transsexual *per se* undermines customary notions of clear-cut gendered identities. Her flamboyant behavior and presentation add to a campy image that especially in the U.S. has widely been accepted as subversive and anti-hegemonic agency.[7] Viewed from within Turkish gender politics, I tend to have doubts, however, as to the exact level of transgression. Although the change in legislation was brought on by Ersoy's court case, resulting in a rather progressive legal regulation,[8] the ensuing situation for transgender people has not been without conflicts. On the contrary, as Deniz Kandiyoti points out, the pressures to eliminate any ambiguity in matters of gender has caused serious problems for transgender people: "Despite these changes, the medical and legal preconditions for sex-change surgery have not yet been fully worked out, creating areas of uncertainty, tension and potential medical malpractice" ("Pink Card Blues" 279). Still today, transsexuals face a life that stereotypically links them to prostitution and makes them subject to frequent and violent police harassment, often forcing them into continued semi-illegal sub-cultural ghettoization. The established hegemonic structure, though somewhat loosened in recent years, still today maintains a strictly dichotomous gender system, denying the existence of homosexual and transgender identifications. Therefore, a male-to-female transsexual like Ersoy is more likely to be considered as an aberrant woman and thus her former biological male sex will simply be ignored. As many cases from Istanbul's transgender scene prove, one of the ways to 'come out' of the prescribed invisibility of closeted sexual behavior still remains the choice of a 'corrective' surgical procedure. Nevertheless, as Kandiyoti argues, gender issues in general and those relating to transgender people in particular have a local specificity due to historically and culturally given mechanisms of exclusion and inclusion that are unyielding to generalizations:

> [T]he identities of male-to-female transsexuals in Turkey are crafted through complex interfaces between their personal biographies, the economic and political pressures of their immediate milieu and the more distant backdrop of international trans-gender and human-rights politics. The interactions of *travestis* with state apparatuses at critical junctures of

---

7 See, for example, Kate Davy's essay "Fe/Male Impersonation: The Discourse of Camp."
8 The Amendment to the 29th clause of law no. 743, Turkish Civil Code, 12 May 1988, 19812, states: "In cases where there has been a change of sex after birth documented by a report from a committee of medical experts, the necessary amendments are made to the birth certificate." According to Kandiyoti, "this ruling *may* appear as more advanced than that of many European countries, where the original record of one's sex of birth is not thus obliterated" ("Pink Card Blues" 291, emphasis added).

their lives—when applying for new identity papers, trying to avoid military service or being handled by police force—communicate powerful messages of their stigmatisation as a deviant minority. [...] On the other hand, the images of fast-track living, glamour and consumption that they project, as well as the market networks in which they circulate, encapsulate the post-1980s mainstream, with its emphasis on material success and "making it fast" (*köşeyi dönmek*) to an uncomfortable degree. ("Pink Card Blues" 290)

This claim of a specifically Turkish mode of living transsexuality accounts not only for the ambiguous fascination that transsexuals evoke in the broad public, but also for the perception of transsexuality as a signifying cultural practice of paradoxical and disparate public performance, especially with regard to highly visible actors like Arabesk singers. Thus, an example like Ersoy's speaks for Arabesk as "all encompassing metaphor" (Öncü, "Global Consumerism" 186) expressing the pervasive identity problem of a Turkish society that is "strangely composite" and as such unwillingly "appropriating and incorporating into its closed circle what does not fit into the existing scheme of things" (Öncü, "Istanbulites and Others" 115).

Orientalized Pop-Export: Tarkan

Turkish singer Tarkan for years has been one of Turkey's most prominent pop exponents and exports. His music style and performance mixes bellydance, rap, break-dance, Turkish classical music and Western pop. Significantly, since the release of his first all-English album *Come Closer* (2006), produced in the U.S., he has been aiming, through his music style and star image, to join the global market forces.

And yet, refocusing the perspective from a global scope back to Turkey, Tarkan is but one example of a booming pop-culture within his homeland Turkey, centered in Istanbul's clubbing scene, and present—via radio, television, internet, cell phones, mobile media players, and music streaming services—in virtually every household throughout the country. Tarkan, who as a child of Turkish *Gastarbeiter* in Germany was relocated to Turkey in his early teens and now lives in Istanbul and New York, is a 'product' of migrant politics due to transnational economics. When viewed solely from a Western perspective, he figures as thoroughly Westernized and highly sexualized Orient-export. Yet, as unlikely as it may seem from that perspective, his music is actually rooted in the Turkish tradition of Arabesk culture that rightfully must be claimed to be of a historically and geographically localizable—non-Western—specificity. An example of his mixture of Western pop and Oriental Arabesk is the bestselling hit song "Kuzu Kuzu" ("Like a Lamb") from his 2001 album *Karma*. As can be seen in the song's video versions, Tarkan not only uses finger cymbals, but also engages in a routine of belly-dance, both of which indicate the music's Arabic sources.

As the lyrics show, this is a love song not necessarily connected to the Arabesk tradition of bemoaning one's bleak destiny. On the contrary, the song's theme of a lover, who has been unfaithful and has betrayed his beloved, but who claims to have changed and is now willing to return humbled "like a lamb," depicts a person who tries to change his destiny. There are even overt sexual allusions like the 'punishment' of hot peppers for forbidden kisses that highlight erotic role play instead of ineffective melancholic yearning:

Bak! Kırıldı kolum kanadım	Look! I'm lost without you
Olmadı, tutunamadım	I couldn't handle it
Zor! Yokluğun çok zor	Hard! Your absence is too hard
Alısamadım	I couldn't get used to
Vur, vur bu akılsız başi	Bang, bang this foolish head
Duvarlara	On the walls
Taşlara vur sevabına	On the rocks for the joy of it
Sonra affet, gel baş bağrına	Then forgive me, come embrace me
Süzüldüm, eridim	I'm changed, melted
Sensiz olamadım	Couldn't do without you
İşte kuzu kuzu geldim	Look I've come meekly as a lamb
Dilediğince kapandım dizlerine	At your knees for as long as you want me
Bu kez gururumu ateşe verdim	This time, I've swallowed my pride
Yaktım da geldim	Threw it away and came
İster at, ister öp beni	Discard me if you wish, kiss me if you want
Ama önce dinle bak gözlerime	But first listen, look into my eyes
İnan, bu defa	Believe me, this time

Anladım durumu (bil), tövbeler ettim	I know the situation (know this), I've repented
Ooofff ooofff	Ooooo ohhhh
Acı biberler sür dilime dudaklarıma	Rub chili peppers on my tongue and lips

(Tarkan, "Kuzu Kuzu". Lyrics see <www.elyrics.net/> and translation—slightly altered—by Ali Yildirim <www.getalyric.com/>.)

Together with the fact that the album's title, *Karma*, plays with Arabesk's notion of fateful destiny, Tarkan both refers to traditional Arabesk traits and in a self-referential, Orientalizing manner moves beyond tradition. This is obvious especially when looking at songs like "Kuzu Kuzu," where he interconnects love lyrics with instrumental pop arrangements and Oriental body performance creating a stylistic cross-over. This move from local tradition to encompass larger, widely differing audiences is also reflected in recent music theory. In her review of the "Politics and Poetics of Dance," Susan Reed refers to ethno-musicology's shift from the category of music to sound in order to incorporate such elements as performance, dance and movement into its field of interest (504). She analyzes the complex ways "in which dance and movement styles are transmitted across class, ethnic, and national lines" (505) and claims that this crossover gives insight into signaling group affiliation and difference. Accordingly, looking at movement through the focal point of class and locality may bring forth a "bodily bilingualism" that Jane Desmond describes in the context of race and class differentiation as a "way of speaking, with the body [that] is used in specific instances, depending on whether class or racial codes are semantically overriding" (46). While Arabesk performance is also situated at the crossroads of class and ethnicity as shown, Desmond's concept here seems equally useful in terms of cultural and gender crossovers. Tarkan's allusion to Oriental belly-dancing can therefore be claimed to be such a bodily bilingualism. On a global terrain, Tarkan is recreating and molding himself into a representation of an Oriental 'Other' which in turn brings him precariously close to feminized, exoticized and colonial notions of the Orient, mostly associated with sexually attractive and available women, but including men as well. It is especially through his movements which include belly-dancing that Tarkan may be said to deliberately allude to such an Orientalism.

Also, his overall bodily presentation leans towards an even higher degree of sexualization compared to Emrah, for example, while conspicuously lacking the exaggerated masculinity of his colleague. And this foregrounding of the sexualized body makes Tarkan even more than Emrah a target of ambiguous adoration within the rock/pop arena. In the history of Western pop music at least, white heterosexual masculinity was the norm on stage or screen, but as such ultimately invisible compared to women or ethnically marked men. Only rarely could "cock rockers" such as Mick Jagger or Iggy Pop be fetishized without endangering their masculine allure: "Cock rock performers are aggressive, dominating and boastful and they constantly seek to remind the audience of their prowess, their control" (Whiteley, qtd. in Kiessling and Stastný 38). Within this discourse of normative white male heterosexuality, dancing men are considered effeminate and gay. Tarkan, however, in his visual representations often looks directly into the camera with an alluring, seductive smile, and his defined, but not too muscled and hard-bodied physique is shown in various stages of semi-nakedness, yet mostly adorned with some symbol of the Orient. His 2005 commercial campaign for the telephone company Avea is a case in point in that it not only confirmed his cult status in Turkey, but also his strikingly ambivalent presentation in terms of masculinity. In one of the ads, he is dressed in a transparent shirt that through various lighting devices seem to be luminously floating about his naked torso while he is moving to fast dance beats. Another video shows him sitting naked in a bath tub—full of foam, of course—singing an a-cappella tune of melancholic yearning. Both ads conspicuously refrain from heterosexual physical contact with the bathtub commercial even suggesting to autoerotic pleasures. Besides, most of the images in his CD booklets underline this stylized Oriental presentation, with some openly alluding to the Islamic art of ornamental calligraphy.

Tarkan's method of adorning his body, seemingly in a self-referential manner, distinguishes himself *and* reaches out, since, as Georg Simmel has claimed, adornment can never remain with the individual alone:

> One adorns oneself for oneself, but can do so only by adornment for others. [Adornment is] an act, which exclusively serves the emphasis and increased significance of the actor, nevertheless attains this goal just as exclusively in the pleasure, in the visual delight it offers to others. (206)

And since his adornment is one that for Western pleasure-takers indistinctly seems 'Oriental,' a sense of individuality gets lost altogether, because such a "foreignness of sensibility does not permit us to grasp the real individuality in the work of art, so that we can only penetrate to its more general and typical features—as is often the case for instance with oriental art," says Simmel.

What emerges, however, instead is the foregrounding of style as "that type of artistic arrangement which, to the extent it carries or helps to carry the impression of a work of art, negates its quite individual nature and value, its uniqueness of meaning" (Simmel 211). Particularity, the artist's very own signature so to speak recedes in favor of an artistic commonality shared by many beyond the individual work.

These are moments of the mentioned "bodily bilingualism," since on the one hand Tarkan situates himself more than the other Arabesk singers within a cultural context of the Middle East, where belly-dancing has long been both a social—or folk—practice as well as a profession performed by women *and* men alike. Dance scholars like Anthony Shay stress the fact that only through colonial rule did the notion of exclusively female belly-dancing become dominant, because especially the male members of the colonial society deemed male dancers as unmoral and feminized, and usually a ban on male dancing was the result of the colonial male sensibilities being offended:

> The European observers came to the Middle East bearing orientalist opinions concerning depraved Moslem morals and looked to have them validated. A closer analysis reveals that male dancers were almost always discernible from females in the iconographic sources. (Shay 70)

Thus, even though a male dancer's sex would be discernible, his male gender was disputable from the viewpoint of cultural outsiders. For the latter, the scandal of the male dancer was his dubious sexual allure as seemingly being available, yet remaining frivolously aloof. As such, and although

> the male dancer continues as an institution, it is an occupation that is fading with the emergence of new concepts of gender and sexuality and the issue of which behaviours may be ascribed as "male" and "female" constitute dynamic and fluid cultural categories. The performances of dancing males can still excite both intense interest and deep-seated feelings of choreophobia. (Shay 82)[9]

On the other hand, Tarkan's body—his style and movements—adheres to the Western discourse of double entendre. In doing so, he covertly uses a second language that is queerly coded, I would claim. It is an 'open secret' within the

---

9 The custom of belly-dancing continues in an informal and impromptu manner in gay bars.

gay community both in Turkey as well as abroad that Tarkan himself is gay.[10] This is not to say that we can automatically conflate his private predilections with his public star *persona*. But I do argue that Tarkan deliberately mixes musical genres of different cultures as well as creates hybrid body images that cover *and* reveal various things simultaneously. Taking a look at his album *Metamorfoz*, for example, there is a noticeable move in terms of music towards rock beats, its stronger Western kick drum rhythm representative of a well-established masculinity in its generic coding. And clearly, with his catering to an international audience Tarkan participates in the rising interest—and sales figures—of Oriental music products on the Western market since the 1990s, as Oliva Bloechl confirms: "British and American consumers' desire to possess cultural artefacts associated with the Middle East must be [...] contextualized as part of the living history of Orientalism" (134). Markus Wyrwich even makes a case that such a living Orientalism has a sedative quality, covering otherwise confrontational situations like the impending Islamist fatwa against the U.S., while paradoxically reproducing offensive Orientalist clichés at the same time (83). Even though Wyrwich mainly refers to Western artists incorporating Oriental elements into their own compositions or performances, in his discussion he also includes pop songs released by transnationally operating labels.

Tarkan's all-Turkish album *Metamorfoz*—as was his preceding all-English album *Come Closer*—was produced by subdivisions of Universal, and not as his prior albums by Istanbul Plak. While his move back to Turkish language has generally been noted as a return to his local roots, this supposed switch back is not as unambiguous as it might seem. Like the non-Turkish production label, the album's conspicuous title suggests that Tarkan plays with the changeability of his stage *personas* offering new and subtle twists. Alternatively dressed up in retro-style business attire and hard-rock jeans-and-leather outfit, his short-trimmed hair and full beard are clearly signs of a re-masculinized rep-

---

10   Gossip about Tarkan's sexuality continues to flourish, in part due to his own contradictory statements. Already in 2006, for example, he claimed in an *Hürriyet* interview: "Bu ülke beni ille de gay yapacak" ("This country will necessarily make me gay") (Arman). And while repeatedly denying to be gay and also asserting not to believe in marriage ("Tarkan: Gay değilim, evliliğe inanmam;" "Leute: Der türkische Popstar Tarkan"), he did marry Pinar Dilek in 2016 and in 2018 their daughter was born.

resentation, making him less Oriental, perhaps more straight acting, but ultimately less gay?

I believe, to quote Amico on his findings analyzing the connection of house music and homosexuality, that Tarkan here takes part in a cultural dilemma where "gay men are forced to resort to re-appropriation, *bricolage*, in their attempts to mine 'straight' society for musical material" (369). At the same time, Tarkan's musical and gendered crossover success accounts for a cultural realization of an East-West synthesis that governmental politics have failed to bring about as the seemingly never-ending bid of Turkey for an entry into the EU shows. Ertuğrul Özkök in an article of the Turkish daily newspaper *Hürriyet* of 1993 even considers Tarkan to be "the first full-blown megastar of the East-West synthesis" who not only unites Turkish people across the age divide but whose musical and visual aesthetics participate in Turkey's efforts in modernization: "The new music that gushes forth from Tarkan's unbuttoned shirt is the first sign that an exodus that had rejected the East without being able to set foot in the West, a mental migration, an aesthetic nomadism is achieving a transition to sedentary life" (Özkök qtd. in Bora 445).

If indeed we take Arabesk as an example of music's capacity of "sounding out," i.e. of constructing trajectories between oneself and elsewhere (Stokes, "Sounding Out" 121), then Arabesk's inherently generic hybrid style of "cut'n'mix" to evoke Dick Hebdige's term speaks of an interplay between power and resistance, metropolitan center and marginal dislocation, global and local, Occident and Orient, mainstream and exoticism, and thus ultimately reflects where Turkey stands in the world at this very moment. While 'Turk Pop' as being part of the all-encompassing label of 'World Music' for many may seem to signify the successful entry of a local music tradition into the global music economy, it risks losing its rootedness in actual migratory history and social turmoil.[11] Arabesk music being globally marketed as "The Sound of Istanbul" grants this music a geographically and visually specific 'sound;' whether this marketing strategy highlights national identification

---

11   See Fatih Aydogdu and Frketic who in an interview on "Türk Pop" as migrant music claim: "Die Transferprozesse der World Music verliefen in eine Richtung, nämlich von einer territorial und ethnisch festgeschriebenen und scheinbar authentischen 'Dritte-Welt-Kultur' hin zu westlichen Metropolen, wo immer Interesse an neuen und 'fremden' Phänomenen besteht. Dass der Transfer von World Music von tatsächlichen Migrationsbewegungen begleitet war, und dass die Quellen der Weltmusik meist selbst von Überlagerungen, Aneignungen und Übersetzungen geprägt waren und sind, wurde völlig ausgeblendet" (95).

or rather blurs it instead, remains to be disputed. As a musical genre, Arabesk both adheres to the stereotype of an Oriental sound signifying longing, beauty, and seduction *and* to the equally prevailing stereotype of anything Oriental being disturbing, ambiguous, or even perverse (Aydoglu and Frketic 98). Today's Arabesk performers, be they Tatlıses, Emrah, Ersoy, or Tarkan, all take part in cross-cultural gender politics and transnational musical syncretism. While moving back and forth between the rootedness within Istanbul's metropolitan culture and the global market of pop culture, the Oriental beats and nomadic tales of these at times subversively hybrid performers ultimately sound out to audiences far beyond their home habitat.

Works Cited

"arabesque." Web. 31 July 2021. *Merriam-Webster Dictionary*. <http://www.merriam-webster.com/dictionary/arabesque>

"Leute: Der türkische Popstar Tarkan als Homosexueller bezeichnet." *Der Tagesspiegel*. 10 June 2021. Web. 4 Dec 2021. <https://www.tagesspiegel.de/gesellschaft/panorama/leute-der-tuerkische-popstar-tarkan-als-homosexueller-bezeichnet-und-weitere-promi-news/233096.html>

"Tarkan: Gay değilim, evliliğe inanmam." *gayhaber.com*. 26 July 2006. Web. 4 Dec 2021. <http://www.gayhaber.com/haber/231/437/tarkan-gay-degilim-evlilige-inanmam-.html>

Amico, Stephen. "'I Want Muscles:' House Music, Homosexuality and Masculine Signification." *Popular Music* 20.3 (2001): 359-378.

Arman, Ayşe. "Bu ülke beni ille de gay yapacak." *Hürriyet*. 12 Nov 2006. Web. 21 Nov 2021. <https://www.hurriyet.com.tr/bu-ulke-beni-ille-de-gay-yapacak-5419770>

Aydoglu, Fatih, and Vlakta Frketic. "'Türk-' und 'Jugo-Pop:' The Sound of . . . Migrantische Musik und ihr Labeling durch die Popindustrie." Interview with Rosa Reitsamer and Rupert Weinzierl. *Female Consequences: Feminismus, Antirassismus, Popmusik*. Eds. Rosa Reitsamer and Rupert Weinzierl. Wien: Löcker, 2006. 93-101.

Bloechl, Oliva. "Orientalism and Hyperreality in 'Desert Rose.'" *Journal of Popular Music Studies* 17.2 (2005): 133-161.

Bora, Tanıl. "Nationalist Discourses in Turkey." *The South Atlantic Quarterly* 102.2/3 (2003): 433-451.

Bozdoğan, Sibel. "The Predicament of Modernism in Turkish Architectural Culture: An Overview." *Rethinking Modernity and National Identity in Turkey.*

Eds. Sibel Bozdoğan and Raşat Kasaba. Seattle and London: U of Washington P, 1997. 133-156
Çınar, Alev. "National History as a Contested Site: The Conquest of Istanbul and Islamist Negotiations of the Nation." *Comparative Studies in Society and History* 43.2 (2001): 364-391.
Cloonan, Martin. "Pop and the Nation-State: Towards a Theorisation." *Popular Music* 18.2 (1999): 193-207.
Coplan, David. "Musics." *International Social Science Journal*. Special Issue *Anthropology—Issues and Perspectives: II. Sounding Out New Possibilities* 154 (1997): 585-595.
Davy, Kate. "Fe/Male Impersonation: The Discourse of Camp." *The Politics and Poetics of Camp*. Ed. Moe Meyer. London and New York: Routledge, 1994. 130-148.
de Certeau, Michel. *The Practice of Everyday Life*. Transl. Steven Rendall. Berkeley: U of California P, 1984.
Desmond, Jane C. "Embodying Difference: Issues in Dance and Cultural Studies." *Cultural Critique* 26 (1993/1994): 33-63.
Gebesmair, Andreas. Die Fabrikation globaler Vielfalt: Struktur und Logik der transnationalen Popmusikindustrie. Bielefeld: transcript, 2008.
Hebdige, Dick. *Subculture: The Meaning of Style*. London: Methuen, 1979.
Kandiyoti, Deniz. "Gendering the Modern: On Missing Dimensions in the Study of Turkish Modernity." *Rethinking Modernity and National Identity in Turkey*. Eds. Sibel Bozdoğan and Raşat Kasaba. Seattle and London: U of Washington P, 1997. 113-132.
—— "Pink Card Blues: Trouble and Strife at the Crossroads of Gender." *Fragments of Culture: The Everyday of Modern Turkey*. Eds. Deniz Kandioyti and Ayşe Saktanber. London: I. B. Tauris, 2002. 277-293.
Kiessling, Stephanie, and Nina Stastný. "'Let's Get Physical.' Körperinszenierungen zwischen Pop & Rock." *Female Consequences: Feminismus, Antirassismus, Popmusik*. Eds. Rosa Reitsamer and Rupert Weinzierl. Wien: Löcker, 2006. 33-43.
Koskoff, Ellen. *Women and Music in Cross-Cultural Perspective*. New York: Greenwood, 1987.
Nalbantoğlu, Gülsüm Baydar. "Silent Interruptions: Urban Encounters with Rural Turkey." *Rethinking Modernity and National Identity in Turkey*. Eds. Sibel Bozdoğan and Raşat Kasaba. Seattle and London: U of Washington P, 1997. 192-210.

Öncü, Ayşe. "Global Consumerism, Sexuality as Public Spectacle, and the Cultural Remapping of Istanbul in the 1990s." *Fragments of Culture: The Everyday of Modern Turkey*. Eds. Deniz Kandioyti and Ayşe Saktanber. London: I. B. Tauris, 2002. 171-190.

———. "Istanbulites and Others: The Cultural Cosmology of Being Middle Class in the Era of Globalism." *Istanbul: Between the Global and the Local*. Ed. Çağlar Keyder. Lanham et al.: Rowman & Littlefield, 1999. 95-119.

Özbek, Meral. "Arabesk Culture: A Case of Modernization and Popular Identity." *Rethinking Modernity and National Identity in Turkey*. Eds. Sibel Bozdoğan and Raşat Kasaba. Seattle and London: U of Washington P, 1997. 211-232.

Railton, Diane. "The Gendered Carnival of Pop." *Popular Music* 20.3 (2001): 321-331.

Reed, Susan A. "The Politics and Poetics of Dance." *Annual Review of Anthropology* 27 (1998): 503-532.

Reitsamer, Rosa. "Walk on the White Side: Weiße maskuline Normativität in der Popkultur." *Female Consequences: Feminismus, Antirassismus, Popmusik*. Eds. Rosa Reitsamer and Rupert Weinzierl. Wien: Löcker, 2006. 169-179.

Shay, Anthony. "The Male Dancer in the Middle East and Central Asia." *Belly Dance: Orientalism, Transnationalism, and Harem Fantasy*. Eds. Anthony Shay and Barbara Sellers-Young. Costa Mesa: Mazda, 2005. 51-84.

Simmel, Georg. *Simmel on Culture: Selected Writings*. Eds. David Frisby and Mike Featherstone. London: Sage 1997.

Stokes, Martin. "Islam, the Turkish State and Arabesk." *Popular Music* 11.2 (1992): 213-227.

———. "Music, Fate and State: Turkey's Arabesk Debate." *Middle East Report: Turkey in the Age of Glasnost* 160 (1989): 27-30.

———. "Sounding Out: The Culture Industries and the Globalization of Istanbul." *Istanbul: Between the Global and the Local*. Ed. Çağlar Keyder. Lanham et al.: Rowman & Littlefield, 1999. 121-139.

Tarkan. "Kuzu Kuzu." *Karma*. Istanbul Plak, 2001.

Tatlıses. "Ayağında Kundura." *Ayağında Kundura*. Türkuola, n.d.

———. "Ağrı Dağı (Cano Cano)." *Bulamadım*. Idobay, 2007.

Tekin, Latife. *Berji Kristin: Tales from the Garbage Hills*. London and New York: M. Boyars, 1996.

Whiteley, Sheila. *Sexing the Groove: Popular Music and Gender*. London and New York: Routledge, 1997.

Wyrwich, Markus. "Lokalisierung im Klischee—Orientalismus in gegenwärtiger Popmusik." *Sound and the City: Populäre Musik im urbanen Kontext*. Eds. Dietrich Helms and Thomas Phleps. Bielefeld: transcript, 2007. 65-85.

Yüksel, Şahika et al. "Group Psychotherapy with Female-to-Male Transsexuals in Turkey." *Archives of Sexual Behavior* 29.3 (2000): 279-290.

Cultural Studies

Gabriele Klein
Pina Bausch's Dance Theater
Company, Artistic Practices and Reception

2020, 440 p., pb., col. ill.
29,99 € (DE), 978-3-8376-5055-6
E-Book:
PDF: 29,99 € (DE), ISBN 978-3-8394-5055-0

Ingrid Hoelzl, Rémi Marie
Common Image
Towards a Larger Than Human Communism

2021, 156 p., pb., ill.
29,50 € (DE), 978-3-8376-5939-9
E-Book:
PDF: 26,99 € (DE), ISBN 978-3-8394-5939-3

Elisa Ganivet
Border Wall Aesthetics
Artworks in Border Spaces

2019, 250 p., hardcover, ill.
79,99 € (DE), 978-3-8376-4777-8
E-Book:
PDF: 79,99 € (DE), ISBN 978-3-8394-4777-2

**All print, e-book and open access versions of the titles in our list
are available in our online shop www.transcript-publishing.com**

Cultural Studies

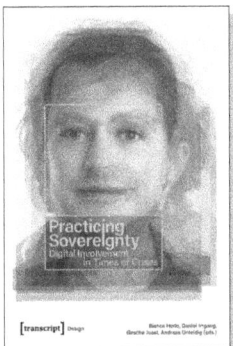

Bianca Herlo, Daniel Irrgang,
Gesche Joost, Andreas Unteidig (eds.)
Practicing Sovereignty
Digital Involvement in Times of Crises

January 2022, 430 p., pb., col. ill.
35,00 € (DE), 978-3-8376-5760-9
E-Book: available as free open access publication
PDF: ISBN 978-3-8394-5760-3

Tatiana Bazzichelli (ed.)
Whistleblowing for Change
Exposing Systems of Power and Injustice

2021, 376 p., pb., ill.
29,50 € (DE), 978-3-8376-5793-7
E-Book: available as free open access publication
PDF: ISBN 978-3-8394-5793-1
ISBN 978-3-7328-5793-7

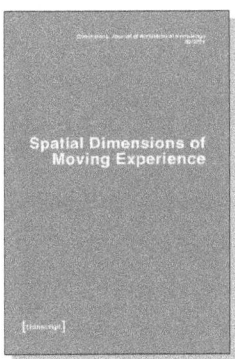

Virginie Roy, Katharina Voigt (eds.)
Dimensions. Journal of Architectural Knowledge
Vol. 1, No. 2/2021:
Spatial Dimensions of Moving Experience

2021, 228 p., pb., ill.
39,00 € (DE), 978-3-8376-5831-6
E-Book: available as free open access publication
PDF: ISBN 978-3-8394-5831-0

**All print, e-book and open access versions of the titles in our list
are available in our online shop www.transcript-publishing.com**

GPSR Authorized Representative: Easy Access System Europe, Mustamäe tee 50, 10621 Tallinn, Estonia, gpsr.requests@easproject.com